DEPLOYMENT

DEPLOYMENT

Strategies for Working with Kids in Military Families

Karen Petty, PhD

Redleaf Press®
www.redleafpress.org
800-423-8309

Published by Redleaf Press
10 Yorkton Court
St. Paul, MN 55117
www.redleafpress.org

First edition 2009
Cover design by Percolator and Jon Letness
Interior design by Mayfly Design
Typeset in Adobe Caslon
Developmental edit by Cathy Broberg
Printed in the United States of America

Library of Congress Cataloging-in-Publication Data
Petty, Karen.
    Deployment : strategies for working with kids in military families / Karen Petty.
       p. cm.
    Includes bibliographical references.
    ISBN 978-1-933653-74-7 (alk. paper)
    1. Children of military personnel—Care—United States. 2. Deployment (Strategy)   I. Title.
  UB403.P387 2009
  355.1'29—dc22
                         2008039423

Printed on acid-free paper   U15-08

To military children everywhere, whose bravery and spirit are a constant source of inspiration to me. And to those who care for them and those who serve and care for our country—you are my heroes.

DEPLOYMENT

Acknowledgments

Much thanks to those who inspired me to write this book. Your work with military children is to be commended. Thanks especially to Kyra Ostendorf and David Heath at Redleaf Press for believing in this book and the need to provide strategies for those who work with and on behalf of military children. Your constant encouragement and guidance through the writing process brought affirmation to my passion for military children and their providers.

Introduction

My dad served in the Navy during World War II on the island of Okinawa, Japan, before I was born. My whole life, I've listened to stories about Okinawa, but only recently was I able to visit a U.S. installation there. During my visit, I tried to envision some of the stories he had told, tried to make them come to life, but it was too far in the past. My friends Barbara and Louis took me to shops where beautiful silk kimonos brightened the windows. The island was too peaceful and too full of wonderful things to see and do for me to imagine what it was like during the war.

Although I missed being a military kid by a few years, my heart has always been with kids whose parents serve in the military and who are separated from them during times of deployment.

I didn't know it when I started my career, but all along I was taking steps to help military families and children. After working as a teacher and caregiver of children for over twenty years, I became a college professor. I taught social-emotional development to students who would one day be advocates for and teachers of children, using my practice and experience to inform my teaching. I then had the good fortune to become a consultant and curriculum writer for military-based programs and was able to visit many installations around the world to see a side of the military child that I had not seen as a classroom teacher. I earned a doctoral degree in curriculum and instruction from Texas A&M University, with emphases in early childhood education and child development. This experience and preparation have given me respect and passion for the thousands of children with military parents and the challenges they face.

Why This Book Is Necessary

One-half of all military personnel are married with children. Almost a half million children under the age of eight live in military families in which one or both parents are deployed (www.military.com). In no other situation are children placed on such high alert for a parent's impending danger and faced with the kinds of stress that living the life of a military kid brings. Transitions that arise when parents and family members face assignment or reassignment and when family relocation separates children from loved ones or moves them into new schools and communities bring challenges and change. It's important not to overlook the unique stressors involved when working with military families. This book provides support and strategies for teachers, caregivers, trainers, and advocates working with military children.

Although this book is written specifically about the challenges children face related to deployment, the coping strategies it outlines will be helpful when working with other children as well. Whenever a parent leaves home for an extended period—whether he is working on temporary duty (TDY) that takes him away from home or he is working in another country—children experience a sense of loss. Of course, not every parent in the military goes to war or even leaves home. Jobs in the community as recruiters and positions on military installations that keep parents close by are common. Much of the information in this book will still be helpful to caregivers in these situations.

If you are a family child care provider, a family member or friend of the family, or a center care provider, know that providing care for the military child is one of the most important jobs you will ever have. This book will help you to provide quality and nurturing care. If you care for military children with special needs, I recommend *Including One, Including All* (Wanerman, Roffman, and Britton 2010).

Whom This Book Is For

Deployment: Strategies for Working with Kids in Military Families is written for those who work with or on behalf of children whose parents serve in the U.S. military—Army, U.S. Marine Corps, Navy, Air Force, National Guard, and Reserves. You may be teaching or caring for military kids on an installation or off, in Department of Defense Schools, public schools, private schools or home schools, or

family child care or center-based child care, or you may be their grandparent or other family member or friend. Social workers, program directors, trainers, and principals can all gain a better sense of the military child by reading this book and thoughtfully reflecting on their programs and the principles that inform or guide their decision making about the military child.

For the purposes of this book, *military child* is defined as one whose parent is serving either in the active-duty forces or in an activated and mobilized National Guard or Reserve unit. The age span for the military child in our discussion includes infants through school-age children. In this book, the term *primary caregiver* refers to the adult who is responsible for the child while the parent or parents are away on military duties. Primary caregivers are often the first point of contact and consultation for children when their parents are deployed. They provide care for the child when out of center or school care. A primary caregiver can be the other parent, a relative, or a close friend of the parents. The terms *caregiver* and *provider* in this book refer to a child care provider (center or home-based care) or teacher who cares for the child in a part-time capacity.

Family Child Care

Family child care supports military parents by providing quality care and education and as an alternative to center-based or kinship care. As a licensed family child care provider, you have decided to provide high-quality early care and education for military children. You know that their needs are unique, and you will be expected to provide for their social, emotional, learning, and physical needs while exercising patience and understanding. When stress levels are high, you focus on temperament and a goodness of fit (Thomas and Chess 1977) where individual children's needs are concerned, providing just the right solution for each child. To increase your own circle of support and to become a member of a large network of family child care providers, visit the National Association for Family Child Care Web site at www.nafcc.org.

Kinship Care

If you are a relative, stepparent, godparent, or any adult who has a bond with a child and you care for that child while his parents are deployed, you are engaging in kinship care. You are not alone! More and more military personnel are relying on kinship care for their children during deployment. (This is also common within the civilian population.) Parents are trusting you to keep their children safe and to carry on established traditions and routines. The responsibility can be overwhelming, especially if you have not cared for children before or have not done so in a long time. Caregivers at child care centers and teachers in schools may be able to help you in this time of transition. See also the agency Web sites listed in appendix B of this book under What Caregivers Can Expect.

Child Development Center Care

Once military parents have been given a departure time, they begin to assess their options for the care of their children. If there are no other trusted family members or friends to care for their children full-time, parents may turn to a child development center for child care. Some of the questions you may be asked are, "Do you have extended hours?" "Do you have experience in caring for military children?" "Can you keep me informed of what my child is doing?" Deployed parents have the added job stress of being separated from their children for long periods of time, and your assistance is critical in helping the parent left behind, or the family or friend who is left to care for the child if both parents are deploying (called *dual deployment*). In the case of dual deployment, you will be in a relationship with the primary caregivers and the deployed parents. Some days it may seem like a thankless job, but just knowing the importance of caring for the youngest, and maybe the bravest, children in itself can be rewarding.

Child development centers on military installations are designed to be a good fit for young children, care providers, and families. The program at such a center addresses the whole child, is developmentally appropriate for children, and provides relevant and significant curricular experiences on a daily basis. Those who work with and on the behalf of young children attend to development in cognitive, language, physical, social, and emotional areas. Music and movement, math, science, social studies, science and technology, as well as nutrition, health, and safety, are at the heart of the curriculum. Learning activities are not left to chance but are carefully planned and implemented based on the needs of the children in care. Care providers are well trained, and provider-to-child ratios are more than adequate. Efforts are made to work with primary caregivers or the non-deployed parents or guardians who take care of military children while the parents are deployed. Child development centers and child care providers play a huge role in assisting primary caregivers during deployment or temporary-duty assignments.

SUGGESTION FOR MILITARY FAMILIES

The Deployment Health and Family Readiness Library, which can be found at http://deploymenthealthlibrary.fhp.osd.mil, is an excellent resource for parents who are getting ready to deploy.

SUGGESTION FOR EARLY CHILDHOOD PROFESSIONALS

The National Association for the Education of Young Children (www.naeyc.org) and the National Association for Family Child Care (www.nafcc.org), both of which have state and local affiliations, are great networks of caregivers that can become your arms of support.

How to Use This Book

Throughout the book you will find strategies for helping military kids and their families cope with deployment issues and challenges. Each chapter features different topics that provide information about the military child and her world, but you do not have to read the chapters in succession to find the information that you need. Based on a sound theoretical foundation, this book is mostly about good practices, and the strategies offered in each chapter attempt to inform you of ways to address the needs of children and their families as they face separation by deployment and other military duties.

Because military children face unusual or irregular hardships, their experiences throughout the stages of deployment must be discussed. At the same time, they are still children and have many of the same experiences that children outside of military families have. Adults outside the military can use this book to learn more about military children and how to support the adults caring for military children. Both nonmilitary adults and adults living and/or working inside the military can use this book to learn more about the stages of children's development and how each stage can be positively fostered and celebrated. Throughout this book, I highlight strategies to advance military children's social, emotional, cognitive, and physical needs.

In chapter 1, I give an overview of what teachers and providers can expect when working with the military child. I provide strategies that will help the child during the parent's absence and address the complex issues that preclude caregivers from offering best practices in care. Since they represent both sides of care for the child, providers and primary caregivers should understand each other's perspective. I encourage you to examine your own practices and explore ways to improve your understanding of kids from military families in your care.

Chapter 2 focuses on how to offer emotional support for children in your care. Its strategies will help you plan emotionally positive environments based on sound child development principles and practices for children from birth through age eight. You will learn about how secure attachments in infants and toddlers are founded as well as how you can provide emotionally supportive environments for babies, preschoolers, and schoolagers. I provide strategies for enhancing patriotism in children, providing peaceful environments, and teaching tolerance through specific activities. I also address the important issue of bullying, which military kids sometimes face, and give strategies for responding to it. The chapter also details strategies to help children with the challenges of being left behind during deployment, with an emphasis on fostering emotional intelligence and resiliency. Finally, I discuss how to use routines and rituals to maintain stability in the environment and provide strategies for celebrating holidays with children.

Chapter 3 addresses the emotional benefits of play and how you can help kids understand their feelings by offering an emotion-centered curriculum. Play is monumentally important for military children, and this chapter helps you to know when it is disrupted and what you can do about it. There are suggestions for how to foster play through music, dance, art, and books. I also discuss how to scaffold children's learning and offer strategies for when a child's behavior is outside the norm (including violent behavior) and needs more attention from outside professionals.

Chapter 4 discusses the social, cognitive, and physical benefits of play. I discuss strategies for setting up outdoor play environments, loose-parts play, and games with rules. The chapter addresses the benefits of play for children of all ages.

In chapter 5, I focus on the benefits of programming in music and literacy. I discuss how to incorporate music and creative movement throughout your curriculum, including using music as part of transitions. I explain how you can use principles of music therapy in your early childhood program.

In discussing literacy programming, I provide many ideas of how to use storytelling, circle time, and environment enhancements, such as a computer center, to provide literacy rich environments.

Chapter 6 focuses on multiple intelligences theory and the Reggio Emilia approach as resources for creating quality child care programs. I discuss Howard Gardner's theory of multiple intelligences and ways to observe children and make curriculum plans using his theory. In the section on Reggio Emilia, I describe how you can make your environment a "third teacher" and how you can use documentation to guide your practice with children. An exciting part of this chapter, inspired by the Reggio Emilia approach, is learning to teach preschool and school-age kids to delve into a topic and make their own projects. As researchers, children can use critical thinking with your guidance and conduct their own investigations of the environment, which can result in in-depth learning.

Chapter 7 concentrates on developing partnerships with parents and primary caregivers and learning to work together in family-centered environments. I provide strategies for verbal and written communication with parents and primary caregivers as well as ideas for preparing family-friendly and useful bulletin boards, newsletters, personal notes, signs, and program-to-home activities that parents or primary caregivers and children can do together.

Chapter 8 explores strategies for staying connected when military children are separated from friends and family after relocation or from a parent or parents after deployment. I suggest ways military children can stay in touch with loved ones, including using technology such as podcasts, wikis, and blogs.

Chapter 9 discusses other important issues that children of military parents face, such as repeat and extended deployments, and addresses children and grief. I offer strategies for you to use when both parents are deployed or when single parents are deployed, and I list signs to alert you when children, parents, or primary caregivers are at risk and what help you can provide. I also offer strategies for helping children grieve the death of a parent.

Many providers, especially in communities away from military installations, have limited experience with military children and are not familiar with the uniforms (including weapons), language, and rituals of the military. A sister of a service member commented that she was surprised the first time she and her children saw her brother in uniform. She had always taught her children not to play with guns; she spent lots of time after her brother was deployed explaining to her children that her brother was going to use his gun to be a peacekeeper. It is a good idea for providers to have at least a basic understanding of the challenges and triumphs that military families (especially children) face. A glossary of common military terms is included at the end of this book.

This book is based on careful research and selection of best practices in child development and early education. As you provide care for military children, I hope it will serve you well.

CHAPTER ONE

What You Can Expect

The impact of deployment on children can be a challenge for the best trained and experienced care providers of military children as well as for those who have taken on a caregiving responsibility without much notice, guidance, or assistance. You may have children in your care who have experienced long-term separation more than once. Or you may have children who are experiencing separation from their parents for the first time. You may have received a call from a military parent who needs immediate child care, and you may not have time to build a relationship with the child prior to the parent's departure. In all of these instances, it's important to immediately put in place strategies that will help the child survive, succeed, and even thrive in the parent's absence. When it comes to preparation, time is of the essence, as the child's world can be changed in a short period of time.

As a former teacher and care provider, I can attest that children handle separation from their parents in different ways. Some already possess the resilience or hardiness to face the separation, while some will need more nurturing, understanding, and kindness while their parents are away. A child's age and stage of development also play a role in determining how well she can cope with separation from parents, but no matter what the child's age or developmental status, deployment is stressful and full of challenges.

Despite these challenges, families can grow stronger during deployment. As a caregiver, you will have many opportunities to help children become stronger communicators and more resilient as they learn about the jobs their parents are doing. It is important for you to understand the changes children go through as they experience separation from their parents through deployment. Trying to find balance between continuing daily routines and keeping connections with the deployed parents is at the heart of caring for children of military families.

Change

Children of all ages endure change at many points in their lives—whether it is moving to a new home, the birth of a sibling, going from one caregiver to another, or transitioning from one school to another. Change is an inevitable part of life. With deployment, the routines that children are accustomed to may be changed, disrupted, or ended all together. For instance, a morning routine might include being woken by Daddy or Mommy, eating breakfast with the family, brushing teeth, and then getting a ride to school or child care with one or both parents. This routine will need to be revised to exclude the parent who is going away and potentially to include other adults or siblings.

Because most children thrive on routine, it is up to the adults in military children's lives to keep their routines as intact as possible. Doing so will help lessen worry, anxiety, and confusion for the child, as routines often represent stability and comfort. Of course, you cannot control the predictability of the child's home life. What you can do is ensure that the child's time with you follows a consistent pattern throughout the deployment period.

It was a cold February morning, and five-year-old Sabrina was not up to playing before the bus took her to school. She attended the before- and after-school program of a child care center. Her teacher asked if she wanted breakfast. She shook her head and continued to draw. The teacher asked if she wanted someone to sit with her. Another head shake. "Do you want to talk?" asked the teacher. A final shake of the head. I observed a while longer and realized that this wasn't an ordinary morning. A provider was also missing from my visit the day before. Finally I asked, "Is something going on? Where is Martha? I was hoping to see her again today in our training." I was told, "There was a big deployment this morning. Martha's husband and Sabrina's dad were among those who had to go."

I learned a lot from this interaction. The way that the providers responded to Sabrina and spoke of Martha clearly indicated the closeness of the caregivers and military families. It also illustrated that it is possible to prepare for days like this, as all providers appeared ready to provide the necessary support for the children left behind. They knew the importance of understanding the child's situation and using nonverbal and verbal communication.

Gina, who is eight, talked about how much she missed her dad and the difficulty of being left with her new stepmom. She said, "I miss my daddy so much, but I know he will come back as soon as he can." Many military children are sent to live with grandparents, aunts and uncles, or close friends during deployment. In all situations, how adults approach change with children strongly influences their acceptance of it and their ability to be resilient.

The most frequent and severe type of change that military kids face is the deployment of one or both parents. While some might dream of a job that requires travel and the ability to live abroad, to the military child, this reality can be frightening and unpredictable. The stress of worrying about their parents in dangerous situations takes a toll on children, as do the frequent moves and expected homecomings or reunions that sometimes never happen. Using practices that are appropriate for each child's age and stage of development can ease the stress and facilitate a positive transition period for military children experiencing deployment.

Common Challenges for Infants, Toddlers, Preschoolers, and Schoolagers

Military children are children first. They have the same basic needs to be loved, feel safe, and experience consistency through routines and rituals as all children do, but their lives with military parents bring an additional set of challenges. They depend on their primary caregiver and you to provide extra emotional support during sustained periods of stress or when they feel that danger is likely to occur.

Primary caregivers who are parenting singly have the additional stressor of trying to take over a second parenting role in the absence of another parent. In addition, many military parents are single parents, and they try to do the best they can under the circumstances. Support groups are critically important at this time. Single parents leave their kids behind with family members or friends and constantly live under the stress of not being there for them.

Under the best circumstances, children will show trying behaviors during deployment. Even with the best parenting practices, military children will endure stress that other children will not. That's why it is crucial that mature and emotionally secure adults provide the best environment of care possible. Children will look to the trusted adults they have become attached to for comfort and peace during times of deployment and separation.

Infants

Babies are constantly interacting with their caregivers, learning about relationships, and increasing their knowledge and skills at rapid rates. Babies need consistent attentive care as they develop their new skills. Infants who are part of military families experience additional changes. You can help alleviate some of the undue stress on babies by becoming aware of attachment issues and stages of development in infancy—the period between birth and eighteen months. Children in this stage may experience changes in sleep, excessive clinginess, and frustration during deployment.

At around nine months, infants begin to experience true sadness, and this emotion is often accompanied by a sense of loss. It is at this time that they become truly aware that a parent is absent or removed from sight, and they feel anxious as they try to determine if or when the parent is returning.

ATTACHMENT

Attachment is an emotionally secure base formed when infants and toddlers receive consistent warm and nurturing care from an adult.

You may wonder how deployment will affect the infant in your care or if it is important which parent is absent. Babies who have experienced strong attachment to at least one parent and even other caregivers or family members will be less affected by deployment and will attach to you if your care is

- nurturing—you are warm and caring, kind and encouraging;
- attentive— you are responsive to their cries, and you do not leave babies unattended for periods of time;
- consistent—you are the one whom the baby receives care from day after day;
- safe—you provide a safe environment with little stress;
- developmentally appropriate—your care is filled with age- and stage-appropriate activities that are inviting and meaningful; learning occurs routinely (Copple and Bredekamp 2009).

If babies are more attached to one parent, then the absence of that parent will have greater effect.

But the baby can also become more attached to the parent left behind. Moreover, you can offer attachment in the absence of the deployed parent. Babies can thrive in your care—that's the beauty of attachment!

STRATEGIES

Providing Infants with a Stable Environment

Keep calm. Always use slow and gentle movements when holding babies or placing them in their cribs or on changing tables (avoid jerky, quick movements as much as possible).

Keep the same routine whenever possible. Infants can begin to predict what comes next or who their caregivers will be at particular times of the day. Talk to the baby, describing changes in location or environment and telling him what will happen next. "You are fussing. Let's change your diaper."

Play soft music or sound machines. Use them to provide gentle rhythms and sounds such as waterfalls and rain falling or waves at stressful times, or you can sing lullabies and rhyming tunes.

Use routines to enhance or encourage language development. Talk to babies during diaper changes or feedings, providing them with outlets for communicating their feelings.

Ask primary caregivers to provide you with the baby's favorite toy or blanket when she is with you. The baby will respond more positively when you are caring for her if she has something familiar to hold or interact with.

Try to bring siblings into the care environment as often as possible. Siblings have a positive effect on babies experiencing separation distress.

Ask primary caregivers to visit the care environment before leaving their infants for the first time. Infants who see their primary caregiver interact with you will separate more readily and positively.

Toddlers

Toddlerhood, usually defined as the ages between eighteen and thirty-six months, is a transition time like no other. Toddlers are on the brink of a language explosion, but their expressive language skills (what they say) are not up to the same level as their receptive language (what they understand). They need your help communicating. As you talk with toddlers, use words to describe how you think they are feeling.

Toddlers are able to think and plan their actions. This means their behavior is reflective of their moods. As they come to know that they are individual persons, separate from their parents or primary caregiver, their "I" or "Me" begins to take control, and all actions stem from this newfound knowledge. They are establishing a sense of self and are claiming all the rights and privileges that accompany this new individuality. In truth, they are entering the thinking twos rather than the terrible twos. Self-awareness is at the root of toddler behavior—a sense of cause and effect that wasn't present in infancy. "If I do this, then I can make that happen." Their often erratic and aggressive behavior stems from an inability to verbalize the countless emotions they have at any given moment. Couple this with the changes that are occurring in a military family facing deployment, and caregivers of toddlers have a recipe for adversity.

Although toddlers are especially vulnerable during deployment, facing the temporary loss of a parent does not have to be disastrous. Caring adults can minimize the challenges by knowing about toddlers and their stages of development as well as adapting to the unique needs of each child. For example, if you know that young toddlers don't have the language to express when they are missing a parent, you can offer extra hugs and opportunities to play their favorite games and sing their favorite songs. The best care environments I've observed (both home-based and center-based) include lots of togetherness or closeness with the children and have many planned activities. (By *best care* I mean settings where children appear the most content.)

Temperament—emotional sensitivity, or overall levels of happiness, fussiness, and general attitude—is always a factor to be considered with any child. For this reason, it may be difficult for a caregiver to easily discern normal toddler behavior from behavior related to the parent's absence. Determining the root cause of a toddler's behavior is important, and it may take more than one observation to discover the grounds for his actions. Learning to regulate his own emotions can begin in late toddlerhood, but it is a lifelong task that is difficult to master, even in the best of circumstances.

Extreme amounts of any negative behavior are the red flags to watch for. Regardless of their circumstances, toddlers in peril or extreme stress who display more than usual fussiness, anger, sadness, or despair are showing that they need help. Toddlers may also exhibit more aggression than before, going through "cranky" periods without cause or evidence, reverting back to earlier behaviors, and having a strong preference for certain foods (preferring the same food for days). You should be alert for all of these signs and act quickly to alleviate the toddler's stress.

You can expect toddlers who are experiencing a loss from deployment to continue displaying many emotions on a daily or almost momentary basis. Again, if a toddler is securely attached to at least one adult who continues to care for her while the deployed parent is away, the negative behaviors should be very similar to those of a toddler who is not experiencing an extreme loss. Without a strong attachment, either to you or a second parent or caring adult left behind, a toddler's behavior may be very demanding. Toddlerhood is a period of great developmental strides for children, but it can be a trying stage for the adults who care for them. Being open to and prepared for the changing needs of the toddlers in your care will help relieve some of the stress.

It is extremely difficult for toddlers to understand when Mommy or Daddy will be coming home. When a parent is absent from their day-to-day lives, toddlers feel a loss of stability and control over the events in their lives—they are often fearful because of this loss. Unlike infants, they understand that people continue to exist outside of their sight, but they cannot grasp geographic concepts such as Mommy serving in Iraq or Daddy working on an installation in Guam. Reassurance from you will provide them much needed comfort. Phrases such as "Your mommy loves you very much, and she is working hard at her job so that she can come home" and "It's okay to miss your daddy while he is at work" are appropriate. It is always important to remind them that Mommy and Daddy are at work, just as if it were any parent working at a job.

If you are taking care of a toddler, you are always on demand. The children look to you as the nurturer, rescuer, teacher, the one who provides a safe zone—an all-around very important person. Military parents and primary caregivers also look to you for assistance, words of advice, and comfort in addition to excellent care for their child. Supporting the family supports the child. It can be an overwhelming job but a rewarding one!

STRATEGIES

Providing a Reassuring, Loving, and Stable Environment for Toddlers

Resist becoming frustrated. Toddlers especially display their emotions through their behaviors. It's important to respond to their outbursts with empathy, patience, and understanding. Talk about the child's feelings by using phrases such as, "I know that you miss your mommy. It's hard not knowing when she's coming back." Or, "Your daddy wants to see you too."

Provide bulletin boards or picture walls. Hang pictures of the children's parents, siblings, grandparents, and close friends. A Velcro strip attached to a low wall allows toddlers to view and remove pictures as they wish.

Avoid making additional major changes such as potty training. Wait for a few weeks after one or more parents deploy before making changes such as moving to another classroom, gaining a new caregiver, or initiating an abrupt change in routine.

Follow a schedule as much as possible. Allow for playtime, meals and snacks, and naptimes to occur at the same time each day. Routines are especially critical for toddlers. They thrive when they know what to expect on a daily basis and may feel that life is predictable and safe. Encourage primary caregivers to drop off and pick up at the same times as much as possible.

Encourage parents to share their family rituals with you and incorporate those into your care as much as possible. Rituals are different from routines in that they are built on customs, religious or spiritual practices, and cultural values. For example, trick-or-treating is a cultural ritual that many U.S. families practice. Check with parents to see if it is part of their rituals before offering a ritual such as trick-or-treating in your program.

Provide many opportunities for play. Toddlers find emotional relief in playing alone, with caregivers, and alongside their peers. Build a schedule around indoor and outdoor play.

Provide opportunities for creative movement. Use stuffed animals, scarves, balls, parachutes, and other soft toys for toddlers to move creatively.

Provide opportunities for creative expression through art activities. Schedule time to paint, draw, color, and knead or sculpt child-safe clay or playdough.

Schedule time each day to put on rock 'n' roll or various kids' music CDs. Music can bring calm and harmony to toddlers. (See chapter 5 for more information on using music throughout the child's day.)

Provide indoor or covered outdoor play spaces to use during inclement weather. Gross motor activities are essential for toddlers. Toddler-sized basketball hoops and riding toys allow toddlers to burn off energy, which in turn can calm their emotions.

Allow rest time each day for toddlers. Most toddlers need between ten and thirteen hours of sleep each day. Overly tired toddlers can have more difficulty falling asleep and staying asleep, so a naptime of two to three hours is essential and should occur at the same time each day. Allow toddlers to choose a stuffed animal or a favorite blanket to sleep with. Play soft music or read stories with gentle, nonaggressive plots just prior to napping.

Encourage story time each day for toddlers. Allow time for toddlers to browse (read) on their own as well as time for you, the caregiver, to read to them. Group story time may not be possible, but you can practice the "If I read it, they will come" motto. Position yourself so that they can walk by or stand to hear the story and see the pictures. They may also continue playing in other areas while stories are being read aloud, paying closer attention to certain parts of the story that are familiar or exciting.

Preschoolers

Children between the ages of thirty-six and sixty months are generally referred to as preschoolers. Their language is flourishing, physical growth spurts are common, and gross motor skills and fine motor skills are developing at rapid rates. Emotionally, they are extremely attached to loved ones, which usually include friends and family, though they also enjoy relationships with peers. Preschoolers have a better chance of developing and keeping friendships with peers if their environment is stable and secure. Military children are no exception. Parents and caregivers can work together to ensure that children have secure bases from which to come and go, even in the midst of deployment and separation. A secure base exists when a parent or caregiver is consistently present, strongly attuned or connected to the child, and a stable influence in the child's life.

A SECURE BASE: ATTACHMENT AND MILITARY KIDS

John Bowlby, author of *Attachment and Loss* (1973) and *A Secure Base* (1988), explains that parents can form a secure base to which a child can return after experiencing the outside world. The base itself provides a place of shelter from harm, fear, and distress in times of peril and during typical, natural explorations. Attachment between adult and child characteristically involves the adult allowing the child to venture and retreat, venture and retreat. Bowlby called this dance of knowing when to allow the child to venture and retreat "attunement" (1988, 18); I call it "at one-ment." In fact, the base is so important that the attached adult and child can withstand any separation, even the death of a parent or significant caregiver. It bears saying again: if one significant adult (in our case, you, a parent, or another family member) is securely attached or has provided a secure base for a child, then the base will be there for the child to retreat to in the case of severe or prolonged separation—either by death, divorce, or deployment.

It is not known if children attach more securely to secondary caregivers when the primary caregiver is male versus when the primary caregiver is female. But young children will readily attach to the parents who spend time with them and communicate with them often. A child will become more comfortable and attach to strangers if the child is securely attached to one parent (male or female). In a two-parent family, the child will fare well with secondary caregivers if an attachment or secure base is in place with the remaining parent. If the child is being reared in a single-parent home, attachments to other adult family members and friends are important, no matter the gender of the parent deploying. A more in-depth discussion on attachment can be found in chapter 2.

Just as preschoolers (and toddlers) often regress to behaviors displayed at younger stages after the birth of a sibling or other life-changing experience, they also regress when facing a temporary separation such as deployment of a parent. During deployment, separation anxiety is not uncommon and may be shown by excessive clinging to the parent left behind or to you, the care provider. Regression can include sleep disturbances such as nightmares, excessive waking during the night, and bed-wetting. Anxiety affects preschoolers in many ways. You should alert primary caregivers of any consistently unusual behaviors shown while in your care, especially if you provide overnight care or extended day care. In other words, *occasional* bed-wetting or using baby talk are not reasons to caution a primary caregiver, but consistent, prolonged, or sustained unusual behaviors should be shared with the primary caregiver.

Preschoolers have reached a stage of development where they may commonly fear a loss of people or things they love. By this time, most young military children have experienced loss through parents going to work in other countries or the death of family members or pets. If they have not faced a loss, then they usually have a friend who has, and they are aware of the possibility. Because of this, both parents, or the people whom the child has the strongest connection with, should tell the child about the deployment, and the news should come as soon as the change is definite. It is a mistake to believe that young children do not know that something is looming or has begun to happen to the family. (Even infants can sense that something is out of place and affecting their providers and their environment.) If children have a chance to become accustomed to the idea that there will be a separation, they will be able to practice the coping skills they will need when the deployment actually occurs.

Preschoolers may also have the language skills to ask, "What's wrong?" or "Why is Mommy crying?" They are able to read cues from parents and discussions that don't include them. The more children are included in conversations about an upcoming deployment—even though they may experience sadness—the easier it will be for them to move through the pre-deployment phase. You can assist parents in providing an environment that says to children, "Your feelings are respected here, and we will help you to understand them."

Of course, each child is unique and develops at an individual pace. Look at the children in your care individually as well as collectively and at overall behaviors to assess their similarities and differences. As you gain experience in helping children face their parents' deployment and separation, you will become more attuned to the varieties of preschoolers' behaviors and learn how to apply the best practice or strategy for each child.

STRATEGIES

Helping Preschoolers

Provide lots of puppets, and allow children to bring them to story or group time daily, using the puppets to "talk for them"—voicing feelings they may otherwise be unable to express. For example, begin group time or a conversation by holding up cards with faces that depict a range of feelings and emotions and ask if anybody's puppet is feeling sad, glad, mad, etc., that day. Children will have the opportunity to project their feelings safely through puppets.

Allow preschoolers to engage in dramatic play, replaying the loss before and during deployment. Use circle time to talk about feelings of loss, and initiate role playing by giving role-play starters such as, "I know that some of your parents are about to be deployed. Can two people show us what that looks like, how that makes you feel?" Also, watch for spontaneous play where children are playing out this scenario, and be ready to intervene if necessary, with prompts such as, "It must be really hard to watch your mom go to work in another country."

Provide sand tables and trays along with small figurines of animals, people, homes, and so on, to allow children to engage in sand play, an emotionally soothing activity that has been used with children who are grieving and suffering a loss.

Provide activities for the military parent and child to do together, either at drop-off or at pickup times. Families who play together are building and strengthening their relationships, and strong relationships are what will help children weather deployment separations more easily. For example, provide a dual-sided easel for a parent and child to paint together or have an adult-size comfortable sofa so that a parent and a child can share a book.

Offer extra support on a daily basis through frequent eye contact, smiling, and nonverbal responsiveness.

Encourage or plan play dates where primary caregivers can become involved in their child's dramatic play, especially where problem solving can occur. Provide props and costumes for adults as well as children.

Encourage the primary caregiver to bring a skill or craft to demonstrate to the children in care. For instance, a parent who plays the guitar will make an exciting guest at music time.

Encourage all primary caregivers to engage in spontaneous play as they bring and pick up their children. An open-door policy to play will encourage the adults to have playful, emotional exchanges with the children that will set the tone for their day or evening together.

Schoolagers

Children between the ages of five and eight experience separation and loss much the same as younger children, but with a greater degree of understanding. They may have many of the same emotions, such as sadness, anger, frustration, blame, and grief. School-age kids understand the meaning of death and war, as they watch television and hear nightly news reports of the day's events, including the number of service members killed or injured.

Shelly, age eight, tells of her fears that her daddy won't come back from war, and she worries every day that he will be killed if he doesn't pay attention. Seven-year-old Mark tells his friends that he is afraid that if his daddy is hurt in the war, he won't be able to coach his baseball team anymore.

The fear of loss is outstanding for many schoolagers. One mom reported that her school-age son had a hard time going to bed each night because of his fear of nightmares about his deployed dad. Also, schoolagers experiencing deployment may show signs of depression such as loss of appetite, loss of sleep, and lack of regard for normal routines and responsibilities. A dad reported that his nine-year-old daughter had lost interest in playing sports since her mom deployed a year ago.

You have the enormous job of supporting these children as well as the primary caregivers who are left behind. Be reassuring as you answer questions. By keeping a watchful eye on the military kids in your care, you can be a second set of eyes and ears for the parent who is deployed and for the one who is left behind.

STRATEGIES

Supporting Schoolagers

Avoid treating schoolagers like little adults. Service members sometimes give the oldest child (especially boys) in the family the charge of taking care of the family while he or she is away. Children can often take this too seriously and try to step out of their role of being children.

Provide journals for school-age kids, and schedule a time each day when they are encouraged to write stories about whatever they are feeling that day. Drawings can be added to the daily journaling to accompany the stories, or used in lieu of them.

Use photos of children with different faces that depict moods such as happy, sad, angry, frustrated, confused, and lonely. Laminate photos for sturdiness, and place them in a container beside a blank poster with binder clips attached (for holding the pictures). Encourage kids to change the faces as often as their feelings change. Alternatively, photos can be glued to magnetic paper or printed on it. Kids can place the magnetic photos on a file cabinet or other metal surface that is designated as the "feelings face place."

Provide brochures and information about community resources for the parents and primary caregivers of schoolagers, such as counseling, spiritual groups or meetings, parent groups, online help such as www.militaryonesource.com, and Family Readiness Support programs on installations. Also, the Military Child Education Coalition Web site (www.militarychild.org) and the Department of Defense installations' Family Support Centers are great resources for military families with children.

Encourage military families to participate in United Through Reading at www.read2kids.org. This program, which creates videos and DVDs of parents reading, helps military parents stay connected to their children, no matter where they are stationed. School-age children especially like the connection through the use of technology.

Be honest when children ask questions. If you don't know the answer, say, "I promise to let you know when I know." Schoolagers can tell when a parent or other trusted adult is upset, and withholding information can make them even more fearful.

Allow plenty of time for play. Play allows military children to be children and possibly forget for a short time the stresses of deployment.

Military kids are in many ways just like any other kids. According to the New York State Department of Social Services, school-age kids "need a program that lets them enjoy their out-of-school time to relax, play, pursue hobbies and other interests, build relationships with trusted adults, and socialize with other children" (New York State Department of Social Services 1993). Most of all, school-age children want a place where someone who cares about them will listen to them and occasionally check in by asking, "How are you doing?" Adjusting to deployment often takes time, and each child is different, but a child's unusual behaviors or symptoms should not last longer than a week without alerting the primary caregiver.

THE NATIONAL MILITARY FAMILY ASSOCIATION

The National Military Family Association Web site, www.nmfa.org, is a good resource for providers who care for school-age children during deployment.

School-age children who show the most positive signs of coping well during deployment have

- a good relationship with their parents;
- a strong sense of self-esteem and self-worth;
- an understanding of the deployed parent's job and why the parent has to go away;
- reliable communication with their parents, even during deployment; and
- a trusted adult who will listen to them and be honest with them.

(Fleet and Family Support Centers of Hampton Roads, VA)

School-age kids are better able than younger children to understand a parent's military job, and you can expect that their fears will also be real. Enable as much video conferencing, instant messaging, and e-mailing as possible in order for them to stay connected and to help them cope with their fears.

Stages of Deployment: What to Expect

For parents in the military, *military readiness* means helping their families prepare for their deployment and for carrying on during a lengthy separation. While *deployment* refers to people who are actively serving in the armed forces, not all military personnel go to war. According to a recruiter I spoke to, "You pick your job when you enlist. If you are a veterinarian in civilian life, you can become a veterinarian in military life, whether you are in the reserves or active duty. You don't have to be a soldier."

Preparing families for separation is one of the key readiness goals for U.S. military personnel. Planning for the care of children in the absence of their military parent or parents is of critical importance. This preparation for separation occurs at several stages, and part of military readiness is knowing what to expect at each stage of deployment.

Deployment usually occurs in four stages: (1) preparing for deployment; (2) active deployment or sustainment; (3) homecomings and reunions; and (4) redeployment. Each stage has its own characteristics and affects all military children in similar ways. It is important that parents and caregivers have the resources and ability to help children approach each stage positively.

Your knowledge of the different stages of deployment will ultimately help you care for military children who are experiencing tensions and stressors at home. Keeping the lines of communication strong with the primary caregiver will also help you stay abreast of changes in the deployment schedule.

Stage One: Preparing for Deployment

Preparation for the deployment of a military parent can occur in the days, weeks, or months leading up to the actual leave. In some instances, because of the nature of the mission, the deployment will occur quickly and without warning, and little time can be given for preparation. In other cases, deployment dates are set months in advance, allowing for more preparation for the expected departure.

During the pre-deployment stage, children of military parents often sense a tension in their home that was not there before. Increased stress, vulnerability, and lots of confusion are common for kids. Children have a way of knowing that something has changed even if parents choose not to talk about it in front of them. Even infants can sense tension in adults. As a provider, you can encourage parents to take care of themselves during this stage; such caretaking can go a long way toward lessening the anxiety of young children. Two- and three-year-old children can understand that Daddy or Mommy is preparing to go to work and will come back as soon as possible. Just as separated grandparents or other family members assure children that they will see them again as soon as they can, deploying parents can honestly do the same. You can reinforce this message.

As they prepare for an upcoming deployment, one of the biggest challenges for parents of young children is to find caring, responsive adults to care for their children. It is critical that they find affordable care where best practices in child care are the standard. Adults who understand separation and anxiety and can empathize with the requirements of prolonged absences of one or both parents are

EXPECTATIONS OF THOSE WHO CARE FOR MILITARY CHILDREN

- Be knowledgeable of, or willing to learn about, military children, and be attentive to their needs.
- Be warm, caring, and culturally sensitive to military children.
- Be well trained and credentialed with a CDA (Child Development Associate) credential from the Council for Professional Recognition (www.cdacouncil.org), an associate's degree in child development from a community college, or a degree in child development from an institute of higher education.
- Have low adult-child ratios. One adult should care for no more than six children under age three. Check the licensing standards for the approved ratios in your state.
- Provide areas for play that enhance all areas of a child's development and activities that are developmentally appropriate for the age and stage of the child (Copple and Bredekamp 2009).
- Maintain safe environments and consistent supervision.
- Be committed to having relationships with military parents, and have an open-door policy that welcomes primary caregivers at any time.

needed. By offering quality care and by understanding the unique needs of military families, you can be the support a deploying family needs.

STRATEGIES

Working with Kids during Pre-deployment

Ask that parents alert you of the possible time or window of deployment (if possible). Talk to the family *before* deployment or talk as soon afterward as possible with the remaining parent or caregivers. Ask how they would like to receive communication and how often. Ask if there are co-parenting agreements for separated or divorced parents in order to help with smooth transitions between the two parents' homes and families.

Be prepared for more emotional outbursts or signs of sadness, aggressiveness, or anger during this time. Watch for signs of stress in children in the form of behavioral problems, reverting back to a former stage of development, excess crying, irritableness, mood swings or changes, loss of appetite, undue fears, and clinginess. Have a plan in place and resources to refer to if this happens.

Plan lots of good play activities for all age groups during this time. More play and less direct teaching may be necessary.

Keep changes in routines to a minimum, as military kids will count on your care and rules to be stable and consistent. Especially avoid changes in caregivers at your home or center if at all possible.

Become an expert listener and observer of children by taking notes and making observations often. Ask, "How are you?" and then really listen to the answer.

Photograph parents and children before deployment, either commercially or with your own camera. Display photos on walls and bulletin boards, and provide each family with individual photos of their own. If a child is in a single-parent home, encourage the parent to include any other significant people in the child's life to join the photo session.

Record the deploying parent on video or voice recorder. The parent can read or tell a favorite story or talk about a favorite time with the child.

Schedule a play day for parents and children to make projects or crafts that can be kept in the center or at home after the parent has deployed.

Provide items in a play center or area that can be packed, unpacked, and repacked to replicate the items that a service member would take on a mission. Make informed decisions about whether or not to include toy weapons. This topic is covered more extensively in chapter 3.

Ask the parent who will be deployed to prepare notes, either on computer or handwritten, that you can place in a container for the child to read each day.

Make a list of each child's family traditions, and include those in your planning.

Listen to children's talk about their deploying parents, and answer questions as openly and honestly as possible. Ask parents how they prefer that news is shared with their children.

Stage Two: Active Deployment or Sustainment

During active deployment, military children miss their parents. The close relationships that young children have formed with their active-duty parents do not end once the parents are gone. When a parent leaves, the comfort she or he provided may not easily be replaced by another adult, no matter how good the intentions. Feelings of anxiety, anger, sadness, depression, and restlessness as well as negative behavior and loss of appetite are common for kids during active deployment. Some kids avoid talking about deployed parents, as it is too painful to discuss the emptiness they now feel.

A child of any age can sense the absence of a parent who was a large part of their care. Infants respond to the emotions of their primary and secondary caregivers, making the care you give all the more important. Preschoolers may become clingy and will need lots of hugs and reassurances from you. Schoolagers can predict what will be missed by the absent parent, such as birthdays and other holidays as well as sporting events like baseball games and soccer. They will need to be assured that these important times in their lives will not be forgotten.

Installation Family Centers are excellent sources of support for parents and caregivers during deployment. In addition, Military One Source, available at www.militaryonesource.com and 800-342-9647, has resources for military parents and their children. Operation: Military Kids (www.operationmilitarykids.org) provides information to support kids as they transition from school to school as well as general coping strategies and ways to connect with other kids who are facing similar situations. A section of Zero to Three, an organization for parents and caregivers of young children, is dedicated to resources for military families and those who care for military kids: www.zerotothree.org. There are resource brochures such as *Little Listeners in an Uncertain World*, about how parents can help infants and toddlers cope with stress.

STRATEGIES

Working with Kids during Active Deployment

Use lots of affirmations with kids: "I can see that you miss your mom," or "I agree. It will be great to hear from your dad."

If you provide overnight care, choose a good-night saying that the child and the deployed parent can say from anywhere, such as "I see the moon and the moon sees me—Daddy sees the moon and Daddy sees me," or "Say good night to the moon wherever you are because everyone can see the moon from wherever they are."

Keep the active-duty parent involved by sending him or her newsletters or photos of recent events. (See chapter 8.)

SUGGESTION FOR MILITARY FAMILIES

One military family practiced "unholidays" when the deployed parent returned for a short visit by choosing a holiday that would be missed during the deployment. For example, Thanksgiving was celebrated in July, or Christmas was celebrated in March. They also held one big birthday celebration and had a cake with everyone's name on it.

Dear Parents,

As you approach deployment, please know that we are here to help your child through the transition of your departure, while you are away, and after your return. Here are a few suggestions to assist your child during this difficult time:

- Try to spend lots of quality time with your child (alone time with each child if you have more than one child) prior to departure.
- Answer all questions (even the tough ones) about your departure and time of separation to the best of your ability. Children can deal with more than we think if we are honest with them.
- Make a point to listen to your child, as fears or concerns may be minimized through lots of talk.
- Capture memories in photos, songs, drawings, and stories before you leave.
- Practice communicating as if from long distances to provide assurance that you can (if you will be able to) keep in touch. For example, send your children letters through the mail or by e-mail, and tell them that this is what they can expect while you are gone.
- Write postdated notes and letters that can be mailed by another parent or family member if you will be out of reach during your mission.
- Keep home routines and rules as consistent as possible during deployment stages.

Remember that you are not alone. We are here to help you in as many ways as possible. Please let us know if you need assistance with any of the above suggestions. We are a phone call, visit, or e-mail away.

Sincerely,

Stage Three:
Homecomings and Reunions

Anticipation of a parent returning home after deployment can be exciting as well as a time of uncertainty for military children. A post-deployment reunion brings much joy to the family but at the same time can disrupt the rhythm that was created in the absence of one or both parents. Routines have been established that now have to be renegotiated or changed, and roles that were taken over by certain family members may now have to be relinquished to the returning parent.

Parents who have been deployed often have to get to know their children all over again, as they have been gone for many months, and sometimes over a year. Birthdays have been celebrated, and for some fathers, new babies have been born in their absence. New dads may feel uneasy if they are becoming a parent for the first time, especially since they were absent during the pregnancy and birth. Other parents may find that the trust and closeness they had with their children before deployment can take time to reestablish upon reentry into the family. Children may need time to warm up to their post-deployed parents.

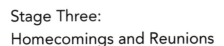

Working with Kids during Homecomings and Reunions

You can aid in the homecomings for military parents and children by taking these steps:

Prepare photo albums with pictures of the deployed parents, and share them with the children often prior to the homecoming.

Provide special activities that include the parents who have returned, such as parent and child lunches or picnics.

Understand that the children may experience behavioral changes once the active-duty parents have returned, and they may require more listening or holding time.

Give the children the words to express these new feelings, such as, "I know that you are feeling happy and upset, and it's okay."

Offer free parenting classes on basic child development that will remind or inform parents of what can be expected of children at different ages and stages, especially when children have relapsed into a former stage.

Encourage parents to talk with their children about the new changes and any new rules.

Location, Location: Home for the Military Child

The lifestyle of most military kids can be more mobile than what civilian kids experience; they may move many times or watch one or both parents leave and return during their time of service. Their home life and the location of their home may vary as well. If military children have parents who are on active duty, they may live on or near military installations, but not necessarily. If their parents are in the Reserves, they might live in towns and cities that are far away from the nearest military installation.

When Kids Live on or near an Installation

There are three main types of child care for families on or near military installations. Child development centers, school-age care programs, and family child care are the triangle of care settings that service men and women have come to rely on. While these are not the only types of care, they tend to be used the most often and are vital to military fami-

lies on a daily basis. Before they are old enough for school, children who live on military installations may attend child care for a fee. If there is no school on the installation, children attend school off the installation in a Department of Defense School or a local public or private school.

CHILD DEVELOPMENT CENTERS

Child development centers, or CDCs, on U.S. military installations worldwide are some of the best in the world, as a great number of them are accredited by the National Association for the Education of Young Children (NAEYC) and meet much more than the minimum standards imposed by a state agency. Many military families depend on these centers to provide the secure base that is so critical to their family's well-being. It is within these child care centers that caring teachers, directors, trainers, cooks, janitorial staff, program directors, administrators of family member programs, and many others take personal interest in ensuring that every child is cared for during separations. Whether it is a typical daily parting, a PCS (permanent change of station or installation), a TDY (temporary duty at a location other than a permanent duty station), or deployment, which can last for months or even more than a year, providers at military CDCs understand what a child is experiencing, as they are often the spouses of service men and women. It has also been my experience that they have some of the best training available; child development trainers often work alongside teachers.

SCHOOL-AGE CARE

Children in kindergarten and early elementary grades living on or near an installation go home to be with an older sibling or to an after-school program until a parent can come for them. Many military installations are affiliated with Boys and Girls Clubs of America to provide programs and support for schoolagers. In short, it isn't necessary for the military school-age child to return to an empty home after a school day. Quality care is often available "just around the corner" in a facility designed for children.

FAMILY CHILD CARE

Some parents seek lower child-to-provider ratios and the privacy and close-knit networking of family child care homes. Military family child care homes can be found on and off installations and have rigorous expectations for quality care, just as in quality accredited child care centers. Trained family child care professionals as well as outside parent educators work together in many areas of the country to provide research-based curricula focused on best practices in child growth and development (including guidance issues) as well as school readiness.

Relocation: When Military Kids Have to Move

Military kids' lives parallel the lives of nonmilitary kids in many ways, but when schoolagers talk about the biggest challenges of being a military kid, they often say, "I wish we didn't have to move so much!" or "I miss my friends at my last base." Children may not be equipped to cope with the drastic changes typical of the military career. Consistency and following established routines are critical to children's well-being and feelings of security. But when relocation occurs often, as it can with military kids, routines may be challenged and are often disrupted altogether.

Think about your ordinary day or week and all of the relationships and resources that you may take for granted: neighborhoods, child care, schools, playgrounds, parks, dry cleaners, restaurants, medical care, dental care, community groups, entertainment, etc. When relocating, all of those must be left behind. Families may sustain their personal relationships, but not in the same manner, and meanwhile they need to find new medical care, child care, and other essential services. Each basic resource that has to be replaced represents a loss, and children—just like their parents—have to find ways to adjust. In fact, the longer children have been in one place having secure attachments and positive experiences, the more difficult it is for them to move. The comfort and security of familiar things such as their soccer team, a dance studio, or their favorite restaurant may be all that the children have known, and the more parents involve the children in planning the upcoming move, the better they will be able to accept it.

Relocating typically involves three stages, and each stage offers opportunities for you to engage the children in your care:

1. Pack-out—the initial stages of packing and making preparations for the move. Provide backpacks and small suitcases in the dramatic play area.
2. The trip from one location to another—often involving air and land travel. Provide books and maps about states and countries that house installations.
3. New location (on or off an installation)—often involving living in temporary quarters on an installation. Set up a dramatic play area that resembles a temporary housing apartment.

Here are some activities you can use to assist military children with their own departure and reentry.

STRATEGIES

Pack-Out

Encourage parents to allow children to help pack their own belongings so they can decide what to take with them personally as well as what can be packed and shipped. Many relocations or moves involve moving companies that pack belongings for the family and then ship them to the next destination. This process can take weeks, depending on whether it is within the United States or in another country. Children will appreciate having a few favorite toys and other belongings with them during the move.

Welcome Wagon

Encourage the children in your care to welcome kids who are arriving:

- E-mail or otherwise contact kids as soon as you know they are coming. Welcome them or their parents (for infants and toddlers) through letters or e-mail.

- Send the family pictures of your program and the kids in the program.

- Add the child's name to visible spaces, such as the birthday bulletin board and his cubby once the child's arrival date is known.

- Assign a buddy or mentor for the incoming kid(s) or new parents, someone who knows the program and can show the new child and his family around and answer questions.

My Friends around the Globe

Use pushpins on a world map to help kids locate their friends and family around the world.

Cooking around the World

Have kids help create a cookbook of recipes from the cultures and countries in which they have lived. Include foods commonly found where you live. The recipes can be retrieved from friends left behind at another installation or found in cookbooks and on Web sites. The kids can help prepare dishes from the cookbook or schedule a taste fair at which many of the recipes can be tried. You can also use cookbooks and taste fairs as fund-raisers for special trips or projects.

Self-Publishing (for Preschoolers and Schoolagers)

Have school-age children write their own books, and have preschoolers write with your assistance. They can tell their military life stories while you record them and then they can illustrate them. These books can be self-published for parents, providers, and other children to read, or the child may wish to keep it as a private and personal reflection. This activity can span several days, weeks, or a whole year.

Here are some ideas to get started with this project. It isn't necessary to complete all the pages. Have the kids pick and choose which ones they would like to try. They may think of additional topics for pages as well.

> Page 1: My family . . .
>
> Page 2: I was born . . .
>
> Page 3: Friends I've known . . .
>
> Page 4: What I do for fun . . .
>
> Page 5: Most days I feel . . .
>
> Page 6: I wish that . . .
>
> Page 7: When I grow up . . .
>
> Page 8: If I could change the world, I would . . .
>
> Page 9: My mom's job . . .
>
> Page 10: My dad's job . . .
>
> Page 11: I wish that people understood . . .
>
> Page 12: My pet . . .
>
> Page 13: My favorite holiday is . . .
>
> Page 14: This is me . . .

Pen Pals (for Schoolagers)

Have older children keep in touch with children who have relocated to other installations or whose military parents have been discharged. E-mail and postal mail are both appropriate.

Plan My Move

Plan My Move is an online tool that service members and their families can use to help the relocation process. Plan My Move acts as both a support structure and an information channel. Go to the Department of Defense Military Homefront Web site at http://apps.mhf.dod.mil and search for "Plan My Move."

_____

When Kids Don't Live on an Installation: National Guard and Reservist Kids

Children of military families who attend schools other than those sponsored by the Department of Defense have lives that are very similar to children in nonmilitary families. They live off the installation in regular housing, their parents don't need special permission or a military ID to enter their neighborhood or town, and they don't live within the fences of a military installation that is protected by armed guards. Children living off installations experience a kind of isolation different from what children living on an installation endure. Their homes may not be located in remote or secluded areas, but they are affected by their parents' departure every bit as much as children living on installations. Their stress, anxiety, anger, and grief are as real to them as to children who live on installations a few hundred yards from a runway where planes take off and land routinely.

Children whose parents are in the Reserves need the same kind of special attention and treatment that children who live on or near a military installation need. The effects of a parent's departure are often unrecognized and may be misunderstood by civilian providers who are in nonmilitary areas and towns.

COMMUNITY-BASED CHILD DEVELOPMENT CENTERS

Tight-knit support groups are evident on and near military installations, but they tend to be missing in remote towns and areas where reservists live and depart from when deployed. Child care centers on installations offer an extra layer of support for military families. But when reservists' families are affected by deployment and their children become "suddenly military," providers may be unaware that a parent is departing. Make it a point to ask about deployment probability on your applications for child care, in newsletters, in electronic and regular communications with parents, and in casual conversations each day. Let parents know that you are willing to be a resource for them and someone who will recognize and appreciate what they and their children are going through. Maybe extra hugs are needed during the week that Mommy deploys; an extra stuffed toy, blanket, or pillow will be needed at naptime.

As a professional care provider, you can maintain a sense of order and predictability for parents and children that will positively influence the way they respond to the hardship of deployment. Use the strategies in this book to assure reservist families that you are committed to helping children during this difficult time.

SCHOOL-AGE CARE

You have the opportunity to respond to reservists' children in your care by using the same developmentally appropriate responses that you already use with children from nonmilitary families. Take care to respond to each child individually, and become a keen observer of his actions each day. Keep the lines of communication open with the primary caregiver to prevent feelings of isolation during this challenging time. As the child looks forward to a homecoming of her deployed parent, take time to share that emotion and to make tangible objects or visuals to aid the child in knowing when the parent will return.

Avoid dismissing the struggles that reservists' children face just because they do not participate in military installation life. Their sense of loss is every bit as real as other military kids' feelings. If you take time to acknowledge those feelings, respond to their questions, and allow them to talk about the events as they absorb them, reservists' children will be able to positively make sense of deployment.

Also, your expertise will go a long way in helping their primary caregivers to assist the child in their care. If children need professional help, talk with the primary caregivers, and have tangible, observed data on hand for them to use as they seek help.

FAMILY CHILD CARE

Family child care providers build close bonds with the parents of the children in their care, even during deployment. Use deployment to continue building these relationships by offering thoughtful, sympathetic, and supportive care. Ask the primary caregiver for regular updates on the deployed parent. Share your daily and weekly schedule so that the primary caregiver can know you have stability in your program. Make it a point to keep your program filled with daily routines and rituals; predictability helps children to feel safe and to experience less stress.

CHAPTER TWO

Offering Emotional Support

Many children under the age of eight are living in military families in which one or both parents are deployed. Military jobs can be some of the most dangerous in the world, and the risks that military parents face can take a toll on their children, bringing much stress and anxiety. Excessive crying (at all ages), clinginess, stomachaches and unexplained pains, and lack of impulse control are a few symptoms of stressed behaviors. Military children need emotional support from family members, friends, care providers, and teachers.

We must respond to the stress that these children experience by supporting their emotional development, thereby helping them form positive relationships with others, feel good about themselves, and develop self-esteem so that throughout childhood and beyond they can live happy and healthy lives.

Emotional Support at Different Ages and Stages (Birth through Age Eight)

Children can grow up to lead successful lives, even if separated during childhood from one or both parents by deployment. Babies will thrive when you willingly and positively accept them into your care. We can encourage preschoolers to share their feelings with us so that they gain confidence and develop trust in adults. Schoolagers can flourish and succeed in school when they are supported emotionally by the adults who care for them as well as by peers in friendly and responsive environments.

You can provide emotional support through responsive interactions that foster secure attachments and by providing a healthy environment that includes predictable routines and rituals. You can also offer an emotion-centered curriculum with enriched play opportunities in which children are free to be emotionally expressive as they play. Their activities "become sources of curiosity, excitement, and sometimes frustration" (Hyson 2003, 5) as the children express their emotions. For example, you can turn a play episode at the sand table into an opportunity for children to express emotions by being accepting, responding positively, and modeling respect for the emotions expressed in children's conversations. Your awareness of children's emotional responses in ordinary play helps them develop positive attitudes about the environment.

Secure Attachments

Children will develop strong attachments to adults who provide positive, caring environments where emotional development is encouraged. Important people in the child's life make her feel safe and loved, even in the absence of her parents. Children

of military parents may experience periods of being in limbo or transition due to reassignment and relocations, which place them in new care environments, schools, and communities. Lifestyles and familiar relationships can change overnight as their parents are called up for duty on short notice. For this reason, consistency in caregivers is necessary for children to have the sense of security that will help them cope successfully with separations.

Parents can develop a secure base for their child to go back to after experiencing the outside world. The military installation or child care setting itself can also provide a place of shelter from harm, fear, and distress in times of separation and deployment. In the case of military children, the secure base can be provided by at least one caring and responsive adult who provides care in the absence of the parents.

Many children don't adjust to new situations easily, and attachment between an adult and a child is a gradual process that may take weeks or months to occur. In these situations, you can stimulate or foster attachment with the child by doing some of the following:

- Provide a warm and trusting environment with consistent routines and rules.
- Respond quickly, consistently, and lovingly to children.
- Provide environments where loud, disruptive noises are absent and children feel safe and secure.
- Provide one-on-one interactions by singing, playing rhyming games, talking, listening, and cuddling.
- Model appropriate behaviors of kindness, generosity, and respect for children and for other adults.
- Avoid propping bottles when feeding babies or leaving older kids unattended while they are eating.
- Smile often, make lots of eye contact, and use gentle touches.

- Use routine care times—such as diapering, feeding, and bathing—to talk to infants and toddlers.
- Avoid overstimulating the child with too many activities without periods of rest or sleep.
- Identify an adult to be the primary daily care provider.

Children who show strong signs of attachment will usually engage in playful interactions with caring adults. They love to be held, hugged, or spoken to and will normally initiate activities to engage you. They come to you easily and willingly and appear to be comfortable in your care. A sense of trust is evident, and prolonged and excessive crying is absent.

There are signs that indicate a child is having a hard time attaching to another adult. If babies refuse to make eye contact, prefer not to be held or do not interact with you, and are extremely undemanding, these may be signs of a lack of attachment. The "too good" baby may fit in this category—the one who shows little emotion and does not cry, even when hungry or wet. Older unattached children may prefer to play or be alone rather than interact with other children or adults. This is not to be confused with separation anxiety, a kind of distress that infants commonly show before they understand that a parent or loved one will return.

Emotionally Supportive Environments for Babies

Emotionally supportive environments include predictable routines and play opportunities with caring and responsive providers. One way to create a healthy environment is to become an intentional and attentional caregiver (Epstein 2007) by following an effective infant/toddler curriculum. You provide the support, and babies will provide the wonder. Intentional caring or teaching comes from knowing the developmental stage of each child individually and acting on that knowledge by providing an environment that promotes attentional caring, or care that purposefully observes and gives

attention to little ones. Babies have the ability to think and learn as early as birth, and you can learn from the children you care for and increase the quality of care you provide to new heights. Babies initiate a kind of accord or harmony with their caregivers, and your program's curriculum should be built around their needs. Gone are the days when child care meant routine care only. Make the environment one that has learning spaces organized around the young child. Everything that a baby experiences from the moment you receive him to the moment he leaves with his parent or primary caregiver can have purpose.

Emotionally Supportive Environments for Preschoolers

Emotionally supportive environments address the whole child and are developmentally appropriate (Copple and Bredekamp 2009), providing important curricular experiences on a daily basis. Music and movement, math, science, social studies, science and technology, as well as nutrition are mainstays—but emotional health and safety are at the heart of an emotion-centered curriculum (Hyson 2003) for preschoolers. It is carefully planned and implemented based on the needs of the individual children in care. Teachers are well trained and child-to-provider ratios are low enough to allow for lots of conversations with children about what they are going through.

Between the ages of three and four, most children have some ideas about war and may be able to talk about them. Each child, at her own level, can be helped to understand the dangers of war and her feelings about losing a parent to deployment. In an emotionally supportive environment, adults answer questions freely and honestly without giving too much information, which can be overwhelming or even frightening. War is a difficult topic to address openly with children: you may fear telling them too much or scaring them, but children appreciate honest answers from adults, even if the answers are tough to hear. Honest answers can sound like this: "I know that war is scary. I'm scared sometimes too. But your mommy and daddy are doing everything they can to be safe." Or, "I am here with you to keep you safe, and your mom has people with her to keep her safe." It is even okay to say, "I don't know the answer, but we can try to find it together."

Millie, a four-year-old whose father was deployed as a Navy Seal, constantly asked her grandmother when her daddy was coming home. Her grandmother responded, "It's hard to know when your daddy will get off work because of his job, but we know that he will be home as soon as he can. Let's write him a letter and let him know how much we miss him."

Sometimes adults aren't sure if it is okay to bring up the subject of war or deployment if kids don't ask. You may think children don't need to know information or won't think about the war if you don't talk about it. Yet such silence can be dangerous to a child's well-being because it is misleading. Many children can't express their fears in words but will welcome your sincere and straightforward approach to discussing sensitive topics. It is a good idea to discuss possible approaches to delicate is-

sues before the parent deploys (if possible). Let parents know that you will be using an honest approach, answering what their children ask and giving them enough information to calm their fears. You may not share military parents' beliefs about the job they do. Different political viewpoints are fine, but it's always important to support the warriors and their children, even if you don't support the war.

Emotionally Supportive Environments for Schoolagers

War is still a difficult concept to understand, even for older children. Schoolagers may be at the age where they are forming their own opinions about violence and do not agree with the jobs their parents do. You are responsible for listening to them and helping them resolve their emotional conflicts as they try to support their parents while not understanding why they had to go away. You do not always have to have an answer, but it's important that you have time for them. Teaching patriotism may help kids understand why it is necessary to protect our country and how important the job their parents do is. There may never be agreement about the politics of war, but we certainly want to support our military children and their family members by respecting the decisions their parents made to join the military.

Teaching Kids Patriotism

Patriotism means different things to different people, but most would agree that it is about having an appreciation and love for one's country. Children of military parents are often exposed to acts of patriotism very early, and it is part of their emotional self-esteem to feel proud of their parents and the job they do for our country. Although children sometimes have difficulty understanding patriotism because it is such an intangible concept, there are lots of tangible activities they can do to further their understanding. Bike parades with child-made flags and decorations, flag making, and writing stories about our country and why we love it are a few of the ways that we can show our patriotism with children. Other projects such as singing patriotic songs or listening to patriotic music during routine times, learning about National History Day, and exploring the emblems that we use in the United States can further a child's knowledge of our country.

The following strategies for developing patriotism are for schoolagers, but they can be adapted for younger children as well. Strategies may include military parents; family members, such as uncles, aunts, cousins, and grandparents; and friends who are important to the military child.

STRATEGIES

Where Does My Family Member or Friend Work?

This activity highlights the person and emphasizes the idea that military men and women are doing a job—just like truck drivers, doctors, teachers, and factory workers. Military personnel work in many different places and do many different jobs—on ships, on jet planes, on land, in submarines, and in buildings. Ask children to draw, paint, sculpt, or write a story about where their military parent, family member, or friend works.

Someone I Know Works in the Military

Provide paper, markers, colored pencils, and other supplies for making portraits. Ask children to draw a portrait of someone they know who is working in the military, such as a parent, grandparent, uncle, aunt, cousin, friend, or neighbor. Provide frames for the portraits made from mat board or posterboard.

Hooray for the USA

Have children create a timeline of the United States and the battles that have been fought to preserve it. Take several months to complete this project, discussing each event and representing events in storytelling, drawings, and role playing.

Our Flag

Provide red, white, and blue paint or markers and rectangular paper. Talk about the colors in our flag and the number of stripes (thirteen, one for each original colony). The colors are the same as those of the British flag that was flown before Betsy Ross sewed the first flag for our country in 1776. The first flag had thirteen five-pointed stars, and a star was added after each state became a part of the United States (we now have fifty).

Our History

- Have children research specific topics from the history of the United States on the Internet or in a local library. For example, children could research the history of the military, the history of flight (from barnstormers to missiles), or the history of lawmaking. Use Web sites such as www.kids.gov and www.pbskids.org.

- Read the Declaration of Independence, and discuss it. Why do we need one? Can you write a new one for today's times?

- Read the Bill of Rights (the first ten amendments to the Constitution), and talk about the rights we have today. If it were written today, would it read the same?

Family Tree

Get families involved by creating a family tree with each child; talk about how their families first came to America or were already here.

Veterans Day

- Build children's self-esteem by sponsoring a "Take a Veteran to School Day." All children love to have their parents involved in their daily activities. When the deployed parent is home on leave or has returned from deployment, make arrangements to have him or her come to school.

- Read books and stories about Veterans Day, such as *Veterans Day* by Jacqueline Cotton (2002), *Pepper's Purple Heart: A Veterans Day Story* by Heather French Henry (2004), and *Veterans Day* by Robin Nelson (2005).

- For more information, visit the History Channel's Take a Veteran to School Day Web site, www.veterans.com, and the History Channel's classroom resources Web site, www.history.com.

Peaceful Classrooms and Environments

In supportive environments, adults model peacefulness. Because military children are exposed to war more often than most children, it is extremely important to counter those experiences with peaceful ones. To military children, a report of violence and war in the news is not just about someone else; it could very well be about a deployed parent or the parent's unit. Peaceful environments help children feel safe. Adults model peacefulness by treating each other with a kindness and respect children can imitate. Kids will also see that peace is valued. When the environment is safe, children can go about their business of play, trying out new ideas, taking risks, and making discoveries. They know they can honestly share their fears with you, even when it is difficult. Children will learn to solve problems, make good choices, and have self-control in a peaceful environment when your actions and words become a model for them. As you act peacefully, they will learn to trust you and know that you are always there for them to talk about anything.

Diane Levin, author of *Teaching Young Children in Violent Times* (2003, 8), refers to the peaceable classroom as a place where "children learn how to live together in a respectful and empowering classroom community," where "trust and safety, responsibility, mutual respect, and cooperation are woven into all aspects of the classroom." When a sense of community is built between military families and schools, family child care providers, or child care centers, children benefit. When important adults resolve conflicts peacefully, children will understand that the violence of war should never be the first response to a conflict. The jobs that military parents do as service members are honorable and deserving of respect but can also be difficult to explain. One military dad describes it like this: "I want my children to see me as a peacekeeper as well as a peacemaker. Those are my most important values. I know they will encounter others who see me as something else, but I do the job that I do because I believe in peace."

Here are some other ideas for building a peaceful environment:

- Avoid using biased terms.
- Have sharing times built into the daily routine.
- Encourage children to bring things from home that will make them feel more securely connected between home and school, such as photos of their family, special toys, or blankets.
- Make a peace table where children can go to "talk it out" when they have disagreements.
- Give children lots of opportunities to make choices.
- Play music that is peaceful in nature, such as *Sweet Dreams: The O'Neill Brothers' Piano Lullabies.*
- Allow children to talk about disturbing news that they have heard or seen in the media. Provide a "Peace Talk" time each day when any subject is okay to bring up.
- Use puppets and role playing as aids to approach tough topics.

Some children are natural-born peacemakers, and some children need lots of encouragement in resolving conflicts. Keep conversations going about why people go to war and how peace should always be our first strategy or option.

Teaching Tolerance

Parents across America hope to keep their children sheltered from the effects of war, but military kids live under the umbrella of war on a daily basis. Whether or not it is being discussed, they know that one or both parents are involved in a job that often deals with violence, and violence can mean trauma or loss. You can adopt a policy of teaching tolerance so that children can feel supported when their lives are disrupted and they are faced with the tragedies of war.

Regardless of your personal beliefs about war, it's important to teach children to be tolerant of one another. One idea is to develop a plan so that all the children in your care can support and assist one another during stressful times, such as separation from their parents during deployment. You can teach tolerance to the children in your care in the following ways:

- Encourage nonmilitary kids to show support for military children by preparing hero packs (see chapter 9 for details) or writing letters to a military child's deployed parent.
- Offer special times when all children can work cooperatively on projects, such as learning about common deployment locations or useful phrases in languages that are spoken where parents are deployed. Also, have nonmilitary and military children share stories about the work their parents do.
- Aid transitions from military installation care to off-installation care by planning outings with military and nonmilitary children and families. Ask the military families to share their experiences with different languages and cultures from the places where they've lived.

STRATEGIES

Understanding Conflict Game (for Schoolagers)

Have kids think of conflicts they have experienced or witnessed and write them on index cards. They can describe times when they were bullied, rules were broken, or they were treated badly. Encourage peacemaking skills by talking through the conflict or having kids share how they felt when someone was being mistreated or they were being mistreated. When kids disagree, help them come up with a compromise. Also, encourage them to make a peace promise that details how they will respond when they are mistreated or witness someone else being mistreated in the future. For example, the peace promise could state that they would honor each others' views. Each kid would then sign it, agreeing to find peaceable solutions to problems. As a visual reminder, create a peacemaking poster with the following actions:

- Talk it out.
- Compromise.
- Make a peace promise.

Divide children into small groups. One person takes the index card and reads it, and then the whole group uses the peacemaking poster to resolve the issue by choosing one of the actions from the poster.

Emotional Support and Bias

Bias can occur when a person lacks understanding or is critical of or takes action against another person because of her racial or ethnic background, religious preference, physical ability, socioeconomic class, linguistic background, gender, or sexual orientation (Byrnes and Kiger 2005). Military children often live in more culturally diverse societies than other children. As many military families live around the world, on and off military installations, their children are often exposed to customs and cultures that are different from those in the United States. Most military children living abroad attend child care on the installation or at Department of Defense Schools; they do not attend schools with the children from the region where their installation is located. This prevents children from becoming a part of the society and can cause bias and misunderstanding of someone else's values and customs.

Children who live in countries where war is ongoing are often targets of bias from American kids, including those from military and nonmilitary families. Keep your emotionally supportive environment bias free by helping children discover how they are similar and different from children in other cultures, societies, and lands. Find common threads or bonds among children by helping them learn about each other's cultural heritages and the various holidays and traditions they celebrate. Your modeling of respect for all people will go a long way toward helping children condemn bias and prejudice. Children learn so much by watching our everyday behavior. We have the ability to set examples that will in turn help the children in our care to stamp out bias.

STRATEGIES

Limit Bias

- Help children appreciate differences and diversity and view them positively.
- Challenge unfair practices and beliefs.
- Confront difficult issues rather than avoid them.
- Make your classroom or environment reflective of every child who is in your care. Post photographs of children with their family members.
- Invite parents and other family members to share their cultures and customs with all the children.
- Avoid tokenism, which occurs by only displaying pictures of people from outside your classroom cultures. Also, avoid bringing in artifacts or materials from other cultures just

to provide "multiculturalism." Make each lesson authentic and culturally relevant to the kids in your care.

- Develop a peace pledge with kids in which they promise not to hurt others.

For more information on antibias and culturally relevant activities, see Tamar Jacobson's *Confronting Our Discomfort: Clearing the Way for Anti-Bias in Early Childhood* (2003), Stacey York's *Roots and Wings: Affirming Culture in Early Childhood Programs* (2003), and Ellen Wolpert's *Start Seeing Diversity: The Basic Guide to an Anti-Bias Curriculum* (2005).

Teaching Kids to Prevent Bullying

Behaviors such as bullying can compromise the supportive environment for military children. Military children are often the targets of bullying because of controversies over U.S. participation in war. Children who bully do not routinely suffer from low self-esteem, as was once thought. Bullying occurs because of a lack of impulse control, a need for power and control, a need to feel smarter, and heightened risk-taking behaviors (Sanders and Phye 2004). Although boys are seen as bullies more often than girls, relational aggression is common in girls today. Just as we practice a "no labeling" policy of children in other aspects of behavior, it is also important to refrain from labeling kids as bullies. Address the bullying behavior instead.

Bullying behavior includes punching or shoving, calling names, negative teasing, spreading rumors, and generally preventing someone from joining a group of their peers. It most often starts with verbal abuse but soon escalates to physical abuse if unattended.

If you see that a child is the target of any of these behaviors or is skipping school without reason, consider whether bullying is occurring. Bullying is actually a form of child abuse and should be treated similarly. Preschool children have refused to go to school or child care because someone is teasing, hitting, or calling them names. Teasing is common among schoolagers but becomes a type of bullying if harm is intended.

In order to prevent or at least reduce bullying, you can take these steps:

- Start a bully behavior prevention club that teaches peacemaking and cooperation. Help all children to recognize bullying behaviors that they may have engaged in themselves. Bullies are not bad; bullying behavior is!
- Insist that children tell you, another adult, or an older sibling if they are being bullied (just as in child abuse).
- Arm them with key phrases to use if bullied, such as, "Cut it out, Stephen," and tell them they can always walk away.
- Have children stay in a group rather than be alone if there is a chance they may be bullied.
- Tell them to stay calm. Bullies gain more power if a child gets upset.
- Assure them that you will do something about it.
- Read books such as *The Recess Queen* by Alexis O'Neill (2002) that address bullying at school and give courage to those being bullied.

Emotional Intelligence and Resiliency

Children who have emotional intelligence show more empathy toward others, have better cooperating behaviors, and appear to be more caring. They practice pro-social behaviors, have lots of friends, and have fewer incidents of violence and risky behaviors.

Daniel Goleman's 1995 book *Emotional Intelligence* popularized the concept of emotional intelligence. Children with high intelligence quotients (IQs) and low emotional quotients (EQs) are at risk for bullying, antisocial, and noncooperative behaviors in general. Children with high EQs tend to become more productive citizens and have lots of friends throughout their lives, regardless of their IQ. Goleman says that we as teachers, family members, and providers can coach our children to resolve conflicts creatively by helping them to understand the stressors that cause them to be frustrated, angry, sad, out of control, impulsive, and hurtful to others. The results are improved sharing, more tolerance for those different from themselves, better self-control, and improvement in social skills, to name a few.

How can we foster emotional intelligence in our children?

- Help kids build a vocabulary for their feelings. If they can recognize and label their emotions, they can take steps to change them.
- Help kids feel proud of their accomplishments. Showcase or highlight their accomplishments in newsletters, on bulletin boards and posters, and in personal notes to them.
- Help kids build empathy to understand or take the perspective of others.
- Teach kids to "self-talk" or manage their feelings by "catching" the feelings before they act on them.
- "Coach" emotional intelligence just as you would if you were coaching T-ball or soccer. Make a plan that includes steps to succeed.

It won't happen at the first practice, but with time and effort, emotional intelligence can be developed.

Resilient Children

Children who possess resiliency are those who show hardiness and persistence as they overcome difficulties in life—even in the midst of the most challenging obstacles, such as separation from or loss of a loved one. In everyday events, resiliency is observed in children who bounce back easily, ask for help, set goals and accomplish them, share their feelings, and are aware of their abilities. They appear to have Teflon coating that keeps challenges from overtaking them, and they are able to bend and stretch like a rubber band in the midst of adversity. In other words, they can keep going even in hard times.

Resiliency can be taught. With certain tools or skills, children can become resilient even if they are not ordinarily strong or hardy.

STRATEGIES

Stretching

Provide large rubber bands for the children. Stretch the bands, and watch them go back to their original state. Talk about resiliency: we may be stretched when we encounter something that is hard for us to grasp or understand, but if we can go back to our original shape or condition, we are resilient.

Developing Resiliency

To help children become more resilient, do one or more of these activities every day:

- Read stories about courage such as *The Little Engine That Could* by Watty Piper (2005) or *The Diary of Anne Frank* (Frank 1973). Talk about how the characters were courageous and how we show signs of courage every day.
- Model resiliency. Show kids that you can face challenges and carry on. Share stories about how you faced challenges and overcame them.
- Be there for them. Be a good listener, and practice key phrases of encouragement such as, "You really know how to comfort your little brother when he is sad," or "Look how brave you are being while your mom is away!"

Courage Necklaces or Bracelets

Provide wooden beads and stringing material for each child. Add a bead to the string each time they are courageous or show resiliency. Have them describe the act every time they add a bead.

Talking about Resiliency

Invite parents and other community members to talk about what has made them resilient and how they have overcome challenges in their lives.

Make a book about famous people or people who are heroes to the children—it may be the parents of military children or other family members who have shown the most resiliency in the children's eyes. Add quotes and photos as well as stories about the heroes.

Stories of Courage

Schoolagers can write their own stories of courage about deployed family members and friends. Provide a Web site such as a blog or wiki (see chapter 8 for information on blogs and wikis) to chronicle their personal stories. Read to younger children picture books about courageous acts such as:

> *Little Owl* by Piers Harper (2004)
>
> *I'm Gonna Like Me: Letting Off a Little Self-Esteem* by Jamie Lee Curtis (2002)
>
> *Little Quack* by Lauren Thompson (2003)
>
> *The Story of Ruby Bridges* by Robert Coles (2004)
>
> *Stuart's Cape* by Sara Pennypacker (2004)

Routines and Rituals

Supportive environments foster resiliency and include consistent and predictable yet flexible routines. These routines are especially important during a difficult time like deployment. Establish stability

for children of all ages by following a reliable and dependable schedule.

Provide schedules that alternate active and passive activities throughout the day. Predictable and stable environments help children to become less stressed and to feel safe. For example, for infants and toddlers, alternate floor time and outdoor time (active) with mealtime or bottle feeding and crib time (passive) to prevent fussiness or excess crying. Take note of the number of passive and active routines that occur throughout the day, and adjust the schedule to fit the needs of the children in your care. When necessary, passive times, like transitioning between activities, can be converted to active times. Hang mobiles safely out of arm's reach over the diaper changing area to focus the baby's attention while you're doing routine care. Sing familiar songs or make up your own lyrics to familiar tunes.

Babies are always communicating their needs, and attentive caregivers can become experts at reading a baby's signals for more or less passive and active moments. A sample daily schedule for infants and toddlers that provides alternating active and passive activities is provided on the following pages. Review your own schedule to ensure that each type of routine is included in the child's day.

Sample Daily Schedule for Infants and Toddlers

MAIN ACTIVITY	ENHANCEMENTS TO ACTIVITY	ATTENTION / DOMAINS OF DEVELOPMENT	ACTIVE (A) PASSIVE (P)
Bottle/meal/ snack time	Talk to child; sing familiar songs; encourage self-feeding.	Language, cognitive, physical	P
Diaper changing time	Count toes and fingers, make eye contact, and move each arm and then each leg across the baby's midline* or the center of his body.	Physical, cognitive, language, social-emotional	P/A
Outside time (early or late in the day is better for sun safety)	Use cognitive concepts in talking with child, such as big, little, round, square, color, fast, slow; provide lots of physical activity by using swings, wheel toys, and open spaces to crawl, walk, or run.	Physical, cognitive	A
Transition time (diapering, toileting, hand washing, traveling, etc.)	Sing songs such as, "Row, Row, Row Your Boat" and change the lyrics to reflect the routine, for example, "Put, put, put the diaper on the baby Sam."	Physical, language	P/A
Naptime	Play soft music with and without lyrics; sing softly (songs that rhyme).	Cognitive, language	P
Floor time	Build towers of blocks or cubes (two to six blocks).	Physical, language, cognitive	A
Transition time	Walk or stroll between areas and count and sing nursery rhymes.	Physical, language, cognitive	P/A
Mealtime	Use placemats with shadows or outlines of familiar mealtime objects. Practice one-to-one correspondence with toddlers by talking about the objects and where they go on the placemats.	Language, cognitive	P
Diaper changing time	Count toes and fingers, make eye contact, and move arms and legs across the baby's midline.*	Physical, cognitive	P/A
Naptime	(See suggestions for first naptime, above.)	Physical	P
Transition time (washing hands or cleaning up)	Listen to music.	Cognitive, language	P/A

MAIN ACTIVITY	ENHANCEMENTS TO ACTIVITY	ATTENTION / DOMAINS OF DEVELOPMENT	ACTIVE (A) PASSIVE (P)
Snacktime	Count plates and napkins with toddlers; sing cleanup song; encourage child to feed self.	Cognitive, language, social-emotional	P/A
Floor time	Give simple directions for picking up an item and placing it in a spot; place lids on boxes and remove; place shapes in puzzles; provide textured puzzles for babies; initiate ball play.	Cognitive, language, physical	A
Transition time (departure, toileting, diaper changing)	Sing a good-bye song.	Social-emotional, language	P/A

* See chapter 4 for more about the importance of crossing the midline.

Extended family members often provide care for military children once parents are deployed. To support primary caregivers, you can begin new routines or continue former or familiar routines for military children. In supportive environments, rituals and routines provide reassurance and predictability, comfort, and a sense of control for children.

I watched as school-age children in a military installation program held a funeral for their pet hamster. A provider told me that the children, ages five to eight, had planned the funeral all by themselves. I listened as one child read a eulogy and several others told stories about the hamster. I asked the provider if this was a common occurrence, and she said, "Yes, we always allow the children to find their own ways to deal with loss. Not all the children came to the service, but that's okay too."

As you care for military children, consider whether you can incorporate any of the following rituals into your program. Allow children the opportunity to help in the planning process when possible, no matter how small a part they may play.

- birthday celebrations: making the cake, decorating, special excursions
- service projects: feeding the homeless, planting flower gardens, collecting gently used toys and clothes for a women and children's shelter
- Halloween: trick-or-treating, making costumes
- Veterans Day parades or Take a Veteran to School Day
- graduations
- funeral services or wakes; memorial services
- weddings
- seasonal celebrations

BEDTIME ROUTINES AND OVERNIGHT CARE

Military parents report that when they know their children are getting the rest they need and have consistent nighttime routines, they feel much better about being away from them. Bedtime can be challenging for those who provide overnight care. Deciding the perfect time for bed is based on a child's need for plenty of rest. Observe him carefully for several nights to see if there are "sleepy clues." Yawning, becoming glassy eyed, increased motor activity (running wild), or even "I'm sleepy!" are all signs. Once you've determined when the child's mood or tempo usually changes, allow an hour to perform a bedtime routine before the child actually goes to sleep.

It is difficult for young children to go to bed and leave the rest of the family "up" playing games, watching TV, and so forth. It is helpful to turn down all lights at a certain time and turn off the TV, music, etc., in order to transition to bedtime. Provide a warm bath with lavender-scented child-friendly soap, and lessen the number of toys for the nighttime bath, as it is the time to wind down. Playtime in the tub can be reserved for a morning or afternoon bath, and nighttime baths can be preludes to sleep. One care provider who cares for military children overnight has a toothbrush and toothpaste ready and gives it to the child to use while he's still in the tub. After a gentle drying with a soft towel and dressing him in comfortable pajamas, she turns down the bedroom lights, gives a quick massage, and reads soothing bedtime stories such as *Goodnight Moon* by Margaret Wise Brown (1991) and *Time for Bed* by Mem Fox (1997).

For older kids, use chapter books, but limit reading to one or two chapters each night. A list of appropriate chapter books for schoolagers is provided in appendix A at the end of this book. In order to induce sleep, one adult reads the same story to her young children every night. Another uses a timer and sets it an hour before bedtime. It provides a beginning and end time for the nighttime routine, and he says it works wonders for his preschoolers and schoolagers.

Make tucking-in time the final ritual. A grandmother pretends that the child's bed is a present, and she wraps the sheets around him, pretends to tape them, and then ties a bow with a final kiss on the cheek. An uncle takes his niece to the window at the same time each night as a final good-night ritual, and together they blow Mommy (his sister) a kiss wherever she is. When possible, Mommy blows them a kiss at the same time. A family child care provider allows a child to look at a small photo album each evening and say a prayer for each member of his family.

Whatever your bedtime routines and rituals may be, keeping them consistent and predictable will give children a sense of security that some things aren't changing, even if they have experienced a loss. You may also use some of the above routines for daytime naps. Naptime can be stressful, as children sometimes are reminded of their separation or loss when activities come to an end. See appendix A for bedtime and naptime books.

RITUALS

Rituals are time-honored traditions that families use to reinforce values or strengthen connections. They may not occur as often as routines, but they can be used to help foster a sense of security and constancy. Rituals are usually rooted in customs or celebrations that are specific to a family's culture or upbringing. Many military families use rituals to help children cope during deployment or separation; they allow children to predict certain events that will bring joy and excitement or to remember the special person who is away from home.

Rituals become more meaningful to children if the children have been encouraged to plan or perform their own ritual, either in addition to or in place of the adult's ritual. Extra meaning can be added to adult rituals if we explain the reasons for them and then allow children to design a ritual that is based on their understanding. For example, funerals are confusing for children, but if they are allowed to assist in the planning, whether for a lost parent or for a pet, appropriate levels of understanding and acceptance can occur.

Holidays and Celebrations

Holidays and celebrations are usually accompanied by important family rituals and can teach children about family values and traditions. Whether it's a Fourth of July picnic and parade, Cinco de Mayo festivities, or an Easter egg hunt, most families spend time together on a holiday, and children come to expect these breaks in everyday life. When family members are deployed, children appreciate it even more when we continue to celebrate their familiar customs such as birthdays and holidays. Every effort to keep things as similar to their pre-deployment lives as possible will reassure children that we care about what they like and need to do.

As you work with children from different backgrounds and cultures, honor the holidays and celebrations of each child. When planning holiday celebrations, consider the importance of the celebration to the children as well as the appropriateness of the activities. For example, celebration of holidays such as Mardi Gras may be unimportant to children who know nothing about its meaning or origin or whose family has not celebrated it in the past. Take a survey of military parents and children to find out which holidays are meaningful to them, and then plan accordingly. As long as celebrations are meaningful and have value for individual children, it's important to continue them during deployment. Avoid celebrating holidays or rituals that are unfamiliar to the youngest children in your care, just to follow a preestablished curriculum. NAEYC (1996) suggests asking the following questions when planning holiday celebrations:

- Should children learn about the particular holiday to be celebrated? Why is it important?
- Does it follow developmentally appropriate practices?
- Does the activity represent specific children and families who are present in the group?
- Have children had a chance to learn about the meaning and significance of the holiday to be celebrated?
- Do the holidays represent the diversity in the group?
- Are the needs of children who are not permitted to celebrate certain holidays for religious reasons recognized?
- Are all children honored at certain times of the year by celebrating holidays and traditions that are culturally meaningful to them?

Use the list on the next page to get started planning holidays appropriate for your group. The children in your care may celebrate other holidays that you can add to your calendar. You may also add birthdays of children and their parents or other important people in their lives.

Children can create their own holiday rituals for special times, such as preparing parades for parents who are being deployed or who are returning home. The celebrations should be planned and implemented by children, bridging home and school values and traditions.

Birthday Celebrations in a Parent's Absence

Deployed parents often miss their children's birthdays, and as we know, birthdays are important to most children. You can continue to create special birthday celebrations by planning activities, such as those that follow, to connect children with their deployed parents:

- Have an "unbirthday" party for children and deployed parents when the parent is home.
- Read birthday books such as *Happy Birthday, Thomas!* by Wilburt Awdry (1990) or *Happy Birthday to You* by Dr. Seuss (1959) on the child's birthday.
- Ask the deployed parent to leave a birthday wish for the child that you can give him on his birthday. For the deployed parent's birthday, help the child make a birthday wish on audio- or videotape, CD-ROM, or DVD, and/or have the child prepare a birthday drawing, poem, or handprint to mail to the deployed parent (unless for security reasons an e-mail or postal address is not available).
- Provide assistance in creating a family Web page where photos or messages can be posted often—especially on birthdays and holidays.

Emotional support is every bit as important to military children as the environments that we create for them. Many programs target language and cognitive activities while emotional support activities sometimes get less priority. As children strive to make sense of the separations they face during deployment, attention to the emotional literacy that can be found through play is fundamental. We explore this topic in the following chapter.

Common Holidays and Celebrations by Month

JANUARY	• New Year's Day (1st) • Japanese New Year (1st) • Martin Luther King Jr.'s birthday (16th—observed on the third Monday) • Chinese New Year (date varies according to Chinese lunar calendar)
FEBRUARY	• National Black History Month • Groundhog Day (2nd) • Mardi Gras or Fat Tuesday (the Tuesday forty-seven days before Easter Sunday; date varies according to Christian lunar calendar) • Valentine's Day (14th)
MARCH	• St. Patrick's Day (17th) • Easter (date varies according to Christian lunar calendar)
APRIL	• Passover (date varies according to Jewish lunar calendar) • Earth Day (22nd) • Take Daughters and Sons to Work Day (date varies; see www.daughtersandsonstowork.org) • Arbor Day (the last Friday)
MAY	• Mothers Day (second Sunday) • Cinco de Mayo (5th) • Armed Forces Day (third Saturday) • Memorial Day (last Monday)

JUNE	• Fathers Day (third Sunday) • Flag Day (14th) • Juneteenth (19th) • America's Kids Day (22nd)
JULY	• Independence Day (4th) • Parents Day (fourth Sunday)
AUGUST	• Ramadan (date varies according to Islamic lunar calendar)
SEPTEMBER	• Labor Day (first Monday) • Grandparents Day (first Sunday after Labor Day) • Patriot Day (11th) • Rosh Hashanah (Jewish New Year, date varies according to Jewish lunar calendar) • Yom Kippur (date varies according to Jewish lunar calendar)
OCTOBER	• Columbus Day (second Monday) • Halloween (31st)
NOVEMBER	• Thanksgiving (fourth Thursday) • Veterans Day (11th)
DECEMBER	• Hanukkah (eight days; dates vary according to Jewish lunar calendar) • Christmas (25th) • New Year's Eve (31st)

CHAPTER THREE

Promoting Play for Emotional Benefits

Helping Kids Understand Their Feelings

Children express their feelings and cope with stress through play, and play is often a healthy way for military children to work through their emotions. Emotionally supportive environments foster this practice. When children make a plan and carry out their own ideas through actions, they play. This can be supported through imaginary stories and situations they create, roles they act out, and rules of games they construct. Children have additional ideas about what play is: "It's fun!" "It's just what we do!" "I like to play every day!" Just mention the word *play* to a young child, and it brings the idea of something fun. But when children face challenges or even disruptions in play, they often turn to adults for help.

Play allows a child to act out her emotions and "make right" what is happening to her. Play has powerful emotional and social characteristics; it's important that you use it to capitalize on the time that children are with you. Foster positive play experiences that will support each child's emotional development. Around ages three or four, children begin social play by interacting with peers. In this stage, children initiate play with each other, sometimes cooperatively and sometimes uncooperatively. Their feelings are on display as they play, reenacting scenes from their own and their parents' lives. When adults encounter traumatic events, we often call a friend or family member to "vent" or debrief, but when young children experience the same events, they tend to act them out in dramatic play.

Observations of children during social play are critically important because they provide insight on the children's emotions. With this insight in mind, you can plan play opportunities that allow children to work through any negative feelings and offer environments that support health and emotional well-being.

Setting Up the Play Environment for Military Children

Set up a supportive play environment for military children by promoting as much interaction between children and adults as possible. Provide space for independent or solitary play as well as for turn taking and sharing opportunities. This will allow young children to practice social skills that are needed throughout life in a very natural way—through play.

The supportive play environment should include marked play spaces for whole group and individual play and for planned and spontaneous play. Bright airy spaces inside and lots of room outside encourage varied activities that promote social and emotional growth. Designated play spaces with areas for alone time as well as peer interactions are best. A "time away" center that houses favorite toys and games for a single child will keep children who need their own space from getting into trouble with peers. To understand this need, consider the difficulty in being housed in a single room with many other people, waiting turns for toys and attention from the one in charge. A time away center would be a welcome space. Children cannot be expected to act pro-socially hour after hour with no place for a personal time-out.

Age- and stage-appropriate toys and materials must be carefully selected, with duplicate toys for younger children and challenging toys for older children. A schedule that allows plenty of time to be creative and interact with peers is necessary. Young preschoolers as well as children in the school-age years need opportunities to become partners in planning their curriculum. It should not be done to them or for them but rather should include their ideas and selections. Consider holding group times when children are asked to assist in planning menus for snacks and meals as well as activities.

Learning or play centers are the most commonly planned areas in classrooms and spaces for young children. They are generally divided into the following centers for a child's cognitive development, but planning them around social-emotional development is key:

- math and manipulatives
- science discovery
- dramatic play
- listening
- art
- literacy
- motor development
- sensory
- computers/technology

Although other centers as well as variations on these themes do exist, these are the basic centers in which play in American preschools is supported. Infant and toddler environments may hold fewer centers, and school-age environments have additional centers such as homework and indoor gardening. Regardless of the concepts or themes that the play centers represent, social and emotional development should always be at the forefront of your planning.

To foster social and emotional development, include for each play space as many of the following ideas as possible:

- Include games and toys that allow children to work alone and with another peer to encourage problem solving.
- Provide materials that are open-ended or have more than one use or outcome in order

for children to create things based on their own feelings.

- Provide props in order for children to engage in high-quality dramatic play.
- Extend children's themes, providing language and vocabulary that are relevant to ongoing play scripts.
- Encourage sharing, cooperating, and turn taking in all play centers by placing side-by-side chairs at the computer, two sheets of paper on one side of the easel, and a timer at the listening and computer centers so turns can be taken at the sound of the timer bell.

Disrupted Play: Helping Kids Understand Their Feelings

Play is often disrupted because of a lack of problem-solving skills as well as low self-image in children of all ages. When children cannot understand the perspectives of others and identify their own feelings when playing, it is difficult for play to begin or continue. Nancy and Jamil's actual experience illustrates this point.

On the playground, four-year-olds Nancy and Jamil were playing. Nancy was sitting in the driver's seat of a child's tractor, and Jamil was pouring sand in-side, on the passenger seat. "Mr. Lee, he hit me," said Nancy. Jamil quickly replied, "Uh-huh, I did, 'cause she won't let me ride." "Are you okay, Nancy?" asked Lee. "I hit her," said Jamil again. "It hurts when you hit," responded Lee. "Can you think of another way to play without hitting?"

Jamil replied, "Nope, and when I get five I'm gonna beat her up." At that point, Aaron, another four-year-old, joined the discussion. "Jamil won't get off so that Nancy and me can ride." "Well, maybe we need to negotiate," said Lee. "What's 'gotiate?" asked Aaron. "That's when you figure out what you want and how to get it without anybody getting hurt," explained Lee. To that, Aaron said, "Come on, Jamil. Let's take turns. First Nancy can ride, and then you can ride."

Lee, the teacher, clearly understood the disrupted play and worked to give it a restart. Young children often find themselves in stymied play situations that need a reframing or assistance from other peers or adults. Never blaming or shaming but always looking forward, care providers who know best practices in emotional development will allow and encourage children to share emotions while interacting with one another.

Emotion-Centered Curriculum

Marilou Hyson reminds us that the curriculum should be emotionally supportive or emotion-centered (2003), one that does more than just teaching children about their feelings. An emotion-centered curriculum encompasses all areas of development and avoids the separation of emotions and cognition, or emotions and physical growth. The fastest way to see whether your curriculum is emotion-centered is to observe the children when they are interacting with one another and see if they are engaged emotionally.

At the meal table, Sam and Kassi are discussing the heights of their juice in the clear glasses in front of them. "Mine is almost gone," says Kassi, while Sam remarks, "Mine is taller than yours 'cause I didn't drink it much till my soup was gone." The teacher begins to sing a clean-up song as lunchtime comes to a close, but Kassi and Sam continue to observe the leftover amounts of juice, making scientific comparisons after each one takes a drink.

At first glance, one might notice only that Kassi and Sam aren't paying attention. A teacher who practices emotion-centered curriculum would instantly recognize the valuable learning that is occurring. The two children were so engaged that their emotions were powering the discussion. This type of learning is referred to as *emotional competence* and cannot be replicated on a worksheet or in a workbook. Their "faces, voices, and bodies indicated a high level of absorption and emotional involvement" (Hyson 2003, 17).

In an emotion-centered curriculum, all emotions—fear, joy, sadness, happiness, etc.—are welcomed, and the curriculum makes room for children to explore or play out their emotions. The environments are safe, and the adult caregivers offer new experiences that allow the children to experiment without fear of failure. When children are experiencing deployment, offering an emotion-centered curriculum is helpful as you provide activities and plans that will center around the needs of the children and prevent fear of failure. Preschool children may feel confused, surprised that everything appears to be different, and guilty, as they sometimes believe that a parent left because of them. They may have trouble separating from the primary caregiver and show anger or have outbursts or bouts of irritability. Let their emotions guide your routines and plans as you offer Mom or Dad's favorite dessert at mealtime or play their favorite songs during mu-

sic time. Allow children time to express themselves and a place to be alone, but in view, for short periods of time. Have more than one pretend phone available for preschoolers to make frequent calls to Mom or Dad, to tell them how they are feeling or just about what is happening in their day.

Schoolagers have a lot of the same reactions as preschoolers, but they also have a deeper sadness about the absence of the parent, as they understand concepts of time better than they did when they were younger and know that a year or several months can be a long time. These older children may have mood swings and engage in clinging behavior, and you can help them feel connected to their absent parents by attending to their emotions. Writing cards and letters or drawing pictures to send on days when kids are missing their deployed parent as well as asking other family members and friends to visit your program to add encouragement and support to schoolagers can help schoolagers feel more connected.

Scaffolding Children's Learning

David Wood, Jerome Bruner, and Gail Ross (1976) used the term *scaffolding* to describe what happens when learning moves forward with support from a more capable or accomplished peer or adult. The support is withdrawn when the learner is satisfied that she no longer needs it. We scaffold children's learning every day by assisting only when necessary and then withdrawing or retreating as the child grasps the concepts or simply says, "I can do it myself!" Respecting the child's needs and feelings, we guide and redirect the child's participation with others. We provide an understanding of what is best for a child in order to help him restore his play. We are careful to balance our support with the child's initiations or self-plans for play, providing just the right amount of scaffolding.

STRATEGIES

Scaffolding Play

Provide "must" and "may" centers each day; centers that children "must" attend to receive the information that your curriculum deems necessary and "may" centers—centers filled with appropriate activities that the children can choose to attend or not. Provide a checklist for children to complete as they visit each center (Pattillo and Vaughan 1992). A large benefit of this system is that children who have a difficult time making choices or getting started once they arrive are quickly assimilated into the program by having a direction to take or follow. You develop a plan based on each child's challenges and strengths.

Four-year-old Matthew loved the computer in his classroom and wanted to spend all of his learning centers time every day at the computer. His teacher, Ben, knew that Matthew could benefit from spending time at the art center as well, to explore color and shape in different media. So at the beginning of the week, Ben made a "must and may" centers plan for Matthew and posted it where Matthew could see it every day throughout learning centers time. He was still able to visit the computer center, but it was on his "may" list, and he was limited to three days a week at the computer.

RELIEVING STRESS THROUGH PLAY

The impending loss of a parent from deployment is very real to military children. They know a separation from one or both parents is coming, but they cannot comprehend how long the separation will actually be. When children experience stressful events such as a parent being deployed or even Mom and Dad arguing, they may begin to role-play what they have seen. Although this may be unpleasant to watch, such a reenactment can be healthy for children. It gives them a way to relieve that pressure or stress that has been mounting from witnessing the events. Once the steam (stress) has been released through reenactment in play, children often continue to play normally or become interested in other role playing.

Environments that are stressful for adults can also cause stress in children. Whether they are in military care overseas or at home in the United States, adults must encourage and protect children's play. Because play tends to decrease or disappear in the most stress-filled environments, it is up to us to ensure that just the opposite occurs with kids of military parents. To promote play, children must be given protected play spaces.

Restoring Play in Children

Play is directly linked to the healthy emotional development of children. When children have lost their love for play, it is important to implement strategies to help them restore it. All children live in a world where many things are beyond their control; fostering emotional health by creating environments that convey the importance of play and its restorative powers is essential. The need to create and to express feelings is at the heart of playing.

At a young age, military children often understand that they will be separated from one or both parents. Good-byes may be for short or long periods of time, and multiple separations are possible. Children in severe distress or pain often lose their love and need for play during these times. In many cases, children will become so distressed that they need to see play therapists and play counselors. Fortunately, you can also play a role in helping children during these stressful periods. You don't have to be a counselor or therapist to use some basic strategies that will help restore a child's need for play. Play therapists suggest the following techniques for us to foster social and emotional health in children: effective listening and using music, books, art, and dance or movement. These ideas are discussed in more detail below.

Effective and Reflective Listening

Children often feel that adults do not listen to them, so they find ways to get attention. Effective and reflective listening involves taking down the barriers to communicating with children while modeling good listening techniques. Show children how to be good listeners by listening to them.

Keys to Effective Listening

- Be interested and attentive.
- Make eye contact.
- Allow the child to finish before responding.
- Refrain from judging, criticizing, blaming, or shaming while the child is speaking.
- Listen intently, and avoid thinking of what you will say as a rebuttal while the child is speaking. (This really takes practice.)
- Pause: "Ummm," "Well," "Let me think about that," and "That's good information" are all expressions that will give you time to make a fair decision rather than a hasty one.
- Ask for clarification by saying, "I'm sorry; could you say that again?" or "Are you saying that . . .?"
- Practice affirmations such as "It was really brave of you to tell me that," "You've made a big decision today," or "I could tell that you wanted to do the right thing."
- Do more listening than talking.

When using reflective listening, you first put aside your own feelings and preconceived ideas of how the child should feel and act. Listen to what the child says, and acknowledge the child's feelings as you understand them. The dialogue below is from a conversation between a six-year-old boy and his teacher, who are in the after-school program's art room. It is time for the children to go outside to play.

Child:	I don't want to go outside—I want to stay and finish my picture.
Adult:	You don't want to go outside?
Child:	I'm not going outside 'cause it's crazy out there.
Adult:	You're afraid there won't be time to finish your picture?
Child:	Yeah, and I'm gonna finish it first before I go outside.
Adult:	This is really important to you. You need to finish it first before you go outside.

Child: Yeah, can I?

Adult: I think that is a great idea!

Counselors and therapists have long used music, dance, art, and books in play to help children deal with grief and sadness from loss, get in touch with their emotions, and jump-start their creativity. Away from the therapy playroom or the counselor's office, teachers and providers can use some of those same techniques to allow children to recognize problems and to take steps toward resuming happy and healthy lives. It should be noted that play therapy rooms and typical child care environments contain many of the same toys and materials (Muro, Petty, and DakoGyeke 2006). Here are several basic techniques you should keep in mind while working with children in any setting:

- Learn to follow and to lead—depending on the needs of the child.
- Develop a warm and friendly relationship with the child.
- Accept the child and start where the child is rather than where you want or expect him to be.
- Allow the child to take risks and to show her feelings completely.
- Try to recognize the feelings the child is expressing and reflect these feelings back so the child can see his behavior.
- Allow the child as many decision-making opportunities as possible.
- Encourage the child to solve her own problems.
- Have faith that with assistance children can improve their own behavior.

Restoring Play through Music

Someone once said, "Music is what feelings sound like." This sentiment provides inspiration for using music with military children, since listening to music helps children and adults alleviate stress and improve their mood. Music has such powerful effects that it can also be used to improve overall emotional health, calm children, and enable them to create relationships with adults and their peers. Playing music can stimulate and bring out the child's imagination while playing alone, with peers, or with you. It can also allow a child to remember painful events and to "play" through them, transporting the child to a musical place where everything is okay and everything is more manageable.

Join in the music making with the children in your care. It doesn't matter if you play an instrument with precision or if you can sing on pitch; it only matters that the child can tap his potential for healing during a musical relationship with you.

Start where the child is. Some children will engage in music play during small- or large-group times, but others will benefit from one-on-one time with you, weekly or as time is available. Music play is not about learning concepts from a lesson plan or the national music standards—it is solely for emotional development. Children who are experiencing trauma or prolonged sadness will appreciate the opportunity to restore their play with music activities by listening, singing, or playing. (For more ideas about using music in your program, see chapter 5.)

STRATEGIES

Music Matching (for Preschoolers and Schoolagers)

Note: This activity is more about relationships than matching the notes with exactness. This can be done with any size group, but younger children need smaller groups or individual time with the adult.

Each person needs the same instrument, such as a xylophone or small keyboard. One person strikes a tone, and the others try to match it. Add an additional tone each time as a challenge. Some children will want to just watch and listen. Remember to allow individual children to begin or participate at whatever level they are able.

Music in Nature

Go for a walk, and listen for music in nature. Ask children to imitate the sound or to re-create the beat or motif (recurring pattern). Bring the music to life by asking, "If the sounds had feelings, what would they be?" "How could we change the sounds to make them happy?" "Sad?" "Scared?" "Angry?"

Restoring Play through Dance

Like music, dance play has been proven to restore healthy emotions and creativity. Dance offers kids the opportunity for emotional expression and to develop self-discipline, concentration, confidence, problem-solving skills, and self-knowledge. It is not just a physical activity but an emotional and social activity as well. Children develop body and spatial awareness as they move their bodies and learn where they exist in relation to others. Dance teaches respect for others and calls for teamwork when dancing together. It is a self-esteem builder as children learn to create movements and even perform them.

Encourage children to move creatively as often as possible. Use balls of various weights and sizes, scarves of different lengths and fabrics, streamers, hats of all kind, and costumes as props, and allow children to harness their own creativity. Provide all kinds of music to lure or entice children to dance. Clear a space for broad sweeping movements as well as small, restricted ones. If emotions are running really high, plan a SEAD time each day, a time when you "Stop Everything and *Dance!*" Everyone participates, even adults. Allow children to participate directly by dancing or moving or indirectly by observing. For some children, watching others dance is helpful in washing away the sadness and pain felt from separation and loss. This is not to say that dance should only be used on sad days. Maintain a healthy diet of creativity for children by regularly dancing in your program.

STRATEGIES

Dancing with the Stars

With toddlers and preschoolers: Make large stars from posterboard. Paint them in bright colors or decorate them with brightly colored fabrics.

> **With toddlers**: Sing "Twinkle, Twinkle, Little Star," and encourage them to move or walk around with the stars as you sing.

> **With preschoolers**: Put on music such as "Everybody Is a Star" from the Sugar Beats album with the same title.

> **With schoolagers**: Ask children to find music with the word *star* in the lyrics. Screen their suggestions for appropriateness, and play the songs while children stand and paint stars on a large piece of butcher paper attached to the classroom wall. Children will move to the music while painting.

Restoring Play through Art

Art play has long been used for self-expression and as a medium for resolving self-conflict and raising self-esteem. It is also used as a stress reducer and a way to draw out thoughts and feelings when children are in emotional pain as a result of trauma, separation and loss, or bereavement. It is also a great way to maintain an emotionally healthy climate in the classroom on a daily basis, as it helps in relieving emotional tension the children may feel during the separation from their deployed parents.

Art play is drawing, painting, collage making, and sculpting. By using simple art materials such as markers, paint, yarn, paper, dough, and clay, you can provide opportunities for children to represent their thoughts and feelings visually. The process is more important than the product. Children don't have to be budding artists to participate. All expressions are accepted in art play, and children need to be able to play with different kinds of media over and over.

STRATEGIES

My Life

Provide lots of collage materials such as feathers, colored and textured papers, wooden miniature letters, appropriate magazines, and foam cutouts. Have children create a "My Life" picture using materials of their choice. Allow them to let feelings surface, and tell them it is okay to talk about their parents who are deployed and how much they miss them. Most of all, make this a supportive space where children know they are cared for.

Restoring Play through Books

Books can help children work through their problems. Reading a book about a common problem, discussing the problem, and then doing follow-up activities can bring peace and comfort to a child who is hurting. Book play (sometimes called *bibliotherapy*) can allow kids to attach emotions to characters experiencing the same situations. Books can take a child on a journey that can match the journey that their parents are on, serving in the military.

When children can read a book about a problem they are having, the story can become a springboard for discussion with a trusted friend or adult. Emotional turmoil often runs high in military children, even if they don't talk about their fears and emotions. Because reading can be therapeutic in general—for adults too—adults can guide children through their crises by selecting books that have cathartic value. There are three general stages for book play that can help children in working through their emotions: identification, catharsis, and insight (Olsen 1975).

IDENTIFICATION

Observe children's behaviors, and listen when they talk about the events that are happening in their lives. Select books that contain characters or events that resemble the children's experiences. Decide if the events are private enough to warrant a personal reading with the child or if several children are facing the same tough times. If this is the case, the book may be read to a group of children experiencing similar circumstances. Find books that deal with grief and loss, divorce, a death in the family, or whatever needs have been identified. (See chapter 9 and appendix A for book titles.)

CATHARSIS

The child wants to read the book over and over again and wants you to read with him to discuss his personal situation. Offer to read to the child, at any age, if that is his preference. Sometimes simply listening to the story is more beneficial in unblocking emotions and relieving emotional pressures than trying to read the book and think about its meaning.

INSIGHT

As you read with the child, you can raise possible solutions to his problems based on what happens in the story. Together you can make plans to address the challenges and look for more books on the same subject. Help the child choose a follow-up activity from the list below that will further release her emotions:

- Draw a picture.
- Paint a mural.
- Videotape a story.
- Make a podcast that can be sent to the deployed parent.
- Create a song to go along with the book. Write the music and/or the lyrics. Perform it for the class.
- Write or improvise a story, and act it out. Use props, music, etc.
- Reconstruct the story using puppets.
- Draw a story map—chronicling the times and events in the story. Compare it with real-life events in the child's life.
- Make up a different ending to the story.

STRATEGIES

Making Discoveries through Books

Find books about locations where parents will be serving. Use geography books with maps of oceans and landforms. What are all the destinations that a parent visits before returning home? What is the path that the parent took to get to the job? If it's on a destroyer in the ocean, read a book about destroyers, or if the deployed parent has gone to another country, learn about the country by providing books and Web sites on its customs and languages. Reading about the deployed parent's daily routines and getting a better picture of where he is can help the child cope with the separation.

Book Play Guide

Use this guide for successful book play experiences:

- Read a book about a problem you have observed. Ask a child to select a puppet that can accompany her while she reads. Provide hats and other props (sunglasses, scarves, headbands with funny eyeballs, etc.) that the child can use while reading about a subject that she has been hesitant to discuss. Putting on reading glasses or other attire before reading can lighten the child's mood and increase her interest in the process.

- Before reading the book you've selected, let the child's primary caregiver know that you would like to share with the child a book that addresses feelings and emotions.

- Share the book with the child privately, and allow plenty of time for reflections, discussion, and questions from the child.

- If a large deployment has occurred, consider sharing a book with a group of affected children.

- Ask local school or installation counselors or chaplains to attend or to share the book and answer questions.

- Provide follow-up activities for the book such as dramatizing, drawing and painting, sculpting, and journal writing.

- Place the book in a visible spot so children can revisit it as often as they need to.

- Reread the book when asked.

The following books are good choices for book play with children experiencing deployment:

I Miss You! A Military Kid's Book about Deployment by Beth Andrews (2007)

Ned and the General: A Lesson about Deployment by Ron Madison (2004)

Deployment Journal for Kids by Rachel Robertson (2005)

My Dad Is Going Away, but He Will Be Back One Day: A Deployment Story by James and Melanie Thomas (2004)

Daddy, You're My Hero! by Michelle Ferguson-Cohen (2002)

Violent Play

When children grow up in settings where talk of war violence is common, it may be difficult for them to understand the negative outcomes of war. You may find it hard to explain how peacemaking—rather than fighting—is the standard behavior to meet our needs. It seems contradictory to teach children that fighting is wrong when the adults they love may solve problems using guns and weapons.

The need to "work it out" is critical when planning children's playtimes. An obsession with war play can simply stem from a parent being deployed to a war zone. A child who has been left behind may feel powerless and weak. In order to restore the control and power that a child needs to feel safe, or to become centered again, he may need to work through the feelings by reenacting what he has seen or heard. This may be quite discomforting if you want play to always be peaceful and fun, but in order for the child to move forward, his feelings cannot be discounted or pushed aside. Dr. Joel Muro, a play therapist in Denton, Texas, encourages teachers and providers to allow war play by providing dolls and toy weapons, doll houses, and planes to children who are displaying challenging behaviors. Allow children to use play to express their feelings, rather than hold them in. When you support children, their emotional pathways will open rather than close, and children will work through the separation from or loss of a parent much more readily. If you are very uncomfortable in allowing war play, know that you're not alone. In some cases, it is better to leave such play to play therapists, especially if you are opposed to war or disagree with U.S. involvement in the war. Redirect the child to a more peaceful type of play, and provide other opportunities to allow the child to express her feelings without reproach or criticism.

STRATEGIES

Address Violent or War Play

Allow children to reenact violent acts they have seen on TV (with supervision and to a degree), and be sure to correct mistaken ideas as you perceive them in play. After the events of September 11, 2001, many children assumed that planes continued to crash into the World Trade Center buildings, over and over. Ask open-ended question such as, "Where did you see that happen?" or "What have you heard about that?" Answer questions to clarify any misconceptions children have.

Provide lots of time to paint, draw, sculpt, pound, and build. Dr. Muro encourages providers to allow children to paint over or cover up their paintings or tear them up if they choose; to pound as often and as hard as they seem to need to; and to build towers of blocks and knock them down repeatedly.

Provide lots of opportunities for children to journal or write about feelings.

Provide a space and table for children to go to make peace. Puppets, journals, books about peacemaking, and assistance from caregivers can turn negative situations into positive ones.

Provide access to sensory play often, as it is soothing and relaxing for all ages. Media for sensory play include sand, water, playdough, and mud.

Provide a dramatic play center in the home or classroom that has uniforms that moms and dads may wear to work as well as backpacks, hats, for example.

Let the primary caregiver know that the child is engaging in violent play. Assure him that you have a plan to allow the child to work through her feelings rather than suppressing them.

Observe children's violent play closely, and watch for frequency and intensity. If it persists for more than a few days or is extremely violent at the onset, talk to the primary caregiver right away, and ask for help from your Family Member Programs Resources if you are on an installation.

The next time a child becomes contentious, disagreeable, or even violent, rather than impose immediate punishment or consequences, try reflecting the feelings of the child to get a sense of where he is coming from at the moment. It can have tremendous benefits for the child in your care.

Media Coverage of Conflicts or Wars

When children come to school and are retelling an event they saw on TV or in a movie, take time to talk with them about what they saw and listen to their story. Ask them how it relates to them and why it is so interesting to them.

Provide a journal for children to draw or write about their fears. Answer questions, and offer reassurance. Ask the kids if they can think of another outcome for the event or an ending that they would like to see happen.

Violent Images

The number of violent images of war on television and the Internet can cause undue fears and anxiety in military kids. It is not often easy to reassure children when the images are so graphic and frightening, but you can take steps to at least minimize the negative effects.

STRATEGIES

Talking to Children about War

- Limit their exposure to images of war and terrorism as well as catastrophic events.
- Accept all conversation about what they have heard and seen. Try to address each fear or question honestly and succinctly (tell them only what they ask for).
- Seek professional help if the conversations are excessive, last longer than usual, and seem to preoccupy the child's thoughts and actions.

In summary, keeping lines of communication open between you and the children in your care, limiting their time watching or hearing nonstop talk of war, and answering questions openly and honestly, keeping in mind age appropriateness, can go far in helping military children feel safe.

When to Refer Children to Outside Resources

Violence is only one way that children act out perceived problems in their lives. Sometimes children may need to be referred for counseling for other behaviors. Watch for the following signs, and use your best judgment in order to make a thoughtful decision:

- behavior that is persistently contentious
- overly anxious behavior
- withdrawal from the adults and other children in the care setting
- depressed behavior, bouts of persistent sadness for unexplained reasons
- increased irritability
- withdrawal from friends and activities that she once enjoyed
- loss of appetite
- sleeplessness
- lack of energy and low activity level
- loss of self-esteem
- difficulty concentrating
- feelings of persistent hopelessness and helplessness

Although the decision to refer to play therapy or counseling is a difficult one to make, children who are truly in need of counseling cannot wait. Use your installation or community resources in determining if the behaviors are beyond your ability to work with. Include the primary caregiver in making the decision to ask for assistance. Children are depending on us to ensure their health and happiness during these challenging times.

All children experience varying amounts of stress during their childhood, but not all children have the resiliency required to handle their sadness, grief, and loss. Levels and degrees of intensity, persistence, and frequency of a child's behaviors can be the best predictors to use in determining when a child should see a professional counselor or therapist. Consider the following questions when determining if more help is needed for a child experiencing deployment:

How long has the behavior been going on?

How often is the child sad, angry, despondent, and so on?

How intense is the feeling?

At whom is the behavior directed?

Again, individual children at different ages respond to stressful events in different ways and some are more resilient than others. If you are offering the open-ended, adult-supported play that is needed for children to thrive, most children can "reset" themselves after stressful or traumatic experiences because of built-in mechanisms of resiliency. For those children who cannot reset or restore their innate play abilities, or who display more than usual episodes of violent play, play therapy or counseling may be necessary. Knowing when to refer a child is important; play therapists would agree that children belong in their normal environment unless they can no longer function there. Violent play cannot be ignored if it continues for more than a few days, and any one extremely intense episode of violent play demands action. When violent play becomes the norm, more help is needed.

As watchful observers of and participants with military children at play, we can take steps to improve their emotional liabilities. Using the strategies found within this chapter can help. By offering a curriculum that is not only mindful of but centered on the child's emotional well-being, you can assist in providing support during disrupted play. When children are emotionally secure, they will benefit even more from social, cognitive, and physical play.

CHAPTER FOUR

Promoting Play for Social, Cognitive, and Physical Benefits

nfants, toddlers, preschoolers, and schoolagers, whether in family child care or center-based care, need play in order to thrive. Children communicate this message to us over and over as they seek out play spaces and situations where they adjust reality and become builders or architects of play experiences.

It is impossible to separate a child from play and the rest of his world. Our attitudes regarding play mean everything to a child. You'll see a child more freely engage in play if you think of play as vital and instrumental to his well-being.

One of the most important aspects of caring for children of all ages is to develop an environment that lays the groundwork for play. With more and more pressure on children to excel on standardized tests as soon as they begin formal schooling, it is important to find ways to support the natural development of children through play. David Elkind wrote, "The consequences of current pressures to include formal academic instruction in early childhood programs and the negative attitudes toward free play are dire" (2006, 39). Developmentally appropriate programs see the need for spontaneous as well as directed play and build daily routines around these important tenets of the child's day. In truth, play can actually help in preparation for future academic accomplishments rather than get in the way of the child obtaining knowledge and skills.

Moreover, playing in a supportive environment is one of the ways that children with chronic stress caused by prolonged separation from someone they love can adapt (Marion 2003). Thus play is important for military children experiencing stress from losing a parent to deployment.

Purpose and General Benefits of Play

We can tell a lot about the development of a child by observing her at play, as it showcases her cognitive, social, physical, and emotional abilities. Play is extremely important in furthering the development of children of all ages and stages. Research has also shown that a lack of play has dire effects on the young child's brain. Providing children with a play toolbox and time and space to play produces long-lasting benefits.

It may appear that infant and toddler play is very simple in nature, but the development that is occurring in all aspects of the young child's life is phenomenal, and the importance of your participation in that development should not be underestimated. Beginning with sensorimotor play, when they practice the use of all their senses, infants and toddlers develop along a continuum, with play being the vehicle for growth.

Most children of preschool age (three or four years old) have had practice interacting in small and large groups. Some call the preschool years the "play years" (Frost, Wortham, and Reifel 2005, 122). Indeed, preschool is a time for pretend play, as a child uses a toy phone to call Dad, who is working in a land far away, or bakes an imaginary cake for Mom, who won't be coming home soon. Children explore and make discoveries at the sand and water center, and of course they engage in physical play on the playground on the swings, slides, and wheeled toys.

By planning a curriculum that has play at its center, caregivers working with preschoolers can take advantage of windows of opportunity to stimulate cognitive, social, and physical development. That is not to say that direct instruction has little place in a preschool program, but you should first look to play when planning activities to boost skills and competencies.

School-age play differs from preschool play because it is more advanced in all areas. Children in this age range still engage in pretend or make-believe play, but for different purposes. Computer games, rough-and-tumble play, chasing games, organized sports activities, and "hanging out" or socializing are all part of the schoolager's need for play. He is much more cognitively, socially, and physically developed than the preschooler, and his need for play is changing.

The emotional benefits of play were addressed in chapter 3; the social, cognitive, and physical benefits of play are discussed in this chapter.

Social Play

Children engage in *social play* when they interact with peers, as opposed to time playing alone or at a TV or computer screen. It is for this reason you must capitalize on the time that children are in your care—fostering positive play experiences that will enhance social development among peers. Research has long supported the importance of friendship making (Corsaro 1985), that is, the importance of making friends to a child's development. Child care settings are an ideal environment to encourage experiences that help develop the necessary skills for healthy social play.

In 1932, psychologist Mildred Parten conducted a classic study on children's social play processes in group settings. Her six stages of play development (unoccupied, solitary, onlooker, parallel, associative, and cooperative) have been used routinely ever since and are the cornerstone of social play study. Parten's interest was mainly in the way that children play or participate with one another in classrooms or social settings. She concluded that the first four categories decline with age, but the last two (associative and cooperative) actually increase as children get older (Frost, Wortham, and Reifel 2005).

In the rooms of a child development center, you might see Jay, a pre-toddler, playing with blocks in a nonsocial or uninvolved way, while Natalee, also a pre-toddler, sits in the provider's lap and watches (onlooker), but is not involved socially with Jay. Kason, a two-year-old, is absorbed in solitary play, diligently connecting pieces of a train track and making a "chugga-chugga-choo-choo" sound, centered on the task and unaware of anyone else in the room. Alonzo, three years old, takes a bucket of toy animals and dumps them just outside the block center, where three other children are playing. He positions himself in parallel fashion to the center and to other children, but he does not encroach upon their play territory. Isabella and Abbie are four years old and are painting at the easel alongside each other. While they share and take turns with brushes and paints (associating), giggling when one drops the red paintbrush into the yellow paint cup, they are working on individual paintings and are not engaged in any kind of cooperative or relational play. Sophia and Jordan, who are six, are planning a skit based on a book they have been reading at school. In this cooperative form of play, they are making a list of the props that will be needed as well as a script for the players (their peers).

Infants and Toddlers

As stated before, children gradually play in three ways during their first two years—solitary, onlooker, and parallel. Each level of development is important for us to observe, understand, and facilitate. Although children of any age may show signs of the stages discussed here for older infants and toddlers, infants and toddlers cannot perform the later stages of play such as cooperative and associative play. The levels seem to progress along a continuum, giving older children the right to revisit a level at any time (Parten 1932).

Solitary play is the beginning level of play and occurs when the child plays alone and appears to be unaware of other children or adults. Provide toys and safe objects for banging, such as drums, plastic pots and pans, plastic tubs and cardboard boxes, musical instruments, as well as books for exploring (board books, peek-a-boo or lift-the-flap books, and large picture books). Avoid trying to force toddlers to share at this stage or to interact with others. It may be premature to have such expectations. Patience and encouragement are called for.

Onlooker play occurs when a young toddler (usually under the age of eighteen months) spends most of her time watching other children play. Onlooker play offers children the opportunity to observe others solving problems and interact with peers and adults. A child may be at this stage of play and be entering the next stage, parallel play, or revert back to the solitary play stage.

In *parallel play* a toddler chooses an activity that brings him close to other children, but he does not interact with them. He may be playing with a similar toy or involved in the same pretend play but plays alone, near other children. Even though there may be eye contact, children in this stage of play are not interacting with one another. No words are exchanged. This is practice in future friendship making as well as sharing and cooperating with others (Smith, Cowie, and Blades 2003).

GENDER DIFFERENCES IN INFANT
AND TODDLER PLAY

Young toddlers begin to notice gender and can identify themselves as male or female sometime between eighteen months and two years and will often choose toys that are typically reserved for boys or girls. We know that little boys are often more hyperkinetic, or movement oriented, and engage in more rough-and-tumble play, and little girls are more nurturing and language oriented, especially after the age of two (Fagot, Rodgers, and Leinbach 2000). This may be due to the possibility for movement that is built into many toys for boys, such as trains and trucks (things that will "go") or balls (things that can be thrown or caught) as opposed to dolls and housekeeping furniture (things that are tended). Most parents don't instruct their infant and toddler boys to play only with boys' toys and little girls to play only with girls' toys. As children get older, parents play a larger role in toy selection and purchases based upon their perceptions of what little boys and girls should play with.

STRATEGIES

Support Social Play in Infants and Toddlers

- Allow children to play within their own developmental level (onlooker, solitary, or parallel).

- Provide duplicates of popular toys.

- Provide learning centers filled with interesting toys and materials to foster exploration and discovery in pairs, such as sand and water tables, fish tanks, and book bags filled with books and companion puppets or props.

- Provide toys that are dual purposed or open-ended in nature, such as dramatic play or pretend toys and props.

Preschoolers

You can find many descriptions of what play encompasses, but in my experience as a teacher, care provider, and observer of preschool children, when preschoolers play,

- they use objects to represent something in the real world;
- they re-create situations or experiences by "re-playing" or reenacting them;
- they often try to engage adults in play;
- they prefer to play in close proximity to adults;
- they make object substitutions if toys aren't present;
- they use nontoys as toys;
- they take risks;
- they attempt to engage other children in their play;
- they make rules;
- they abandon and reenter play often;
- they change emotional frames often—forgetting the "rules" or the fight they had only moments ago;
- they value play and are sorry when it must end;
- they need time to develop play themes;
- they need opportunities to go back and revisit or re-create a play theme from the day before or week before;
- they seek out adults who value and embrace play;
- they recognize leaders of play and seek to play with them;
- they look for different materials and media for play;
- they look for different spaces and places to play;
- they tire of the same spaces and places if after a few play episodes nothing novel is presented;
- they barely notice weather or noise or anything else when deeply involved in a play experience.

Planes were routinely landing and taking off, but inside the child development center, Keenan was busily stringing wooden beads, unaware of the loud noises. Military installations have sights and sounds that are seldom experienced by most children or civilian adults. Runways for airplanes are so common on installations that they are often part of the common arena where military kids play every day. Whether on an installation in Germany or South Korea, Oklahoma or California, children play.

It is amazing to watch preschoolers continue symbolic play but extend it to socio-dramatic or pretend play. Social play is an important way for preschoolers to spend their time, as they can express feelings and emotions as well as build friendships while playing. To help children develop healthy ways of seeking relationships with others, you can offer time and space for children to interact with one another in play.

Associative play is the fourth level in Parten's stages of social play (Parten 1932). Three- and four-year-olds associate with their peers in play by engaging in an activity with someone else, borrowing items for play, and following others in play. Observe them as they attempt to lead the play, develop play themes, and assign parts to the play. Playing with other children is a new adventure for preschoolers, as they have primarily been playing by themselves or alongside others before this point.

Socio-dramatic play. When children play make-believe, provide roles for one another, and develop a play theme such as "Mommy and Daddy," they have begun to engage in socio-dramatic play. Watch how they engage in one of the highest levels of play. Preschoolers will begin to practice dramatizing and socializing with others, and then as young school-agers, they perfect it. Language development, turn taking and sharing, leading and following, and empathy and perspective taking are all skills that you can observe in action as they extend their socio-dramatic play.

The themes kids develop in play are often based on a current event such as the rodeo coming to town or a recent trip to the beach. Provide prop boxes to enhance or expand the play with symbols. Place items connected with the themes in picture-labeled or transparent boxes, and bring them out when appropriate. Keep the boxes in plain sight for children to choose themes that correspond with their interests.

Social play is an important outlet for feelings and emotions, but it is not always positive. Children work through issues and challenges—including challenges related to deployment—through their play, and they develop a sense of control or mastery over their lives through fantasy and make-believe. Observe children at play to determine if they need your assistance. Ask if you can enter the play, or find a role that you as the adult can add to the ongoing play in order to gain entrance. Be prepared to be banished or prevented from entering if your presence presents a perceived threat to their play. Children often rebuff or deny entry to other children as well as adults if they think the play will be disrupted or stymied by the added person (Petty 1993).

GENDER DIFFERENCES IN PRESCHOOL PLAY

In most cases, little boys and little girls get different treatment from the time they are born. Many parents have set ideas on how their children should dress, toys they should play with, and activities they should engage in. While researchers haven't determined whether these preset ideas actually cause boys and girls to bring gender differences to their play, it is known that boys are usually more active than girls at the preschool stage and that girls are more verbal (Fagot, Rodgers, and Leinbach 2000). In child care in the United States, we often cater to parental suggestions, as the following story about a tutu illustrates.

It was almost closing time at the child care center, and providers Peggy and Diane were preparing children for pickup. "Oh no, he has that tutu on again. His dad is going to blow his top when he sees that!" said Peggy. "You know it!" said Diane. "Let's get that off him before Dad gets here. He got so mad the last time that I thought we were going to lose our jobs." "Kelson loves that tutu so much, and it seems the more his dad gets upset, the more he chooses to wear it. I think we just need to put it away," replied Peggy.

We, as a society, cater to these suggestions too. Consider this advertisement for tutus: "Tutus for Dress-up Games for Little Girls and Baby Girls." Notice that the tutus *are not* advertised for little boys. Clothing and toys can cause issues when adults impose distinct gender preferences upon children.

Carefully consider whole child development as well as parental perspectives when providing sociodramatic play props as well as toys and games in your program. Develop strong bonds with parents and research current topics on gender differences in order to work effectively with parents. Our goal should be to help boys and girls develop healthy understandings of themselves and that their body, not their behavior, makes them a boy or girl (Derman-Sparks 1997).

Use the following ideas in planning activities that will address the whole child and provide appropriate experiences for healthy gender development:

- Address gender bias and stereotyping by reading books such as *William's Doll* (Zolotow 1985) and *Daddy Makes the Best Spaghetti* (Hines 1999).
- Provide themed props or prop boxes with costumes that address different times of

year or events and are based on children's interests and needs.

- Offer assistance or redirection when children who are playing in gender-biased ways need to return to positive play. For example, if a girl says, "He can't play with us, he's a boy," use this as a teachable moment by talking about all of the things that boys *and* girls can do.
- Provide unit blocks and large hollow blocks to assist preschool children in fantasy play as well as positive social behaviors. Add props such as people, vehicles, buildings, and pets to extend non-gender-specific play.
- Provide learning centers that address areas of skill development filled with toys and materials that are age appropriate for both boys and girls. Give children the opportunity to interact with one another and to solve social problems such as "I had it first" or "When will it be my turn?"

Schoolagers

It is easy to see that school-age play differs from preschool play, because it is more advanced in all areas. Children in this age range still engage in pretend or make-believe play, but for different purposes. Computer games, rough-and-tumble play, chasing games, organized sports activities, and "hanging out" are all part of the schoolager's need for play. He is much more cognitively, socially, and physically developed than the preschooler, and his need for play is changing.

Many people expect children, once they enter elementary school, to leave their need for play and become totally immersed in schoolwork. Physical activity in the form of physical education has often replaced the opportunity to engage in free play or even assisted play. High-stakes testing and student accountability have reduced the time available for school-age children to develop through play. Yet play is still extremely important for this age group. If you provide care for school-age children, be sure to offer the important spaces and times for them to play, either before or after school.

You may have noticed that schoolagers care more about peer relationships than preschoolers do, and it is at this time that their social selves begin to emerge and play a big part in their lives. They know who is "popular" and part of the "in crowd" and who is not. They seek to be a part of a larger group and feel left out if denied. Feeling left out may lower their self-image and prevent them from seeking other group admittance, which may also begin a cycle of social helplessness. This can be especially true in schools or communities that are away from installations, where children can feel isolation because their parent is the only one deployed. Give children opportunities to expand their possibilities and to see where their "gifts" are. Groups such as Boys and Girls Clubs, 4-H clubs, and Operation: Military Kids (to name a few) can provide projects and activities that include rather than exclude the military child. These are great places for schoolagers to excel, meet friends, and have positive adult guidance outside the home. Sometimes aggressive play is a part of being a schoolager, as are superhero play and playing war. For most schoolagers, their need for cooperative play or to be with each other in positive play relationships has replaced the need to be with adults, and they can especially benefit from being with other children who are experiencing separation from a parent who is deployed.

COOPERATIVE PLAY

Older preschoolers and schoolagers engage in Parten's most advanced level of play, called cooperative play (Parten 1932). It is often organized and activity-focused and lasts long after childhood, into adulthood. Participants have defined roles, and they plan their goals as they engage in dramatic or pretend play as well as group games.

BULLYING

More than half of all schoolagers report that bullying is a problem in school. At one time it was believed that children who bully (avoid using the term *bullies*) had low self-esteem and that bullying increased their esteem by inflicting pain or hardship on their victims, but recent research has found other reasons for this behavior. Some children have been bullied themselves, at home or in other places. They continue behaviors such as teasing, name-calling, shouting, or physical abuse because this is what they have experienced. Some children bully because they are angry and life is hard for them. They seek to inflict their own pain upon other children who appear to be weaker or are different in other ways and who will probably not retaliate (Sanders and Phye 2004).

It is important to realize that all children may bully at one time or another and therefore need to know the characteristics of bullying in order to avoid those behaviors. Here are some suggestions for minimizing bullying:

- Call out the bullying, not the bully.
- Refrain from labeling children as bullies. This perpetuates the problem.
- Help children identify behaviors that are hurtful to others and then make plans to stop.
- Develop individual as well as group plans to stamp out bullying. Post charts and posters of appropriate phrases to use when feeling angry, mad, sad, etc.
- Listen to children who display bullying behaviors, and make time to check in with them on a daily basis. Let them know that they are not alone in whatever it is that is causing the behavior.
- Begin a no-bullying program before bullying even starts. Let children know that there is zero tolerance for bullying and that you treasure them but not the behavior.
- Notice bullying behaviors:
  - name-calling
  - mocking
  - teasing
  - excluding others from activities
  - spreading rumors
  - physical abuse such as hitting, kicking, pulling hair, tripping, slapping
  - threatening harm
- Be open and available for children who are being bullied. Take the claims seriously, and work quickly with the child or children who are doing the bullying to stop it.

Possible signs that a child is being bullied:

- mysterious stomachaches and illnesses that occur when it is time to go to school
- more than usual distancing from parents or adults—irritability
- consistent loss of lunch money or money for other things
- unfamiliar bruises or scrapes on the child
- sleep problems
- bed-wetting
- problems in completing schoolwork or homework—concentration disrupted

ROUGH-AND-TUMBLE PLAY

Rough-and-tumble play is sometimes referred to as *horseplay* by adults and *play fighting* by children; those who care for schoolagers can find it challenging to cope with. You might ask, Should I stop it? Should I let it go on? Is it okay for kids to play this way? Some think that rough-and-tumble play can have value if it is monitored and a safe place is provided. It has been known to help schoolagers learn to self-regulate, make rules about their own behaviors, and provide an outlet for being physical. It is often a program decision not to allow it. With adult supervision, however, the need for physical play can be provided through arm wrestling and pat-clap-slap rhyming games. These activities do *not* have to lead to aggressive behavior. Assure children that they can withdraw from play at any time if they feel threatened or uncomfortable.

GENDER DIFFERENCES IN SCHOOL-AGE PLAY

Between the years of six and ten, boys and girls play differently. Girls generally enjoy indoor, verbal play or conversations with their friends, and boys enjoy outdoor games and activities in pairs or larger groups. Even when there are many opportunities for both boys and girls to participate in play, girls still most often prefer to play indoors and in less organized activities. This may occur because of influences in our society or from parents (Derman-Sparks 1997), but there are particular strategies that we can use to help children develop in healthy ways.

STRATEGIES

Supporting Social Play in School-Age Children

- Work with all children to be inclusive in their peer play. Hold group meetings either daily or weekly to discuss ways that all children can feel welcome in the program.

- Provide opportunities for children to engage in creative drama in which they must solve problems as a group to produce a product or show.

- Model positive social interactions and communication with peers.

- Make charts and posters that provide pro-social phrases or actions. Post them in the classroom and hallways or on playgrounds as reminders.

- Include games and activities that provide opportunities for both boys and girls to participate.

Cognitive Play

When young children play, they develop in their brains information highways called neural pathways that carry along "news" of the events they are experiencing. The more a child experiences a non-stressful environment filled with interesting and challenging activities and objects, the more connections are made in the brain. These connections continue to synapse, or help the brain to become "wired," according to Rima Shore in her landmark book, *Rethinking the Brain* (1997). "Connectivity is a crucial feature of brain development, because the neural pathways formed during the early years carry signals and allow us to process information throughout our lives," writes Shore (22). In addition, Shore reports that when problem solving occurs, brain strategy surges. Marian Diamond and Janet Hopson call this process the growth of "magic trees," referring to the dendrite growth that occurs during play when children engage in problem-solving events. In their book, *Magic Trees of the Mind* (1998), they write that children who are encouraged to solve problems during play benefit immensely by growing more magic trees.

Infants and Toddlers

In the first year of life, as babies engage in cognitive play, they learn important concepts. They learn cause and effect by turning the knob on a jack-in-the-box and watching the clown jump out when the music stops or by watching their spoon fall to the floor each time they push it too close to the edge of the high chair; they learn problem solving by reaching for a toy that is too far away, rocking their bodies until it is within their grasp; and they learn that the rattle underneath the blanket is still there even when they can't see it.

STRATEGIES

Listening Walk

Take a listening walk with babies. Stop each time you hear a different sound, and put your hands to your ears. Talk to the babies about what they are hearing; describe each sound as loud or soft, high or low. Listen for loud cars and barking dogs, meowing cats and singing birds.

Touching Walk

Plan a touching day or walk with infants or toddlers. Give them opportunities to safely touch flower petals and leaves, tree bark, blades of grass, small stones, and large rocks. Talk about the attributes of each object: small, large, soft, round, hard, crinkly, prickly, or smooth.

OBJECT PLAY

During the first three months, babies keep their hands in a fist, but they then begin to notice objects they can feel. Squeezing, crumpling, and throwing take the place of just touching by six months, as their actions become much more intentional. Provide toy rattles and rings, objects they can bat and swing, and sound cubes and mirrors.

Babies approach toys cautiously at first, exploring all properties of the object with their senses. After the exploration period, a baby will begin to play with the object and appear less serious about it. The next time you offer a new toy to an infant, observe her interactions with the toy and how her mood changes from seriousness to lightheartedness.

For older infants, pound-a-pegs, shape and color sorters, stack-and-sorts, soft balls, and snapping beads will promote their cognitive play. Alternate or change toys frequently to provide novelty and newness, thereby preventing boredom and increasing thinking skills. Learning to manipulate objects is an important part of play during the first year.

SYMBOLIC PLAY

When children can use symbols to represent ideas or objects, it is called *symbolic play*. It is the beginning of pretend or dramatic play. Swiss psychologist Jean Piaget (1954) proposed that symbolic play occurs during what he calls the stage of preoperational development, when two- to seven-year-olds use lots of imagination during their play, but children as young as one or two have been observed using one thing to stand for another, sometimes in the absence of objects.

Two-year-old Mariah runs to her mom and holds out her hand, saying, "Do you want some 'Donald's french fries?" and two-year-old Jessica pretends to buy a toy by placing pretend money in her teacher's hand. These acts of symbolic play have been tied to school readiness, and the more symbolic play that care providers and teachers encourage as well as participate in, the better off children will be. They can exchange pretend money for real money and toy people for real people. As children get older, other acts of symbolic play may include pretending to go on shopping trips, visits to the doctor, or outings to the rodeo or circus.

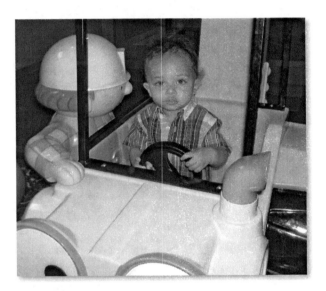

STRATEGIES

Supporting Cognitive Play in Infants and Toddlers

- Allow infants and toddlers time to explore various art materials with and without your assistance, such as painting or scribbling with markers and pens.

- Make available art materials and experiences such as edible dough and nontoxic paints.

- Provide games that encourage bringing both hands to the midline of the body or crossing the midline, such as "Itsy-Bitsy Spider" and "Pat-a-Cake."

- Provide learning experiences with color, such as pointing out a yellow sweater.
- Create an obstacle course with boxes and pillows. Encourage children to crawl through, walk or crawl around, and jump or step over the objects.

Preschoolers

Play stimulates brain growth and development during critical periods of the preschool years. Encourage cognitive play by offering activities and materials that children will manipulate in their environment. For instance, if a child repeatedly chooses to play with a train and tracks, you can stimulate more advanced play by introducing a book about trains and recalling the storyline to the child.

I am reminded of Donald Crews's Freight Train *(1996) and a conversation I had with my two-year-old grandson, who loves trains and plays with them often. After reading the book, I asked, "Do you remember when the freight train went through the tunnel and it was dark? Do we have a tunnel?" I asked him not only to recall the events of the book but also to use his imagination. And let's not forget the language enrichment opportunity when I used the word* tunnel *with a two-year-old. He pointed underneath the sofa and said, "Over there, Grammy. Tunnel under there!"*

STRATEGIES

Supporting Cognitive Play in Preschool Children

- Engage children in counting activities.
- Provide opportunities for sorting: Sort fruits and vegetables by size or shape. Sort toys by color, shape, size, or number.

- Provide discovery centers that house live animals such as fish, hermit crabs, and insects as well as rabbits, guinea pigs, and hamsters. Encourage children to observe behaviors of animals and make projections or predictions based on their observations. Terrariums and aquariums are great discovery-provoking additions to an environment.
- Set up a manipulative center with attribute (blocks with different sizes, shapes, and colors) and pattern blocks for observing patterns. Help children to find naturally occurring patterns in the classroom and on the playground.

Schoolagers

Preschool children and school-age children think differently. School-age children are better able to focus and concentrate as well as make plans and carry them out. They are not as easily distracted and think much more concretely than preschoolers. Their ability and love for games with rules set them apart from preschoolers, as they are now able to interact with peers and adults cognitively and socially when playing. Because of their enhanced cognitive ability, many children at this age spend a lot of time with computers and video games.

COMPUTERS AND VIDEO GAMES

In recent years, computers and video games have replaced traditional outside play activities for many school-age children. Children now have access to cell phones and MP3 players, which can download video games, photos, television shows, podcasts, audiobooks, and music from the Internet. In-ear headphones are a common sight on schoolagers during leisure time. In some areas, schools have even adopted podcasting and vodcasting as common mediums for viewing and listening to lectures and missed schoolwork. Technology is fast becoming a second playscape for school-age children, while teachers, parents, and providers are feeling the pressure to strike a balance between physical activities involving whole-body movement and sedentary cognitive play with technology toys.

Offer schoolagers an abundance of choices for activities that include but are not limited to electronic toys and software. One school-age program offers tickets for twenty minutes of computer game time each afternoon and none before school. A provider remarked that a couple of boys in her care would not go to any other activities if she did not limit their use of the computer room. Another program limits the number of days each week that computers are available, while providers make every effort to play with or assist schoolagers as they investigate topics of interest, play board games, and play in the gym or on the playground.

MULTIPLE INTELLIGENCES THEORY

In 1983, Howard Gardner introduced his theory of multiple intelligences, in which he originally identified seven basic intelligences: musical, bodily-kinesthetic, spatial, interpersonal, intrapersonal, logical-mathematical, and verbal-linguistic. In essence, the theory argues that optimum brain development occurs when all areas of intelligence are stimulated. Gardner identified two more specific areas of intelligence (naturalistic and existential), but tells us that there is not a fixed number of intelligences (Armstrong 1999). Understanding how closely play and cognition (or knowing) are related is beneficial for caregivers when planning curriculum. School-age programs, in particular, can offer activities in each area of Gardner's theory. Chapter 6 gives more detail on program development using multiple intelligences theory.

STRATEGIES

Supporting Cognitive Play in School-Age Children

- Allow school-age children to create additions to the playground based on their interests, needs, and sense of wonder.

- Provide games with rules. Assist younger schoolagers in rule games, but allow older children to play in small and large groups.

- Provide a balance of technological play with other types of play, such as physical and social.

- See that schoolagers attend plays, begin writing their own scripts, and have the opportunity to perform them.

Build leisure time into your schedule to allow for problem solving and project planning. Allow projects that take several days, weeks, or even months to complete. School-age children can plan and implement projects such as planning a camping trip or building a playground structure for younger children. Model flexibility; children of deployed parents may need to take time from school to visit with Mom or Dad on leave, and classmates will need to either move on to different parts of a project that don't exclude the military child or suspend the work on the project until the child comes back. Allow children to post signs on their work that read, "Mary's Work," "Wait for me!" or "I'll be back."

Play and Physical Development

Physical development in young children occurs in four categories: (1) sensorimotor, (2) fine motor, (3) perceptual motor, and (4) gross motor. When planning play experiences it is important to create opportunities for physical growth, as play is central to stimulating all four areas of physical development. Running, walking, climbing, jumping, and crawling are all important components in brain development and actually aid the learning process (Jensen 2005). A child who has strong, frequent physical play experiences from infancy through early childhood is setting the stage for a healthy future.

Appropriate play spaces (indoors and outdoors) and carefully selected materials can easily kindle physical play, as children will heartily explore the environment when given ample time. A child's natural curiosity and innate need to make discoveries (large and small) in his environment is a natural occurrence that is often exhausting even to watch! Besides being just plain fun, physical play can promote physical health and fitness. It develops muscles (large and small), strengthens bones, strengthens perceptual pathways (information highways) in the brain, and strengthens cardiovascular systems (Owens 2002).

Sensorimotor Development

Up to about the age of two, infants and toddlers play with objects, caring adults, and their own bodies in sensorimotor play. As they realize that they can make their bodies move in different directions, they gain confidence and begin to create more movements. As they make eye contact with adults and see an adult smile when they make a particular sound, they begin to realize the control that their sounds can have over adults. Getting a response from objects that they bang or shake, or toys that make noises or movements guides sensorimotor play and causes the child to practice the movements over and over again. As you provide toys, objects, and interactions that stimulate the child's senses, you provide her with an important piece of her overall development. Tasting, touching, and hearing are fundamental components to think about when choosing activities and toys for children in the sensorimotor stage of play.

STRATEGIES

Toys and Activities for Sensorimotor Development in Play

- grasping toys (mobiles)
- noisy toys (rattles, bells)
- blocks
- push-pull toys
- toys with textures and sounds
- wheeled-toys
- slides and swings
- simple household items (cups, pans, spoons)

Fine Motor Development

Fine motor development occurs when a child's hands move with purpose, and the child learns a skill in the process. As the youngest children tend to have the fewest of fine motor skills, they need much practice (and patience) to develop coordination of hands and fingers. Although handwriting is an important fine motor skill, much can be done prior to the child's need to write formally. Provide children with writing or drawing tools, and they will use them voluntarily. Paintbrushes, crayons, pencils, pens, and markers are all instruments that children do not need to be pressured to use. Adding color to a page is enough to tempt children to practice and improve their fine motor skills. Shaking maracas, holding drumsticks, playing a keyboard, and turning a switch off and on are other ways to get lots of practice long before formal writing is required. Fine motor skills can begin to develop through authentic everyday experiences including zipping or buttoning pants, shirts, and coats and lacing and tying shoes.

Once a child has passed the discovery and manipulative stages of play, or just "messing around" for sheer pleasure, you can extend the play by asking questions about the process. For example, "How many cups of water will it take to fill this pitcher?" and "Which basket will hold the most buttons?"

STRATEGIES

Support Fine Motor Development

- Sand play: Indoors, use a sand table or large plastic container with sand. Outdoors, provide a shaded sandbox or play area.

  - Provide toy people who live and work in the sand. If the deployed parents are in a desert, talk with the children about how Mom and Dad are living and working in the sand.

  - Bury objects in sand, and have children scavenge for them. Provide sieves, shovels, scoops, measuring cups, etc., for digging, scooping, and measuring.

  - Use sand molds or cookie cutters to explore volume, size, and shape.

- Provide construction materials and toy cars and trucks for building roads in the sand.

- Water play: To develop hand-eye coordination and to increase fine motor skills, use a water table or large plastic container filled with clean water. (Don't forget the smocks!)

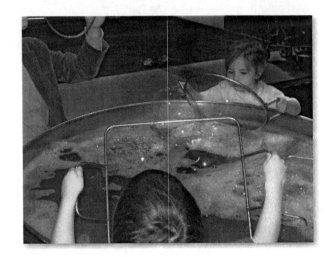

  - Add liquid dish soap, and allow children to experience the texture of bubbles. Bubble blowing is also a great way to calm an upset child.

  - Provide sieves, cups, pitchers, and other items such as small rubber bath toys that children can fill and squirt.

  - Provide a water wheel (available from many toy companies), and allow children to explore.

  - Provide objects that float and sink. Ask open-ended questions about the objects. Have the children guess which objects will sink and which will float. Make a chart to hang alongside the water table to track the children's guesses.

  - Provide sponges of all shapes, thicknesses, and types. Have children explore the water with each sponge, and talk about the process. Take photos, and make a documentation board (see chapter 6 on applying the Reggio Emilia approach for more information).

- Provide materials or objects that dissolve in water and ones that do not. For example, use flour, sugar, powdered drink mixes, baking soda, salt, gelatin, marbles, leaves, rock salt, and antacid tablets (if teacher assisted).

- Provide straws, strainers, eggbeaters, medicine droppers, plastic syringes, turkey basters, and any other kitchen gadgets that are safe for child play.

- Provide plastic dishes, pots, and pans for children to wash with detergent, sponges, brushes, and cloths.

- Bathe the baby dolls! Provide dolls that are washable, along with baby soap or soap that is gentle enough for children to use, washcloths, towels, gentle lotion, etc. Scaffold (assist) the activity as long as any child needs it, and then allow older children to work independently.

- Manipulatives: For daily exploration and use, provide manipulatives such as Legos, blocks, markers and crayons, easels and paint, playdough, and clay to encourage sculpting and other use.

- Zipping, buttoning, and tying: These are important fine motor activities that can be done with real clothing. Look for opportunities to assist a child in all of these activities in order to expand development in this area.

- Create a woodworking bench or large cable spool with safety glasses, woodworking tools, and wood to promote fine motor skill development.

Perceptual Motor Development

Perceptual motor development occurs when children combine perception, senses, and motor skills during play. During such development, children become aware of space, time, direction, and their body. Perceptual motor development is usually paired with a type of movement and most commonly includes the following: (1) using the senses to learn from the environment, (2) learning how to balance or maintain balance with ease, (3) learning where your body is in space, (4) learning how far objects are from you, (5) learning time concepts, and (6) learning directions (Kostelnik, Soderman, and Whiren 2004).

CROSSING THE MIDLINE

For optimum brain development, offer activities that encourage young children to cross their midline as often as possible. The *midline* refers to an imaginary line drawn down the center of the body from the head to the toes; crossing the midline involves moving a hand over the middle of the body to pick up an object on the other side of the body. In order for the left and right hemispheres of the brain to develop appropriately and to work well together, babies must be able to use their arms and hands together. This skill is not only a developmental milestone in infancy but also a first step in having full sensory integration, which is critical for learning to walk, read, and write at later stages.

STRATEGIES

Body Awareness

Learning how to balance

- Provide low balance beams, and each day children as young as two can walk across with assistance, if necessary. Walking on a balance beam requires crossing the midline, a must for brain development. If a balance beam is not available or you do not have space for one, use wide tape in straight and curved lines on the floor.

Learning where your body is in space

- Have children lie down on the floor and make letters of the alphabet with their whole bodies. Have them stand and make letters with arms and hands.

- Place small hula hoops on the floor, and let children practice moving inside to get a sense of where their bodies are. Now have them bring the hula hoops up to their waist and walk around the room, trying not to bump into one another.

- Before turning on the music, have children stand with outstretched hands without touching each other. Refer to their personal space as "hoop" space.

- With eyes open, have children crawl to a designated spot. Then, with eyes closed, repeat the activity.

Learning how far objects are from you

- Draw maps with pictures when traveling on field trips with children. Have the children chart or color in landmarks along the way to give them a sense of when they will get to their destination.

Time Awareness (concepts such as speed and rhythm)

- Play a musical instrument very fast and then very slow. Have children move their bodies to the music by clapping, jumping, or running in place to mirror the speed of the instrument when you play.

- Ask children to pretend they are washing machines and are spinning fast and then slow.

- Clap very simple rhythm patterns with young preschoolers, and then extend to more complex rhythms with school-age children.

Directional Awareness

- Use brightly colored long scarves or streamer rings to teach up, down, front, and back to very young children. Delay teaching left and right until children have a firm grasp of the initial concepts of direction. Young school-age children are usually ready for left and right directions or are aware of the left and right sides of their bodies.

- Tell the children: Wiggle your foot. Wiggle the other foot. Move this way. Now move the other way.

- Play or sing songs that give directions for movement from side to side, backward, and forward.

Spatial Awareness

- Use tumbling mats and balance beams to provide practice in spatial awareness.

- In order for a child to gain a sense of distance, direction, and location, play catch with him often.

- Discuss the location of things: Where is the ball? Where is your house?

- Ask children: How many steps is it to walk to the playground?

Toys for Perceptual Motor Development in Play

- pattern blocks
- puzzles
- sound cylinders
- rhythm and percussion instruments
- balance beams
- hula hoops
- metronomes
- balance boards
- balls

Gross Motor Development

We have all seen the face of a child who has mastered throwing a ball with speed and accuracy or who can climb to the top of the tallest playground structure without assistance. We have seen the face of the toddler who runs into his mother's arms at the end of the day. Gross motor skills are required for each of these activities, and acquiring those skills brings an unparalleled sense of self-competence to a child. Gross motor development can occur through movements such as walking, marching, jumping, climbing, skipping, hopping, rolling, crawling, galloping, leaping, and trotting. Using large muscles in movement and motion will aid in the development of the whole body of the young child.

STRATEGIES

Support Gross Motor Development

- Climbers, slides, basketball hoops and balls, and tumbling mats provide opportunities for young children to develop their gross motor skills in a fun and safe way. Provide assistance to those who are not yet ready to slide, climb, or tumble alone. Lower the basketball hoop for the youngest children, and allow them to place the ball in the net. Raise the hoop as needed for older children who can shoot baskets.

- Throwing activities are excellent for gross motor development. Beanbags and baskets can easily be used inside or outside.

- Use soft balls and beanbags to practice catching. During group time, throw or roll a soft ball or a sponge ball to the children to dismiss them from group or to check for mastery of concepts. For instance, after rolling or throwing the ball to the child, chant, "Chicka, chicka, one, two, three; Janie, spell your name for me." To encourage participation, accept any letter found within the child's name.

- Play a march, such as Hap Palmer's "We're Marching around the Alphabet," any of John Philip Sousa's marches, or circus marches.

- To aid in developing large muscles, have kids run or ride wheeled vehicles up and down grassy mounds or small hills.

- Create circle eights or circular paths made of concrete to facilitate wheeled toy riding. To foster dramatic play, add stop signs, gas pumps, and areas of interest, such as small buildings that can serve as gas stations, drive-through stores, or restaurants.

- For easily facilitated indoor or outdoor activities, try parachute games. When possible, sit, stand, kneel, or walk in a circle between activities. Try the following parachute games:

  - "Weather Report": Young preschoolers through early schoolagers will enjoy sitting around an open parachute (large or small). Begin with a comment such as, "I heard there is going to be a small breeze today. What would that look like?" Encourage children to make the parachute represent the weather report. You can advance to weather reports such as stormy, rainy, cloudy, calm, thunder, and so on, depending upon the children's ages.

  - "Ship at Sea": Discuss the words *choppy*, *windy*, *hurricane*, *breezy*, and *calm*. Place the opened parachute on the floor, and allow children to grasp handles and gently raise the "sea" midway to their bodies in the "calm" position. Place a beach ball or other soft ball in the middle of the parachute to represent the sailboat, and say, "Ship at sea, ship at sea—what will the sea do to me?" As each child takes a turn in calling out a weather word, everyone makes the ship behave accordingly.

  - "Washing Machine": Have early schoolage children stand around an open parachute. Tell them that the parachute is their washing machine and that at first it will wash very slowly. Everyone moves to the right, and then to the left. To facilitate synchronized movements, count, "one, two; one, two; one, two," to the speed of the desired movements, progressing to fast movements and then decreasing until the machine comes to a stop.

- "Popcorn": Children move the parachute to model popcorn popping without spilling any. Soft balls represent popcorn. Use different speeds of popping corn.

TIP

Fitness activities are an important part of care for military children. They differ from regular physical play activities by being more focused and purposeful. The Boys and Girls Clubs of America offer fitness programs that involve the whole family and make physical play fun. You can find more information on their Web site: www.bgca.org.

Planning an Outdoor Play Space

Just as you plan your inside spaces, you should give the outside space due attention. Children's out-

door play spaces have been called the playground, habitat, garden, play space, outdoor classroom, and third teacher, among other names. Under any label, outdoor play and the area where it is performed are just as beneficial as any indoor play environment for children. We have come a long way from the two swings, monkey bars, and slide from my day. Providers are realizing the advantages in providing creative and inviting outdoor places for a child's imagination to develop and thrive.

LOOSE PARTS IN OUTDOOR PLAY

Transportable materials and toys for children that have infinite possibilities for make-believe or sociodramatic play are called "loose parts" and provide a welcome addition to outdoor play. Have children make a list of toys and items that they want to play with on the playground. Place the items in containers or on trays. For my preschoolers, I bought a garden cart at a local home improvement store and used it to wheel our loose parts out to the playground each day. Our loose parts consisted of child-sized gardening tools, art materials, literacy bags, sand and water tools, and costumes with hats for the dramatic play area. Yours can be anything that children use that is not stationery on the playground, such as pipes, phones, cameras, construction toys, transportation toys, housekeeping equipment, blocks, stackable boxes, soap bubbles, shells, and items for planting and digging as well as for ball play.

When children can move the parts around, rearrange them into something else, build them up and tear them down, and incorporate loose parts into their activities, they engage in playground play much more readily and for longer periods of time. Playground experts Joe Frost and Eric Strickland (1985) state that all types of play require loose parts because of the flexibility, diversity, and novelty that they provide. They should be used in conjunction with other materials and playground structures.

STRATEGIES

Supporting Physical Play

- Use loose parts in playground play to provide flexibility and novelty to daily activities.

- Provide interest areas as well as props and simple costumes that assist in a child's need for make-believe play.

- Provide wheeled toys to foster gross motor development.

- Balance free play and planned activities that involve running, climbing, jumping, balancing, swinging, hopping, and walking, and participate often in physical activities alongside children.

- Discuss good nutrition, and offer nutritious meals and snacks to the children in your care. Model good eating habits as well.

- Provide quality indoor and outdoor play spaces for children that are developmentally appropriate, challenging, and engaging.

- Plan outdoor environments that have lots of natural elements such as gardens, hills, grassy areas, shaded areas, and water (fountains, waterfalls).

- Provide balance in physical play and inactive or sedentary play (computers, board games, TV).

- Provide large indoor spaces such as playrooms and gyms in order to support physical play during unfavorable weather.

- Spend the same amount of time planning outdoor play and indoor play.

- Where possible, spend time on nature walks, hiking trails, and climbing hills. Walk rather than ride when possible.

Lyndsay, a provider at a school-age program in California, took delight in sharing her love for the outdoors and how she planned regular outings for the children in her care. She could point to object after object that had been obtained on numerous walks around the installation and on excursions that the youth program had funded. She regularly shared her interest in photography and science with the children. They took pictures of rocks and flowers, shrubs and trees, and an occasional small animal that they met along the way. After they returned from their outings, they studied, categorized, and then cataloged the photos for future reference. I was in awe of Lyndsay's ability to cultivate in the children a high level of interest in her guided tours. She created a sign-up sheet for each excursion and publicized it well in advance. "Have you ever failed to get a group to go with you?" I asked. "No, I actually have a waiting list each time," she responded. Her experience helped me realize the enormous benefits of taking the classroom outdoors.

GAMES WITH RULES

School-age children around six or seven years old are drawn to games with rules, such as soccer, baseball or T-ball, basketball, and dodge ball. Their need to socialize in organized games and sports increases at this time. They are generally more physically adept and have a need to interact physically with their peers (especially boys). Their fine motor and gross motor skills are more refined than those of preschoolers, and they have greater balance and agility than their younger peers. They often make up games and rules for playing.

STRATEGIES

Supporting Play in School-Age Groups

- Provide a balance of unstructured playtime, time for homework, and planned activities appropriate for children of school age.

- Link to the school-day curriculum as much as possible.

- Plan challenging and stimulating activities that are specifically for schoolagers and are more challenging and stimulating when they are away from infants, toddlers, and/or preschoolers.

- Encourage peer tutoring and scaffolding between younger peers and older or school-age peers.

This chapter has presented many strategies for using play to promote social, cognitive, and physical development, underscoring the way children move through their world. A child's need for safe and developmentally appropriate play spaces is central to her development as a whole individual. As you plan environments for children birth through school age, take time to enjoy the unique and special nuances that occur at every age and stage of development.

CHAPTER FIVE

Benefits of Music and Literacy Programming

Music and literacy are closely intertwined and have a significant impact on children. You can promote literacy through music making when you sing a song about a book such as Bill Martin Jr.'s *Brown Bear, Brown Bear, What Do You See?* (1992) and when you chant the letters to the alphabet in the alphabet song.

You can find many books that are companions to familiar songs, such as "The Itsy-Bitsy Spider" (Trapani 1998), "Five Little Ducks" (Raffi 1992), and "Down by the Bay" (Raffi 1998). Nadine Bernard Westcott has a whole series of storybooks made from songs, including *The Lady with the Alligator Purse* (1998), *There's a Hole in the Bucket* (1990), and *I Know an Old Lady Who Swallowed a Fly* (2003). Other books based on songs include *The Wheels on the Bus* (Zelinsky 1990) and *The Seals on the Bus* (Hort 2003). These wonderful picture books, with words to songs the children already know, will encourage children to read and acquire vocabulary and language as you read to them.

Music and literacy also can be integrated to promote creativity, language skills, math skills, and thinking. Information that is ordinarily difficult to remember can more easily be retained if it is couched within a song, rhyme, or chant. You can use music and books to develop children's receptors for skills and concepts in music, language, and literacy. Music and books are also outlets for expression that military children need as they face either short or long separations from parents or family members.

Playing hopscotch, jumping rope, and chanting swinging rhymes are common activities on the playground. As a young child growing up in a small, rural area in the South, I had no access to extensive playground equipment, so my classmates and I spent most days at recess engaged in ball bouncing, hand clapping, and jumping rope to rhymes such as "Georgie, Porgie" and "K-I-S-S-I-N-G."

At the time, it didn't occur to us that this was a form of play. Now I realize that this experience met all the requirements for the definitions of play. Even when there is ample opportunity to play on playgrounds, children still use these rhymes to create, communicate, and build relationships.

Shakey, Shakey

Grammy, Grammy sick in bed (pretend to be sick).

Called for the doctor and the doctor said (pretend to make a phone call).

Get up Grammy (both hands move upward); *you're not sick* (point at Grammy).

All you need is an exercise trick (point at Grammy).

Stand up: Shakey Shakey; Shakey Shakey (shake body from side to side).

Turn around: Shakey Shakey; Shakey Shakey.

To the side: Shakey Shakey; Shakey Shakey.

Sit down! Shakey Shakey; Shakey Shakey.

(Repeat song, replacing "Grammy" with children's names.)

There are several types of play that build upon language, including singing rhymes and songs and acting out characters from stories. With assistance, children can learn language concepts, develop their language skills, and increase their vocabulary through play. Leading conversations, allowing uninterrupted play, vocalizing rhymes and songs, and reading books aloud that create excitement and provide opportuni-

ties for role playing or reenactment are all ways that you can provide language-rich experiences that will benefit children for years to come (Henniger 2005).

An infant plays with sounds as he coos and imitates the sounds he hears from his adult caregivers. The toddler also plays with private language or imitates adult speech as she tries out her new vocabulary; for example, a two-year-old is playing with the word *bicycle* when he calls it a "sicklebike." A preschooler plays with language when she calls a guardian angel her "angel gardener."

I'm often asked, "Do we correct children when they make those mispronunciations?" and my answer is always the same: "They are saying what they think you have said—it sounds like the same word to them, so they haven't said it incorrectly." As adults, we can continue to make the correct pronunciations when talking to children rather than pronouncing it the way they say it. They will in time change the mistaken pronunciations to the correct ones. Such play with words goes something like this:

Adult:	Are you going to ride your bicycle today?
Toddler:	Gonna ride sicklebike.
Adult:	I'll get the bicycle for you from the garage.
Toddler:	Get sicklebike!
Adult:	[singing to the tune of "Mulberry Bush"]:

We're going to get the bicycle out, the bicycle out, the bicycle out.

We're going to get the bicycle out, the bicycle out today.

Wordplay is incredibly important in the development of language and engages the child in a way that is part of his world—through playfulness and acceptance. Other ways to facilitate language development through play include role-playing make-believe characters. When you read high-interest action stories, children will instinctively and routinely reenact them. For example, by providing props, such as a flashlight and a backpack, after reading *We're Going on a Bear Hunt* (Rosen 1997) or many colored caps when reading *Caps for Sale* (Slobodkina 1987), you are inviting children to plan for language play experiences—in and out of your presence.

Music and Creative Movement

When training care providers in military child care, I'm often asked, "But how do we get our director or parents to understand how important music is?" My response is, "First, you have to know why it is important." On that note, it's important to really know why we do the things we do with children. For example, are we offering music time with instruments in our program because the instruments were on sale in the latest catalog and we needed to spend the last of the budget money quickly? Or are we offering musical experiences because they have developmental benefits, based on years of research and expert knowledge in our field? Let's try to practice the latter!

Music is one of the most integral parts of the early childhood curriculum. It is a natural motivator and backdrop for the child's day. All of us have a musical ability, whether large or small, performing or listening. Whether music is offered directly through music concepts being taught at a group time or indirectly through available listening experiences and playing of instruments in a music center, music is a must for every child, from the youngest child in care to the oldest. What would a day be without music?

Music and the Brain

In *Magic Trees of the Mind* (Diamond and Hopson 1998), the authors write that a stimulating environment for preschoolers provides a backdrop for brain growth. They go on to explain that magic trees (dendrite growth) occur most often when children are intentionally provided enrichment experiences

that enhance the different areas of development such as language, cognitive, physical, social, and emotional. There is a distinct window of opportunity not only for acquiring language but also for acquiring music skills (Diamond and Hopson 1998). Taking advantage of these critical periods in early childhood offers children the best opportunity for growth.

Embedding Music within the Curriculum

I have witnessed excellent and expensive musical instruments sitting idle in child care centers. "When does the music teacher come?" I've asked. "We are currently without one, so that wonderful piano doesn't get used much anymore." Or, when observing a nice set of drums, I've commented, "These are awesome. Who plays the drums?" "Well, nobody right now—we just got those but aren't sure what we'll do with them."

Imagine that a single experience can influence the choices a child will make for a lifetime. It's true! A seemingly random experience, such as having a musician visit the after-school program for an afternoon and play the piano, can inspire a child to become involved with music for a lifetime. Even if a music teacher can't be provided, the act of bringing talent from inside or outside the program can affect the way a child regards playing the piano (or the drums) and whether or not the child will pursue a musical career or even a recreational experience with music.

Goals for Child-Centered Music Experiences

You can help young children develop music competence by offering appropriate music experiences in small and large settings as well as with individual children. Building music into the daily curriculum is one of the best things a caregiver can do to fulfill this innate need. Developing the musical intelligence (Gardner 1983) that is within all of us is a right and a privilege for children.

In setting goals for musical experiences, take the "process over product" approach, especially when working with young children. In other words, it is okay to have skills or concepts in mind when planning and facilitating music experiences or setting up the musical environment, but the needs and desires of the children should come first. The innate need to move creatively and to respond to music in creative ways can provide a curriculum that is age, stage, and culturally appropriate (Copple and Bredekamp 2009). In addition, it is important to note the difference between teaching music *to* children and teaching *with* music in early child settings. The early childhood environment can offer opportunities for children to experience music in many ways.

Infants, toddlers, and preschoolers may

- sing;
- play instruments;
- move to rhythms or respond to simple beats;
- compose rhythms;
- use music throughout the day, including transitioning through daily routines;
- learn basic music concepts;
- dance to music of all kinds and genres;
- listen to music of all kinds and genres.

In addition to the above activities, schoolagers may

- perform or present, privately or in front of audiences;
- sing in duets and groups;
- listen to and identify different types of instruments such as woodwinds, brass, percussion, and strings;
- become familiar with major works of operas, chamber music, and ballets as well as traditional and contemporary works such as folk, hip-hop, rock, techno, world, country, and pop;
- use technology to play instruments online and with software.

Singing

Joe's mom asked, "What's that song that you've been singing at school? He comes home singing it every day and tells me that I need to sing with him. It's something about Monday."

"Oh, you mean, 'Today Is Monday,'" I replied, and I began to sing for Joe's mom, "Today is Monday, today is Monday, Monday string beans, all you hungry children, come and eat it up" (Carle 1997).

Teaching a child to sing a song is one of the most powerful kinds of literacy in early childhood. If I were to name only one important ingredient in teaching songs to children, it would be *enthusiasm*! Almost every teacher or provider has a singing voice in a range that is comfortable for him or her. The value of singing with young children is hard to identify, as it touches their very core. I've heard the shyest child humming a song that the rest of the class had been singing during transition times.

At the block center, five-year-old Sashi was singing. I started to hum alongside her as I began building my own tower of blocks. Sashi smiled. A connection had been made that might not have been accomplished with only spoken words.

STRATEGIES

Teaching Songs to Very Young Children

- SING! Enthusiastically!
- Sing some more! (Rather than teaching by rote and breaking the song into parts.)
- Sing songs that are fun!
- Sing songs that are genuine or real to children, such as ones that contain the names of the children in your care.
- Read books such as *I Know an Old Lady Who Swallowed a Fly* (Westcott 2003) that contain opportunities for singing. (Other appropriate titles are listed at the end of this book.)
- Sing during routines and transitions as well as at a defined music time each day. For example, at cleanup time, sing the following song to the tune of "La Cucaracha":

It's Time to Clean Up

It's time to clean up;

It's time to clean up;

It is time to clean up now.

It's time to clean up;

It's time to clean up;

It is time to clean up now!

Another cleanup song can be sung to the tune of "Twinkle, Twinkle, Little Star":

It's Time to Clean Up Now

It is time to clean up now; it is time to clean our room.

We will tidy up the place—use the dustpan; use the broom.

It is time to clean up now. It is time to clean our room.

- Sing songs that are predictable and repetitive, such as "Pop Goes the Weasel."
- Sing songs that can be echoed, such as Ella Jenkins's "No More Pie" (Jenkins 1989).
- Piggyback new songs with old tunes. For example, a new cleanup song can be devised by putting words to a familiar tune.
- When using prerecorded tunes, play the song as background music several times before singing it or teaching it to children.

Refrain from repeating the song over and over and teaching the song part by part. If the song has a good beat that is appealing and captivating to children, there will be no need for drill. Think about how children learn songs that they hear their older siblings sing or when they listen to CDs or the radio. They casually and effortlessly learn every word to the song. Singing a song repetitiously will be enough.

Bob, age four, was struggling in acquiring concepts and skills in language development. One warm sunny afternoon he was swinging on the playground. As I moved closer, I realized he was singing a popular rap tune. He knew every word and kept the beat as well as the tune. It changed the way I looked at children and their ability to memorize as well as learn language. Bob had surely learned this song easily and very naturally in an environment that provided no pressure to memorize it. I began paying attention to how children made emotional connections when singing.

Children thrive on the familiar and the novel. On one hand, children come to expect the familiar, such as the same care provider each day, the same schedule, the same person picking them up, predictable activities, and so on, but on the other hand, children thrive on novelty, the little changes that can occur each day, either spontaneously or directed. For this reason, songs should get a makeover from time to time, especially if they have been sung for a while and have lost their "luster." Try the following activities to spruce up your familiar tunes:

- Use freezes: Eric Carle's book *Today Is Monday* (1997) has chronological events (days of the week) that can be made into a "freeze" or series of connected pictures that tell the story. As you point to each picture, the children sing that part of the story.
- Use puppets: Provide puppet materials for the children to make a character from the song so the song can become interactive.
- Sing it in your head: After singing a song, I ask the children to sing it in their heads—doing the motions to the song, but not singing the words or making any sounds at all. It's hilarious! Try this technique with "This Old Man," "Wheels on the Bus," or "Bringing Home a Baby Bumblebee"—any songs with accompanying motions.
- Use books with songs: Alternate reading a book with singing it. For example, use the book *There Was an Old Lady Who Swallowed a Fly* by Simms Taback (1997). Add puppets to the song and you get three ways to tell the story with children, coupling novelty with familiarity.
- Sing songs with movements: For example, sing "The Itsy Bitsy Spider," adding accompanying actions.

Chants and Rhymes

Sing chants with children that have lively, predictable, and strong beats such as "Miss Mary Mack" (Cole and Calmenson 1990) and repetitive rhymes such as "A, My Name is Alice" (Taylor 2005). Young children can easily memorize chants like these. For instance, "We're Going on a Bear Hunt" is a good example of a chant that young children enjoy. Chants have real value in providing a setting for children who would not otherwise feel comfortable joining the group.

Boom-Chicka-Boom

I said a boom chick a boom (echo)

I said a boom chick a boom (echo)

I said a boom chick a rocka chicka rocka chicka boom (echo)

Oh yea (echo)

Uh huh (echo)

Now smile (echo)

Different style (echo)

(Replace "different" with a new style such as loud, whisper, fast, slow, and sing in the new style.)

Real Cool Cat

Hey there Zaidon, you're a real cool cat (point to child).

You got a lot of this and a lot of that (shake from side to side).

We all think that you are really neat (point to child).

So come on down and do the chicka chicka beat (waving motion to come).

To the side (move to one side in dance motion) *chicka-chicka; the other side* (move to other side in dance motion) *chicka-chicka.*

(Choose another child to take Zaidon's place.)

Jump rope rhymes are familiar chants heard on playgrounds and on city sidewalks. Children blend rhythm, rhyme, and movement together. Jump rope rhymes have cognitive, social, and physical benefits and are great ways for children to play and learn.

The following are traditional chants that can still be heard today:

- "Miss Mary Mack"
- "May-Ree Mack"
- "Anna Banana"
- "A, My Name Is Alice"
- "Sittin' in a Tree"
- "I Like Coffee"
- "Tiny Tim"
- "Doctor, Doctor"
- "Cinderella"

Playing Instruments

As a beginning teacher and care provider, I was challenged when children asked to use rhythm band musical instruments. I would reluctantly agree to get them out of the box, pass them out, and immediately begin thinking that I'd made a mistake. As music wasn't new to me, it shouldn't have been such a stretch. I wasn't alone. Many of my fellow teachers either didn't own a set of rhythm band instruments (intentionally) or seemed to have the same lack of competence I had. I made all the usual mistakes—passing out the instruments to the whole (large) group and telling the children to "wait" until I gave the command to play or handing out a few instruments to "the quiet ones."

This all-too-familiar scene can be eliminated. Once I began trying the following ideas from many successful teachers and providers, music became one of my favorite activities of the day:

- Introduce instruments in very small groups rather than in large groups of ten or more children. In the beginning, use the ages of the children as a rule of thumb: age two = two-person group, age three = three-person group, and so on. Increase group sizes as competence in playing grows.
- Prior to introducing instruments, get a small bell for each child. Practice ringing the bell in unison, fast and slow, and stop and start until children have shown competence in holding their bell and ringing it when prompted.
- Introduce one instrument at a time, such as tambourines. Play a beat for children to echo such as one, two, three, four; one, two, three, four; or one, two, shh, shh; one, two, shh, shh.
- In the beginning, provide lots of time for experimentation. Place a small number of bells or instruments in the music center for exploration and playing prior to using them in groups and for playing outside of group time.
- Allow older children to make up beats and then rhythms for others to echo.
- Encourage instrument identification by using two sets of identical rhythm instruments. Cover or hide the instrument that is being played, and let the children look at the second set and guess which instrument they hear.
- Provide a "home" for each instrument rather than a box that contains a hodgepodge of instruments. Routinely remove the instruments from their homes, and then place them back in their homes when finished. This treats the instruments with respect and conveys that all instruments—large, small, expensive, or inexpensive—are important.
- Use instruments often when singing. Begin with simple beats, and then move on to more complex ones, depending on the ages of the children.

Music and Transitions

Music is not only for group time; it can be used throughout the day as an integral part of the curriculum. It has been my experience that the most important transitioning periods of the nonmilitary child's day are also the most important for military kids in care. They are (1) arriving and departing, (2)

Music and Transitions throughout the Day

ACTIVITIES	MONDAY SAMPLE
Arrival	Classical music plays in background
Art	Paint to music
Music (Group time: creative movement)	Move to music with instruments, scarves, and streamers
Gross motor music play	Jump-rope chants
Fine motor music play	"This Is the Way We Tie Our Shoes"
Story time	Sing song prior to reading story: "Five Little Speckled Frogs" from *Jump, Frog, Jump* (Kalan and Barton 1995)
Waiting transitions	"The Beaver Chant"
Naptime	Soft music, such as that from *Sweet Dreams: The O'Neill Brothers' Lullabies*
Snack, meals	"Sittin' in My High Chair"
Cleanup	Piggyback songs: "Clean Up Better!" "Clean Up Now"

waiting, (3) group time, (4) snacks and mealtime, (5) care routines/hygiene, (6) transferring or transporting from one place to another, and (7) cleaning the environment.

Daily routines offer an abundance of opportunities for musical experiences. Build transition activities into your daily schedule. The planning sheet shown above can help.

WAITING TRANSITIONS SONG

The Beaver Chant

Beaver one, beaver all
Let's all do the beaver crawl

Refrain:

Ch, Ch, Ch, Ch, Ch
Ch, Ch, Ch, Ch, Ch

Beaver two, beaver three
Let's all climb the beaver tree

(Repeat refrain; make motions of beaver climbing a tree.)

Beaver four, beaver five
Let's all do the beaver jive

(Repeat refrain; make disco motions.)

Beaver six, beaver seven,
Let's all fly to beaver heaven (or: Let's all make number eleven)

(Repeat refrain; make motions of beaver flying.)

Beaver eight, beaver nine.
STOP! It's beaver time! (or: Let's all make a beaver line!)

Go beaver; go beaver; go beaver.

CLEANUP SONGS

Clean Up Better!

(To the tune of "Peanut, Peanut Butter")

> *Clean up, clean up better! Clean up, clean up better!* (Repeat)
>
> *First we take the toys, and we clean 'em; we clean 'em. We clean 'em, clean 'em, clean 'em.* (Repeat)
>
> *Clean up, clean up better!* (Repeat)
>
> *Then we take the broom, and we sweep it; we sweep it. We sweep it, sweep it, sweep it.* (Repeat)
>
> *Clean up, clean up better! Clean up, clean up better!*

Clean Up Now

(To the tune of "London Bridge Is Falling Down")

> *It is time to clean up now, clean up now, clean up now. It is time to clean up now. Let's put the toys away.*

Concepts of Music

All kids have a propensity for music on some level. Simple music concepts such as loud and soft, patterns, pitch, rhythm, and tempo can be experienced through singing, rhyming, playing instruments, and listening to music. Be sure to include songs with repeating patterns, predictable patterns, and extensions such as "I Know an Old Lady Who Swallowed a Fly." Teach children to identify motifs or recurring musical phrases or sounds in a song as soon as they can identify and remember patterns (usually at about age five).

STRATEGIES

Music Themes and Motifs

1. Select a song. The following songs are only a few of the wonderful pieces written by male and female composers based on motifs and themes.

   - The first movement of Beethoven's Symphony No. 5
   - "The Ride of the Valkyries" by Richard Wagner
   - *Three Shakespeare Songs*, op. 44 by Amy Beach
   - "Toccatina" and "Scherzo and Trio" by Claire Schumann
   - The overture to *The Flying Dutchman* by Richard Wagner
   - Theme from *Close Encounters of the Third Kind* by John Williams
   - "Maple Leaf Rag" by Scott Joplin
   - Fanny Mendelssohn Hensel, "Schwanenlied" or "Swan Song"
   - "Kind of Blue" by Miles Davis
   - "Viola Sonata" and "Piano Trio" by Rebecca Clarke
   - "Waltz of the Snowflakes" and "Arabian Dance" in Tchaikovsky's *Nutcracker Suite*
   - Theme from *Star Wars* by John Williams
   - "Peter and the Wolf" by Sergei Prokofiev

2. Listen to the music you select to find the motifs before you begin this activity with children.

3. Play the selection during homework time, arrival and/or departure, snack time, etc., so the children can become familiar with it prior to your introducing the concept of motifs.

4. Play a selection to the children in your care. Shorten the piece for younger children.

5. Ask children to signal when they hear a pattern in the song.

6. Play the selection again, and ask children to count how many times they hear it in a song.

7. Ask children to begin listening for motifs in the music they listen to outside of your program.

Ask any child if he would prefer to sit in a desk and learn to count by rote or to dance to music and learn to count; dancing to music while counting is sure to be his response. Language development and creative expression can be advanced with music through rhythm and rhyme coupled with strong beats.

> **THE WOLF TRAP INSTITUTE FOR EARLY LEARNING THROUGH THE ARTS**
>
> For almost thirty years, the Wolf Trap Institute for Early Learning through the Arts has provided arts-in-education services for children ages three through five and their teachers and families through the disciplines of drama, music, and movement. For more information, see the Web site www.wolf-trap.org.

Infants and Toddlers and Music

There's a reason that babies attune to "tunes" that are rhythmic and rhyming. Alan Fogel writes that babies respond to the voice of an adult over pre-recorded songs and music (2001). This universal "parentese" or baby talk, which is presented in a sing-song, high-pitched voice by adults when talking to children, didn't arise by chance. It appears that babies are more attuned when parents use baby talk and actually prefer it over regular speech. What does this have to do with music? Moving in a rhythmic fashion from high to low tones and then from low to high tones when speaking to infants offers them an early experience with singing.

Familiar songs such as "The Itsy-Bitsy Spider" and "Rock-a-Bye Baby" get a baby's attention for a reason. The bi-directional play that the adult engages in with the baby is not only fun but just what a baby needs for proper development of cognitive, social, and language skills. The more exaggerated sing-song voice and repetition the adult offers, the better is the baby's response (Bjorklund 2005).

In addition to preferring adult sounds, infants as young as four months have shown attraction to music being played. Couple music with adult interaction, and you have a winner every time!

Cultural Diversity in Music

You can embrace cultural diversity by first considering the children who are already in your care and the ethnicities and cultures they represent before introducing new cultures. Share recognition of and regard for their families' traditions and experiences first, before introducing songs and dances from other cultures. Military children have often been on installations around the world and have many musical experiences to share. Many military kids live mobile lives and are often in transit. As new children join your group, add activities that highlight or showcase their personal experiences with different cultures. Cutbacks in school funding have diminished the opportunity for many children in school-age classrooms to engage in music of any sort, but military kids can enjoy the benefits and long-term effects of good music opportunities outside the school classroom and inside the school-age program (before or after school and during the summer). Putumayo has teacher's guides to go with the extensive collection of world music they sell (www.putumayo.com).

Schoolagers and Music

Older military kids are ready to have their experiences with different styles of music broadened. By showing enthusiasm, interest, and knowledge of different periods and forms of music, you may go far in enticing schoolagers to expand their own knowledge of music. If you start where their interests lie and build on them, composers such as Haydn, Bach, and Ravel may become as familiar to them as Elvis, the Beatles, and Chicago were to me at a young age.

Schoolagers will appreciate your participation, involvement, and excitement related to music from historical periods. Introduce composers from contemporary and historical periods of music, and bring them to life for children. Consider the following activities built around periods of music and the composers who made them famous. Take a whole year to introduce the music of composers and engage children in appreciation of historical music.

- Find tracks of music and books about composers on the Internet and at your local library. Web sites to visit include www.teacheroz.com/music.htm and www.dsokids.com. Use a project approach for each period of music, allowing children to learn the names of the different composers as well as at least one work from each period.
- Bring in guests to play instruments that were played during the various music periods.
- Provide instruments for children to experiment with on more than one occasion.
- Encourage children to write simple melodies; provide staff paper and basic music notation instruction. Ask local musicians and teachers to assist if possible.
- Play a musical guessing game by having the children listen and attempt to identify the period, the piece, and the composer.
- Play a composition periodically throughout the time that schoolagers are with you. Have a small prize for the child who guesses the name of the piece and its composer, or let the child pick the selection for the next "name that historical tune."

Making a Music Center

The music center or area can also double as the group time area. Plays and miniconcerts or performances can occur there. Small elevated platforms can serve as stages. When I was a preschool teacher, I liked having the CD or tape player close to the group time rug so dance and creative movement could occur daily without extra preparation. A typical music center for preschool and school-age children will have appropriate music; a place to move creatively or dance; and opportunities to sing, play instruments, and create music.

Here is a checklist for the music center:

- daily music objectives
- ample time allotted for music play
- ample space prepared for all types of music play, away from quiet areas
- shelves to house musical instruments, music paper, CDs, headphones, microphones, costumes, and books about music and instruments

Fill your music center and group time with good music for children that encourages language development and self-expression while teaching them musical concepts through rhythms, rhymes, and singing. Listed on the following page are some of my favorite musical artists and their songs as well as Web sites. Use the list to help get your collection started or to try new artists. Add more to your collection as you attend concerts and seminars that showcase the best in children's music. Also, you may use the following sites to find children's music on the Web: www.pbskids.org/music and kids.niehs.nih.gov/games/songs/index.htm.

- Hap Palmer: "This Is a Song about Colors"; "Feelings"; "Sammy"; "Witches' Brew" (www.happalmer.com)
- Greg and Steve: "Limbo Rock"; "Freeze"; "The Three Little Pigs" (www.gregandsteve .com)
- Ella Jenkins: "No More Pie"; "You'll Sing a Song"; "This Train"; "May-Ree Mack"; "Did You Feed My Cow?" (www.ellajenkins.com)
- Dr. Jean: "Tooty-ta"; "I Like You"; "Cool Bear Hunt" (www.drjean.org)
- Thomas Moore: "Humpty Dumpty"; "I Am Special"; "BINGO" (www.drthomasmoore .com)
- Charlotte Diamond: "I Am a Pizza"; "Octopus"; "Spider's Web" (www.charlotte diamond.com)
- Sugar Beats: "Everybody Is a Star"; "Na Na Hey Hey Kiss Her Goodbye"; "Sugar Pie Honey Bunch" (www.sugar-beats.com)
- Jive Bunny and the Mixmasters: "Rock Around the Clock"; "At the Hop"; "Shake, Rattle, and Roll"; "Wake Up Little Susie" (www.rhapsody.com/artist/jive-bunny-and -the-mastermixers/tracks)
- Raffi: "If You're Happy and You Know It"; "Wheels on the Bus"; "Baby Beluga"; "Shalom, Shalom"; "Turn This World Around"; (www.raffinews.com)
- Nelson Gill: "One World, One Light"; "Everybody Limbo"; "Ten Little Ducks" (www .nelsongill.com)

STRATEGIES

Supporting Music in Infants and Toddlers

- Provide music that fosters crossing the midline. For babies, sing songs such as "The Itsy-Bitsy Spider," "Pat-a-Cake," and "Where Is Thumbkin?" crossing the midline with baby's hands and arms on as many occasions as possible.

- Sing songs often, and play soothing music during transition and routine care periods of the day.
- Echo sounds that babies make. Add new sounds for babies to hear and imitate.
- Provide instruments appropriate for infants and toddlers, such as shakers, maracas, drums, and bells. Add musical toys too.
- Develop language through music—play songs that have simple, repetitive lyrics with bouncy tunes.
- Make fingerplays and games a part of each baby's day to foster motor and cognitive development through music and rhyme.
- Make a musical mobile out of small shakers and hang it in a safe place anywhere infants and toddlers are in care: changing table, play space, restroom, patio, entrance, and so on. Touch the mobile to make a soft sound.

Supporting Music in Preschoolers

- Sing songs such as "Going on a Bear Hunt," "The Three Bears in Rhyme," and "The Itsy-Bitsy Spider," demonstrating crossing the midline on as many occasions as possible.
- For preschoolers and young schoolagers, play music that is appropriate for marching, such as "The Ants Go Marching One by One," and ask children to march in a circle or path while raising a knee to be touched by the opposite elbow (for example, right knee, left elbow).
- Play singing and movement games such as "London Bridge Is Falling Down," "The Farmer in the Dell," "Ring around the Rosy," "Hokey Pokey," and "Here We Go Looby Lou."
- Coordinate your curriculum, musical objectives, and goals with the standards of NAEYC and MENC: The National Association for Music Education, which can be found at www.naeyc.org and www.menc.org.

- Provide rhythm instruments, such as sand blocks, ankle bells, castanets, tone blocks, cymbals, triangles, wrist bells, and rhythm sticks, for play during structured and un-structured time. Add percussion instruments (drums, shakers, and gongs) gradually, al-lowing children time to gain respect for real instruments.

Supporting Music in Schoolagers

- Use the project approach to develop an ex-tended look at historical periods of music. Internet access is needed. Have students search the Internet for sites that offer infor-mation about different music periods. Many sites have recordings that kids can listen to. Suggested sites include the San Francisco Symphony Kids Site at www.sfskids.org, the New York Philharmonic Kidzone at www .nyphilkids.org, and the Dallas Symphony Orchestra Kids Music Room at www.dsokids .com.

- Practice crossing the midline. For young schoolagers, provide balance beams or lines on the floor to walk on while music plays. Start with slow music and then advance to faster music as they walk the line.

- Provide materials for dancing, such as paper plates and shoe boxes for skates. Country-and-western music appropriate for children with a strong beat is an excellent choice for paper-plate skating.

- Make the music area a place for performing miniconcerts. Schoolagers love to perform with microphones, costumes, and music or karaoke machines. Record the performances, and share them with parents or use them as a fund-raising source.

- Explore instruments from other countries and cultures such as the Kalimba thumb piano and Djembe drum from Africa, maracas from Peru, rainsticks from South America, guiros from Central America, caxixi from Brazil, cas-tanets from Spain, and gongs and cymbals from China.

- Provide music videos for children that show different dance steps and moves.

- Encourage children to compose music by visiting Web sites such as www.creating music.com or the San Francisco Symphony Kids Site at www.sfskids.org.

- Provide lined music notation paper for re-cording notes and beats composing music.

Literacy

When children of military parents are in our care, we have the unique opportunity to lay the founda-tion for a lifetime of achievement. The debate con-tinues on what constitutes readiness, yet we can all agree that children are born ready to learn and that we must be prepared to foster that learning. The more children in our society have reading and writ-ing opportunities, the better their chances of being ready for school and having school success. This section will offer ideas to help in accomplishing that goal.

Becoming literate begins very early, as children learn to use symbols in place of real things. When a toddler hands an adult a cookie but no cookie is in sight, he has already begun to substitute the unreal for the real. "Want bite?" with a little hand outstretched. "Mmm. That's a good cookie," says the adult. Acquiring language paves the road for reading. This emerging literacy takes place as the child begins to listen, speak, read, and write. Babies play with sounds by simply making them over and over, imitating what they hear in conversations with significant adults in their lives. They are able to understand language, or receive it, long before they can express it in words that adults can understand. Never doubt that they "know" what they are saying.

Fourteen-month-old Jay uses a phrase over and over that sounds like, "A-duh-a-duh-a-duh-a-duh" to his mom and dad. "What is he talking about?" they ask over and over. It is clear that as he points to different objects and repeats the phrase, Jay knows that the sounds stand for something important to him. In time, this phrase will come to mean something like, "I want that."

Literacy Concepts

Use literacy concepts when planning activities for children that will foster reading and pre-reading skills, providing a link between school and care centers or environments. The following concepts, adapted from the *Head Start Child Outcomes Framework* (National Head Start Child Development Institute 2004, 2), are excellent literacy objectives for four-year-olds and are expectations for Head Start children upon entering kindergarten. The complete list can be found at www.hsnrc.org/cdi and can serve as a guide for language and literacy activities in your preschool program.

SPEAKING
The child

- responds to discussions and conversations with peers and adults;
- initiates conversations with peers and adults;
- increases vocabulary (in understanding and speaking);
- uses clear pronunciation and longer and more grammatically correct and complex sentences.

LISTENING AND UNDERSTANDING
The child

- listens to conversations, poems, stories, and songs with interest;
- understands and can carry out one and then multistep directions.

SOUND AND SPEECH AWARENESS
The child

- shows ability to discriminate and identify sounds through spoken language;
- shows awareness of beginning and ending sounds;
- matches sounds and rhymes in familiar words, games, songs, stories, and poems;
- hears and discriminates separate syllables in words;
- recognizes words that begin with the same sounds.

BOOK AWARENESS
The child

- shows growing interest in books;
- shows interest in reading;
- retells and dictates stories;
- can handle and care for books.

PRINT AWARENESS AND CONCEPTS OF PRINT
The child

- shows awareness of print (in community, home, and school);

- is developing an understanding of forms of print in signs, letters, e-mail, newspapers, lists, messages, menus, recipes;
- follows print as it is read;
- recognizes a word as a unit of print;
- shows awareness of letters grouped to form words and of how words are differentiated by spaces between them.

EARLY WRITING
The child

- understands that writing has a purpose;
- uses different writing tools such as computers, markers, pens, pencils, and crayons;
- has progressed from scribbling to using letters as symbols;
- writes own name and the names of others;
- tells stories or records events on paper with text or pictures or both.

ALPHABET KNOWLEDGE
The child

- associates names of letters with their shape and sound;
- notices beginning letters in familiar words (especially in her own name and the names of others who are special to her).

STRATEGIES

Promote Reading and Writing

- Talk to children. Have conversations with them about the events in their lives that can be written or read about such as what a deployed parent may be doing or seeing.
- Let children see you write.
- Let children see you read.
- Create a book nook.
- Create a writing center.
- Include books in all areas of the room or home.
- Include writing (and scribbling) as an important part of the curriculum.

Literacy-Rich Environments

Classrooms, centers, and homes filled with lots of materials and activities that show our knowledge of the importance of language and print can help military children. Although conventional reading and writing are taught to most young children during formal schooling, there are lots of exciting things you can do to get them under way. When children live in a society that reveres reading and writing, it is common for them to be curious about print. Print is everywhere! Children need to become part of this important way of communicating as you prepare the environment for developing literacy.

Literacy Center

The library, writing, language, and computer centers can be combined into one literacy center that fosters the development of literacy skills. Use name-guessing games, letter-sorting mats, and books categorized in bins for reading and sorting. Headphones, taped stories, and different surfaces to write on such as a chalkboard, a whiteboard, and small hand-held writing boards encourage informal writing. Computers with developmentally appropriate software and safe Internet sites are perfect lures to a schoolager to increase writing and reading skills. Chapter 8 has ideas to help kids stay connected to loved ones and friends while they practice their literacy skills.

Rather than having a stand-alone computer center, why not place a computer in or near your writing center as well as in the housekeeping or dramatic play center? If we truly want to integrate our curriculum and make it a part of the child's real life, think about ways we use everyday items and how many of the same ones are used in different areas. The following table offers examples of elements in an environment that supports reading readiness:

Literacy-Rich Environment Checklist

FURNISHINGS

- ☐ comfortable chairs in child and adult sizes
- ☐ tables and chairs
- ☐ rugs

WRITING TOOLS AND MATERIALS

- ☐ paper of all sizes, colors, shapes, and thicknesses
- ☐ markers, pencils, erasers, and crayons
- ☐ staplers, glue, string, hole punches, tape, paper clips, and scissors
- ☐ clipboards and carbon paper
- ☐ word banks, a word wall, or letter stamps
- ☐ blank books
- ☐ envelopes
- ☐ stationery
- ☐ sticky notes
- ☐ stamps and stamp pads
- ☐ invitations
- ☐ notepads
- ☐ coupons
- ☐ index cards of different sizes
- ☐ computer
- ☐ whiteboards
- ☐ chalkboards
- ☐ magnetic letters
- ☐ stencils
- ☐ magic slates
- ☐ cookie cutter alphabet

READING TOOLS

- ☐ recordings of ongoing activities in the home or room, such as stories of gardening experiences, field trips, recordings of plant or animal growth in pictures and words, letters from deployed parents or old friends, and labels on prop boxes and other tools
- ☐ attendance charts, daily schedule and plans, newsletters, and weather charts
- ☐ documentation boards with pictures and child-authored materials visible and on display for several days or weeks
- ☐ picture-book posters
- ☐ old magazines
- ☐ phone books
- ☐ posters
- ☐ maps
- ☐ globes
- ☐ children's magazines
- ☐ newspapers
- ☐ calendars
- ☐ catalogs
- ☐ alphabet posters and charts
- ☐ bulletin boards for display
- ☐ dictionaries
- ☐ menus
- ☐ appointment books
- ☐ message pads
- ☐ business cards
- ☐ order blanks
- ☐ old checks
- ☐ address books

LITERACY ACTIVITIES

Children can

- ☐ listen to books recorded and read by familiar adults or children;
- ☐ write in personal journals, illustrating their stories;
- ☐ write signs, messages, stories, notes; journal;
- ☐ make lists for cooking activities, recipes, purchases for the class, things they did over the weekend, their summer vacation, and so on;
- ☐ dictate a story for the teacher or another child to write;
- ☐ make sign-up lists;
- ☐ make signs, posters, flyers, brochures, and newsletters;
- ☐ write articles for the local newspaper;
- ☐ make recipe books;
- ☐ make documentation boards;
- ☐ create a Web site;
- ☐ draw with text;
- ☐ write stories to accompany dolls in the dramatic play center;
- ☐ label block constructions, for example, "Leaning Tower of Elmendorff;"
- ☐ write notes to peers, for example, block center signs such as "Save this for tomorrow;"
- ☐ make Time 1 and Time 2 drawings (the same drawing done over the course of a month or a year).

LANGUAGE BATHS

In an environment filled with children and adults conversing, singing, and reading aloud, children develop language and literacy skills that help make them good readers and writers. Language baths occur when they engage in socio-dramatic play, build blocks and describe how tall the tower is, and respond to the cleanup song or receive directions in song. For instance, rather than telling the children in my care to "take turns," I would sing their names in this piggyback song: "Bella and John Will Take a Turn" to the tune of "Here We Go 'Round the Mulberry Bush."

The Importance of Children's Literature

Shared reading between two children or between a care provider and a child is irreplaceable when it comes to providing best practices in achieving early literacy skills. Baby books, lift-the-flap and pop-up books, picture books and concept books, and early readers or chapter books are a few of the many types of books that can be provided for children.

READING ALOUD

Read aloud, often, to infants and toddlers to develop early literacy skills. Encourage parents or primary caregivers to begin at home, and you can continue reading aloud while children are in your care. I like to call this approach "Read five and thrive!" Just as five fruits and vegetables should be eaten every day in order to have a healthy diet, I believe that every young child should have a minimum of five books read to him every day in order to fulfill his literary diet. Considering that the average book for very young children can be read in three to five minutes, this goal can be reached in as little as fifteen minutes a day. Even if your toddlers won't sit for story time, practice the motto, "If I read it, they will come!"

A young teacher of toddlers practiced "If I read it, they will come" by preparing props for the book Draw Me a Star *by Eric Carle (1998). She prepared cardboard cutouts of a large star and other things from the story. She had tried holding a toddler story time in the past and wanted to try something new that she hoped would be more successful. She sat down in the middle of the room, props beside her, and began to read. Toddlers would stop and watch from across the room or chime in when they heard predictable or familiar words. Some walked over and picked up a prop and took it to another part of the room. Some sat down, listened, and responded to the story. As she said the words "The end," a toddler yelled, "Read it 'gin."*

STRATEGIES

Reading Aloud to Children

- Just read! Make it a part of your daily routine or schedule.

- Select books that are age appropriate: picture books for younger children and chapter books for older children.

- Select books with real photographs that can become discussion starters.

- Select books that contain interactive parts so that children can become part of the read-aloud process.

- Allow children to select books, and don't be afraid to condense books brought from home that are a bit long. Affirm the child's efforts to contribute to the read-aloud time.

- Stop before the end of the book, and ask, "What do you think happened next?"

- Ask for different endings to the book, such as, "What could the Little Red Hen do differently next time?"

- Ask for more pro-social endings to the book such as, "How could the billy goats Gruff and the troll be friends?"

- Read to children for the pleasure of reading and instilling the love of reading in them rather than for "teaching" them to read. Again, "If we read it, they will come!"

BOOKS FOR CHILDREN

Children need all types of books in the classroom or home. Having several books per child will ensure that you have enough to keep the child interested, especially if you change them at least once per month and more often if needed. Keep a "rainy day" box of books for that day when the unexpected occurs and you need a high-interest activity. The following list provides an overview of the wide range of books that are available for children of all ages. Try to provide a few from each category.

- concept books
- picture books
- number books
- wordless books
- predictable books
- informational books
- alphabet books
- poetry books
- nursery rhymes
- fairy tales
- folktales
- mysteries
- teacher-made environmental print books or books with photos or copies of print found in advertisements of common items children use or places that they visit
- dictionaries
- functional print items, such as name tags, helpers' charts, exit signs, stop signs, cereal boxes, and birthday cards (Fields and Spangler 2000, 119)
- encyclopedias
- real-life photo books

Literacy through Music

Songs are a great way to increase language skills and foster literacy skills. The rhythm and rhyme found in the songs of early childhood are natural lures for children. Strong beats, upbeat tempos, and fun language are all components of good songs for children and can become a part of instilling a love for school (or child care environments in our case) and learning. It is beyond explanation how powerful and pleasurable music is to all of us, especially children. So it just makes sense that we use it to help children acquire literacy, as they seem to have a natural wiring for rhythmic sounds. Music can extend a child's vocabulary as well as blend physical and cognitive exercises into enjoyable experiences, as music often evokes emotions in children and the adults who work with them.

STRATEGIES

Enhance Listening

- Bounce large exercise balls to music.
- Mirror the teacher's and then each other's movements to slow music.
- Use visual posters or cards for children to mirror during music, such as stick figures pointing in different directions and doing different actions.
- Play "Freeze." Have children move to music such as Greg and Steve's "Freeze." Have them freeze into selected or specified shapes such as a pretzel, a triangle, a statue, or a letter of the alphabet.
- Use scarves made of thin fabric as extensions of the body to move during music.
- As part of group or circle time, play music and ask older children to raise their hands when they hear a rhythmic or repeating pattern.
- Using rhythm sticks, have children mirror the beats that you play. Begin with simple and then move to more complex rhythms.
- Read and sing stories such as *Over in the Meadow* (Keats 1999), *And the Green Grass Grew All Around* (Schwartz 1999), and *Shake My Sillies Out* (Raffi 1988).
- Make animal movements while listening to music such as "Dance of the Mosquito" by Liatov or "Flight of the Bumblebee" by Rimsky-Korsakoff.

- Try these Web sites for some fun listening activities that will teach sound discrimination:
  - www.creatingmusic.com
  - www.sfskids.org
  - kids.niehs.nih.gov/games/songs/index.htm

Storytelling

Storytelling is a language-rich experience, especially when we tell lots of stories and engage children in the storytelling process. Stories that have animation possibilities, such as *Caps for Sale* (Slobodkina 1987), are a hit with young children. If children are given props to use during storytelling, they will both listen and actively participate. For instance, the peddler's caps in *Caps for Sale* can be constructed from cardboard and then colored to represent the different caps that the monkeys toss from the tree.

Round-robin stories are fun when you provide a story starter such as, "I went walking down the street, and . . ." Children can then add sentences one at a time, building the story as they continue. Pictures of animals or people can be used as silent story starters. For example, you can hold up a picture of a boy walking down a road, and then have each preschooler or young schoolager add one part to the story about the boy:

Child 1: He's going to see his horse at his grandmother's.

Child 2: And then he's going to stay with his gramma while his mama is deployed.

Child 3: That's John, and he's running away 'cause he thinks he can go and find his dad.

Child 4: He's just taking a walk to a friend's house.

Grab-bag stories are lots of fun: children can take a familiar object or toy from the bag and tell a story about it. Good items to place in the bag are clocks, whistles, small books, small rhythm instruments, play money, toy trains, small globes, airline ticket stubs, play food, stuffed animals, dolls, cars, trucks, and telephones.

Circle Time

When children are preschool age, circle time (often called group time) is a great way to bring the group together each day. It can foster development in all domains as well as build community among children. Preschoolers can sit for about ten to fifteen minutes, depending upon the group and the planned activities, and schoolagers can sit for up to thirty minutes, depending upon interest. If your groups are larger than ten children, have more than one circle time each day, alternating attendance. It is important to give children as much opportunity for participation as possible by having smaller groups.

Give circle time a literacy agenda that is predictable, opening with a song, chant, fingerplay, or rhythmic dance each day. Provide planned activities that foster listening, stimulate thinking, and build creativity as a concept development. Follow the APAP (active, passive, active, passive) pattern to keep children engaged. Close with a recap of the concept activity, and then transition to the next activity by singing a song, chant, or rhyme or going over the rest of the daily schedule using rebus (picture/word) charts.

An appropriate schedule with sample activities for concept development follows:

Concept: Dinosaurs

Introduction of concept: Read a book about dinosaurs.

Development of concept: Show pictures of one or two dinosaurs and discuss different properties or characteristics of each.

Closing: Roll a soft ball to individual children, asking them to tell the group one thing they know about dinosaurs.

Transition to the next activity: Sing the following songs about dinosaurs.

Dinosaurs
(To the tune of "Farmer in the Dell")

He's stegosaurus; he's stegosaurus.

Clickety clack, down his bony back.

He's stegosaurus.

T-Rex
(To the tune of "Did You Ever See a Lassie?")

Did you ever see a T-Rex, a T-Rex, a T-Rex?

Did you ever see a T-Rex, go this way and that?

Go this way and that way.

Go this way and that way.

Did you ever see a T-Rex, go this way and that?

Ask open-ended or divergent questions to stimulate language and thinking during circle time. Continue with a skill to be developed, such as the one in this cognitive activity:

Adult: Where do butterflies go when it rains?

Child 1: They hide in bushes.

Child 2: They go back to Canada.

Child 3: I hope they don't get wet.

Child 4: To my house!

Child 5:   To their mommies and daddies.

Child 6:   I had a butterfly umbrella.

Child 7:   Under a leaf.

STRATEGIES

Successful Circle Times

- Begin an activity the moment the children arrive.

- Choose books and materials with pictures that all the children can see.

- Start by keeping circle time to a minimum. Lengthen the time as the children mature in their ability to listen and follow instructions. Continue only as long as the children are engaged.

- Keep routine activities such as calendar, weather, or assigning jobs, and so forth, to a minimum—weekly rather than daily.

Promoting Literacy for Preschoolers at Circle Time

Storytelling and story reading: use picture books. Use props to tell stories without books.

Use puppets to add fun and excitement to circle time. Puppets can add a dimension of language by "speaking" for the shy child and increasing turn taking for the spirited or dynamic (talkative) child. Give each child a puppet to hold and have each take a turn talking in the group.

Use fingerplays, such as "The Three Bears in Rhyme" or "Going on a Bear Hunt," that provide language play and development.

Do an "object lesson" once or twice a week. Bring in an object to represent a concept you want to teach, such as a coconut for the concepts of touch, color, taste, and smell. Have children and parents supply objects from interesting places they have been.

What's in the box? Place an object in a decorated box or bag (out of sight), and give clues about what it is. Ask for guesses after each clue.

What's in a name? Young children begin to learn the names of their peers through activities such as the following: Print each child's name on a rectangular card or tagboard. Punch a hole in the end of each name card. Place the cards on a ring. During group time each day, hold up each card for all children to see, and sing something like "A is for Alice; where will she play today?" Alice then claims her name and selects a center for play. Sing each child's name until all children have selected a place to play.

Promoting Literacy for Schoolagers at Circle Time

Listening game: Start the game by saying, "I'm going fishing, and I am taking a boat." The next child has to add another item to the trip, as well as remembering the items listed before her turn. "I'm going fishing, and I'm taking a boat and a fishing pole." Continue the game until all children have had a chance to play. For large groups, allow children to ask for assistance. This keeps everyone engaged for the whole game. Avoid putting people "out" for making mistakes; instead find ways to keep them "in." Use "I'm going, and I'm taking . . ." as the story starter for future listening games. Allow a child to make up the first line.

Promote speaking through performance. Creative dramatics or plays, joke telling (including riddles), tongue twisters, rapping, reading a story, reciting poetry, or singing jingles are all important ways that children improve their literacy skills. Encourage children to make up their own to perform. J. Patrick Lewis is an author of children's poetry and rhymes and an excellent source for riddles, tongue twisters, and poems.

Bring in guest speakers to read or tell a story or to recite poetry. Find others who have authored books, stories, or poems, and ask them to share their love for reading and writing with schoolagers. Keep group times to about thirty minutes.

Drawing and Writing

It is as comfortable for children to draw as it is for them to write. Many of their productions on paper are a combination of the two. At around five or six years of age, children usually begin combining drawing and writing and still communicate with inaccurate representations. Accept this work as self-expression, and encourage all drawing that extends the thoughts and ideas of the child, with or without text. Some children begin with a drawing and then write emerging text to explain or extend their thinking. Others begin with text and draw to illustrate the story. Either is okay; both provide a framework for a child's thinking and way of communicating. It is *not* necessary to label a child's drawing in order to provide meaning to the picture unless a child asks you to. Instead, say, "Make your mark here to tell about your picture" or "Do you want any writing on the picture?" If you have trouble identifying children's work, you could invest in a name stamp for each child and allow children to stamp the backs (or fronts) of the drawings, or you

could just let them know that you will be writing their names on their work. Ask if they prefer back or front.

Learning to write occurs in stages, and in the beginning, children will make marks and scribbles that don't resemble writing as we know it. These early attempts at communicating in print are not to be discounted; they should be celebrated and appreciated. Once fine motor skills and letter-sound association develop in young children, writing will not be such a daunting task. The most basic stage of writing is much like pretend reading, where the child practices writing-like behaviors. Children are actually copying or attempting to reproduce what they have seen written, just as children who preread try to read the way the grown-ups do. Again, this pre-writing stage is important, as it lays the foundation for later conventional writing.

You can offer a variety of activities that will promote the fine motor development, hand-eye coordination, and cognitive development that are necessary for writing. For example, provide lots of writing tools as well as paints and brushes, glue sticks, puzzles, ball tossing opportunities, and fingerplays. Making alphabetic letters and symbols can come later, once the child has an interest in writing the ABCs.

I've observed four distinct stages of writing with a few substages that are common to young children. Young children usually experience the following stages in a sequential order, but much overlap can occur between stages, and children progress through the stages at different rates:

1. Manipulative stage (two to three years)
   a. Mark making, scribbling
   b. Lines, dots, marks, and shapes
2. Drawing stage (three to four years)
   a. Symbol making
   b. Drawings that don't depict reality
3. Alphabetic symbol writing (three to five years)
   a. Scribbles convert to circles and straight lines
   b. Letters begin to emerge
   c. Name writing begins
   d. Invented spelling/writing begins (lots of misspelled words)
   e. Blending text and drawings to communicate ideas
4. Conventional spelling/writing (four to seven years to adult)
   a. Correct spelling is important
   b. Phonics, grammar, and vocabulary all become important
   e. Drawings become more accurate and depict reality

As young toddlers, children will take a pen or marker and scribble on walls, furniture, floors, and themselves rather than on paper. In this stage, making marks on available surfaces is much more appealing than waiting for paper or an appropriate writing space. In the very earliest stages of writing mark making is impulsive and done solely for the pleasure of seeing the effects of placing a pen or marker on a surface and watching marks appear. During this manipulative stage children explore with materials, often in a random fashion, while taking control of their environment in this small way. Encourage mark making as often as possible, and provide appropriate large spaces such as walls and tables covered in large rolls of paper where more than one child can "write."

Scribbling or mark making is a precursor to the next stage, which begins at around age three or four. Children in the drawing stage will symbolically represent objects that they have seen in their environment. At first, only the child may be able to determine what is symbolized.

FUNCTIONAL PRINT

Darius was preoccupied with being the leader and asked several times a day if he would be next. As his prekindergarten teacher, I wanted to foster reading as much as possible and meet Darius's needs as well. I printed each child's name on a card and placed all the cards in a vertical column down a corner of my blackboard. Darius could instantly see where his name was located in relation to the leader's each day. To designate the leader, a red arrow was placed to the left of the name. As Darius watched for his turn, he began counting the number of people who were ahead of him, often telling them how many days they had to wait until it was their turn. His counting skills improved dramatically, and he learned to read the names of twenty-one classmates in a short period of time.

As the above example illustrates, functional print can be an important classroom tool for children in military care, as it conveys information in an emerging literacy fashion. As children move from activity to activity throughout the day, functional print can provide directions and help with classroom management. Also, information can be recorded after an event such as a trip to an amusement park or carnival on a "My Favorite Ride" chart. "Whose Birthday Is It Today?" and "Whose Turn to Feed the Fish?" are other functional print charts commonly used to keep everyone informed. Any attempts to get children to read and write will make a difference when they begin practicing these skills (in the form of scribbling at first).

You can also use functional print when labeling classroom or home objects as well as when providing notes to children around the house or room as reminders of activities or events. Functional print is often a combination of symbols, pictures, and printed text. More symbols and pictures are necessary for younger children, and more text can be included for schoolagers. Functional print is a form of communication, so avoid correcting children's writing as it emerges, and continue to model appropriate spelling, pronunciation, and word use for children in your care. Some providers write a new letter to their children every day and place it in a special spot so that everyone will see it. Other providers write individual notes to children and place them in a communication box as often as possible. The idea is to get kids to read and write without concern for making errors. I have used the following functional print ideas repeatedly in classrooms with young children.

STRATEGIES

Sign for Daily Participation in Centers

Reading and Writing Center	
WHO CAME TODAY? MAKE YOUR MARK.	
LORI	
JAMES	
MESHA	
SUSAN	
HAMID	
CAM	
JULES	
LYDIA	
MIOKI	
SANTANA	
KWAN	

Clipboard Sign-in Sheets

Materials: Printed names of children (make multiple copies, as one is needed for each day) and a clipboard

1. Place a sheet of printed names on the clipboard; date the sheet.

2. Have each child sign in each day by writing his name beside the printed name.

3. Save the printed sheets, and assess progress in name writing after several weeks or months.

Note: I made the names large enough to cut them apart after a few days and place them in the children's portfolios.

We Lost a Tooth!

Early school-age children lose teeth. I made a large tooth shape and printed, "We Lost a Tooth!" on it. I then drew smaller teeth and laminated both the large poster and the smaller teeth. When children lost a tooth, they would write their name on a smaller tooth and stick it on the poster. I placed a small treasure chest with inexpensive toys on a shelf so that when children lost a tooth, they could retrieve a treasure from the box.

Functional Print Posters

To celebrate other events in the lives of the children in your care, make posters with the following statements:

- "My dad/mom is away," or "My dad/mom is home."

- "I know my address."

- "I know my phone number."

- "We're moving!" (Make a countdown or visible reminder for children who are being transferred to another installation or who are leaving the military for civilian life.)

Author Study

After reading several of his books over and over, I chose Eric Carle for an author study with prekindergartners. I made a poster showing three book jackets in three columns. Children chose their favorite Eric Carle book and wrote their names in the respective column.

HAVE YOU SEEN MY CAT? (1996)	TODAY IS MONDAY (1997)	THE VERY HUNGRY CATERPILLAR (1974)

Note: Schoolagers can choose their favorite author and make a poster with drawings, favorite lines from the books, reflection statements about the books, etc. Hang the posters for all to enjoy and for documentation of the study.

Recipe Chart for "No-Cook" Pizza Saucers

To teach reading skills, offer this rebus cooking activity with words and pictures.

1. Toast one half of an English muffin.

2. Spread pizza sauce over the muffin half.

3. Sprinkle cheese on top.

4. Add pepperoni slices or other toppings.

5. Place on metal tray, and toast in the oven for about three to five minutes.

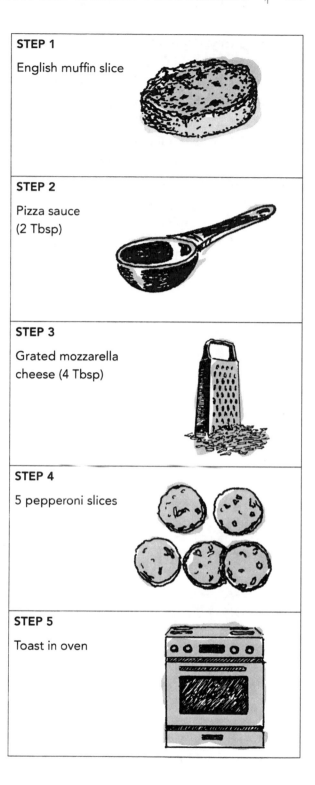

STEP 1
English muffin slice

STEP 2
Pizza sauce
(2 Tbsp)

STEP 3
Grated mozzarella cheese (4 Tbsp)

STEP 4
5 pepperoni slices

STEP 5
Toast in oven

Promoting creativity through music and movement fosters "out of the box" thinking, which is critical to children's development. Music and movement activities should be related to skills children need to develop and planned with specific outcomes in mind. It doesn't take a lot to modify your curriculum to include music and movement in planned or serendipitous moments with children. Children tend to have a more positive attitude about their play environments when music and creative activities are included; such activities are often child-directed and give children opportunities to expand their learning.

Creative language experiences are another facet of a well-rounded program that shows appreciation for the arts and their value to a child's education and care. *Emerging literacy* is a term that we often hear used to refer to a child's development in language learning and the more formal aspects of reading. In this chapter, I gave a much broader vision of emerging literacy. Verbal and nonverbal communication, written words and symbols, gestures and movements are all considered a part of language learning that promotes the child's holistic development.

CHAPTER SIX

Resources for Quality Programs: Multiple Intelligences and Reggio Emilia

Many educators look to multiple intelligences theory and the Reggio Emilia philosophy as two important views of best practices in early education. You can use the information found in this chapter to make curriculum decisions for the military children in your care.

Multiple intelligences theory has been put into practice in many schools across America. With the theory in mind, teachers and providers look carefully at what a child's strengths or propensities appear to be, even at an early age. Building upon these strengths is central to the theory, and curriculum plans and strategies can be based upon the individual strengths of the military kids you work with every day. You can also assess your program to see which of the intelligences are being overlooked and make efforts to provide activities that foster development in those areas as well, especially since traditional approaches to early care primarily address language and math skills.

If you plan your curriculum around principles of the Reggio Emilia philosophy, you will be valuing culture, community, and parent involvement as you show appreciation and respect for each child in your care. A Reggio-based curriculum encourages strong relationships between children and adults and promotes projects that stem from a child's natural curiosity. Using Reggio principles will help highlight and nurture the strong ties that members of military families have with one another.

Multiple Intelligences

When planning environments for children, multiple intelligences theory (MI) can be a good tool to use. According to the theory's creator, Howard Gardner, all children possess more than one intelligence, all children learn in different ways, and it is possible to design a program that addresses those ways of learning. Gardner has identified nine different ways of knowing (Armstrong 1999 and Gardner 2006). Thomas Armstrong describes each intelligence in his book, *7 (Seven) Kinds of Smart* (1999, 224). Armstrong refers to the intelligences as types of "smart" such as picture smart, word smart, and body smart, and I like to use these as they are sometimes easier to remember. Each of his terms, along with Howard Gardner's original terms, are included below:

- spatial intelligence, or picture smart
- linguistic intellegence, or word smart
- logical-mathematical intelligence, or number smart
- musical intelligence, or music smart
- bodily-kinesthetic intelligence, or movement smart
- interpersonal intelligence, or we smart
- intrapersonal intelligence, or me smart
- naturalistic intelligence, or nature smart
- existential intelligence, or wonder smart

Gardner, a Harvard psychologist, describes his theory as a propensity for (or leaning toward) a particular behavior or way of thinking, based on what is valued in a person's own society or culture (1983). In other words, when we encounter schoolagers who routinely ask to go outside and play baseball or to go to the computer room and play video games, we may be seeing body smart (bodily-kinesthetic intelligence) and picture smart (spatial intelligence) in action. When preschoolers select the music center day after day to sing, listen to music, or play an instrument, they are applying their musical intelligence.

One of the most important benefits of this theory is that it leads teachers, parents, providers, diagnosticians, and all others who work with or on behalf of children to look at children's strengths rather than their weaknesses. The traditional report card that outlines only a child's deficits isn't helpful because it only addresses lack of ability, whereas the theory of multiple intelligences addresses abilities or capabilities. In addition, care providers who are aware of this theory can draw from each other's strengths or intelligences when working with children in order to more effectively meet all needs. For example, one teacher, Stacie, loves to garden and routinely asks to be part of outside play, where she has engaged schoolagers in planting and weeding the outdoor garden (naturalistic intelligence), while

Jawan, who plays the guitar, prefers to interact with kids inside the music center (musical intelligence) when he is working in a preschool program.

Recognizing your own strengths or intelligences will enable you to plan more effectively and better understand the intelligences that children possess. Gardner asserts that we can have more than one strength and that those strengths often act in concert with one another (1983). The most effective teaching comes from finding ways to help the child tap into more than one intelligence at a time, which is how the best learning occurs.

As you make weekly plans, word smart or linguistic intelligence is probably a staple in your plans, as it has such value in our curriculum. Standardized tests are traditionally focused or built around only two of the intelligences—linguistic intelligence and logical-mathematical intelligence. Because these two have been at the forefront of testing children and adults, the other seven intelligences have often been ignored, underused, or neglected. It is a watchful planner who takes care in providing a balanced curriculum to include all nine intelligences. Easy? No! But you can learn about each intelligence and how to plan in order to draw upon as many intelligences as possible for the children in your care. Children should never be labeled "at risk" but instead should be considered "with promise"!

Multiple Intelligences and Preschool Children

A child's strengths can often be observed at a very young age. Unlike traditional reporting systems that focus on weaknesses, multiple intelligences (MI) theory uses a strengths model to assess children. You can use MI to make plans to enhance their strengths. By offering a variety of activities, you can afford children opportunities to grow and enhance their strengths while also inviting them to "beef up" their areas of weakness or challenge.

Reporting to parents using a deficit model such as negative progress reports just doesn't work. Such reports aren't good for parents, and they sure aren't good for children. Reporting negative observations only gives one side of the whole picture of a child. They tell what is wrong, rather than what is right and what can be built on.

Preschool programs can reflect the theory of multiple intelligences. Existing learning centers can be linked to the intelligences and planned around them.

Traditional Learning Centers and Multiple Intelligences

TRADITIONAL LEARNING CENTERS IN PRESCHOOL	MULTIPLE INTELLIGENCES	ACTIVITIES
Blocks	Spatial Interpersonal Logical-mathematical Bodily-kinesthetic Linguistic	Unit blocks Hollow blocks Props for block play Books that enhance block play themes
Manipulatives/math	Logical-mathematical Interpersonal Intrapersonal Spatial Linguistic	Puzzles Math games Board games Maps Math journals Counting objects Construction materials Classifying objects
Art	Interpersonal Intrapersonal Spatial Bodily-kinesthetic	Painting Drawing Making signs Story illustrations Clay and dough sculptures Murals Print making Collages Dioramas 3-D objects

TRADITIONAL LEARNING CENTERS IN PRESCHOOL	MULTIPLE INTELLIGENCES	ACTIVITIES
Music	Bodily-kinesthetic Musical Logical-mathematical	Raps Rhymes Dance steps Creative movement with puppets, scarves, ribbons, streamers Song cards Rhythm instruments Acoustic instruments String instruments
Outdoor play	Interpersonal Intrapersonal Bodily-kinesthetic	Jumping rope Hopscotch Wheeled toy play Climbing play Swinging Running Ball play Sandbox digging
Computer	Interpersonal Intrapersonal Spatial Bodily-kinesthetic Musical Logical-mathematical	Desktop publishing E-mail Notes to peers Music site interactions Journaling
Science/discovery	Logical-mathematical Naturalistic Interpersonal Intrapersonal	Sand and water play Weather charts Project learning Cooking Recycling Going "green" (walk instead of ride; grow a garden) Caring for live plants Caring for live animals Caring for insects such as butterflies, ants, silkworms, and earthworms

TRADITIONAL LEARNING CENTERS IN PRESCHOOL	MULTIPLE INTELLIGENCES	ACTIVITIES
Library/listening	Linguistic Interpersonal Intrapersonal	Author studies Silly sayings Jokes and riddles Vocabulary cards Word banks Tales and stories Audiotapes of storytelling Puppet play Book and story illustrations Child-authored books Flannelboard stories Journals Questionnaires Checklists Rhymes Rebus stories Diaries Role play
Dramatic play	Linguistic Interpersonal Intrapersonal	Books about play themes (families, restaurants, transportation) Recipes and menus Phones and computers Calculators and cash registers Prop boxes filled with thematic items
Gross motor	Bodily-kinesthetic Interpersonal	Basketball hoop and ball Inside bowling Small climber and slide Loft
Woodworking	Logical-mathematical Bodily-kinesthetic Naturalistic Interpersonal Intrapersonal	Woodworking bench or table with tools Tree stump and tools Large table made from cable spools

Planning Your School-Age Program around the Intelligences

Most likely, your school-age program has already carefully acquired materials and resources that can be used in planning a program around multiple intelligences theory and practice. Standards in place from resources such as NAEYC (National Association for the Education of Young Children), NAA (National AfterSchool Association), and NAFCC (National Association for Family Child Care) do not need to be replaced with MI theory; rather, they can be an integral part of planning outcome-based activities using the nine intelligences. Planning around MI theory will enhance your existing pro-

Possibilities for MI Theory in School-Age Programs

INTELLIGENCE ADDRESSED	COMMON SCHOOL-AGE PROGRAMS
Word smart	Homework Career programs
Picture smart	Arts programs Art center or room Photography clubs
Number smart	Homework Cooking club Math/science clubs
Body smart	Outside play Gym play Organized sports Martial arts
Music smart	Music center or room Playing musical instruments Music lessons

INTELLIGENCE ADDRESSED	COMMON SCHOOL-AGE PROGRAMS
We smart	Leadership opportunities in character and career programs Drug awareness programs 4-H life skills Boys and Girls Club programs
Me smart	Health and life skill programs Self-esteem development programs
Nature smart	Hikes Field trips Nature walks Pets Gardening (terrariums and hothouses inside and gardens outside)
Wonder smart	Pet funerals Family member funerals

gram and ensure that all children's needs or intelligences are being challenged and fulfilled. Because traditional school programs devote so much attention to logical-mathematical and linguistic intelligences, programs for military youth can fill a need by structuring their programs to ensure that *all* areas of intelligence can be experienced and children can express themselves individually every day.

Color Coding MI Planning Sheets

As a preschool teacher in a child care center, I was interested in using MI theory to ensure that my planning was meeting the needs of all the children in my care. After studying MI theory in a doctoral program, I decided to put it into practice. I first wanted to plan backward; it was important for me to see which of the intelligences I was offering routinely, either daily or weekly. I obtained permission from my center director to replace the standard lesson plan with my newly improved MI lesson plan. I placed circles (seven at the time) at the top of the plan and used a code for each intelligence. Note that naturalistic and existential intelligences are added here, even though they were not part of Gardner's theory until after my preschool teaching days were over.

Each circle was colored with a different pen or marker as the colors represented the intelligences found on my lesson plans. For several weeks, I color coded the plans and discovered where opportunities for children to develop each intelligence were present or absent. This exercise allowed me to identify patterns in my curriculum where too much was being planned around one intelligence, such as linguistic, or not enough was being planned for another intelligence, such as intrapersonal. It was a great start to planning the MI way! At a glance, I could assess my planning and add more to areas that were lacking or plan fewer activities in areas that were overflowing. I also began to see that my plans reflected my strengths, too, and that it wasn't

good to have music activities (my favorite) in every part of the day if they excluded activities based on other intelligences.

As a consultant for military school-age programs, I use the color coding system to frame the existing weekly plans with MI theory. Providers may use the codes to identify areas of strength or where they are offering activities and skill-related programming associated with MI. After looking at several plans and assigning colors to each of the intelligences represented (often two or more per activity or program), it becomes clear where the programming and planning can use assistance. Below I provide the color coding for use with your existing plans, whether in preschool or school-age programs, on or off an installation, and in center or home-based care.

O BLUE	Word smart (Linguistic intelligence)
O RED	Picture smart (Spatial intelligence)
O GREEN	We smart (Interpersonal intelligence)
O YELLOW	Me smart (Intrapersonal intelligence)
O BROWN	Nature smart (Naturalistic intelligence)
O ORANGE	Number smart (Logical-mathematical intelligence)
O BLACK	Body smart (Bodily-kinesthetic intelligence)
O PURPLE	Music smart (Musical intelligence)
O PINK	Wonder smart (Existential intelligence)

Strategies for Using MI in Planning

WORD SMART (LINGUISTIC INTELLIGENCE)

Linguistic intelligence includes recognizing and using sounds in words or utterances (phonology), using words in sentences correctly (syntax), knowing meanings of words (semantics), and using words to achieve a purpose or to solve a problem (pragmatics). Because this particular intelligence begins to develop at birth and is used our whole lives, it gets a lot of attention. Use rhythm and rhyme often while singing or reading to infants and toddlers. Have conversations during routines such as diapering, feeding, and transitioning to sleep. Songs like "Head, Shoulders, Knees, and Toes" are good for the toddlers in your care. For preschoolers, ask lots of open-ended questions that will solve problems, such as, "How many blocks can you stack? or "Can you put the toy on the shelf?" Schoolagers will benefit from lots of communication with you and with their peers by sharing jokes and tongue twisters such as:

She Sells Sea Shells

She sells sea shells by the sea shore.

The shells she sells are surely sea shells.

So if she sells shells on the sea shore,

I'm sure she sells sea shore shells.

Other opportunities that you can give schoolagers to develop their verbal intelligence include, "half-a-story time": you start the story or tell half of it and then ask them to finish it. Make key-word rings with schoolagers that contain their favorite words as well as definitions or drawings. Supply metal rings and cards that are cut in uniform sizes with punched holes for children to write their words each day. Ask them to write a story using their key words for the week. Also, post a word of the day as they arrive and use it in conversation with them.

STRATEGIES

Newsletters (for Schoolagers)

Bring out the roving reporter in the children by providing desktop publishing opportunities. Elicit the help of a parent or primary caregiver who can come by each week or month to retrieve the news and publish it (preferably on-site with the assistance of the children). Ask for drawings, jokes, news of family members, pictures of parents who are deployed, pictures of pets, etc.

NUMBER SMART (LOGICAL-MATHEMATICAL INTELLIGENCE)

As young children begin to classify objects by placing them in categories such as big and little, hard and soft, or sink and float, they are using logical-mathematical intelligence, or number smart. As they perceive patterns in art, everyday objects, and books, they are systematically applying their number smart to make sense of their world. They are always asking how something works or taking it apart to see how it was put together. In order to extend logical-mathematical intelligence in children, plan activities that support growth in logical thinking.

To foster number smart with infants and toddlers, provide lots of toys to manipulate that have more than one purpose or have open-ended play value and come in many shapes and sizes. Preschoolers can discover patterns when you give them differently colored and shaped beads and safe string. Start with simple AB, AB, AB patterns, and then progress to ABC, ABC, ABC and finally to more complex patterns such as AB, ABC, AB, ABC. Also, promote counting by providing concrete objects and math puzzles and games with geometric shapes and different attributes in color, shape, size, and thickness. Provide schoolagers with opportunities to plan and run a class store, solve a math problem of the day, and do logic puzzles, math games, and word problems related to their interests.

STRATEGIES

One-Two-Three, Let's Count! (for Preschoolers)

Find a wall, an empty corner, some shelves, or a large box or trunk to house the following counting materials. Add to the list as often as possible. Spend time each day assisting children with counting.

- abacus or counting frame
- Geo Stix
- measuring cups and spoons
- cone-shaped funnels
- geometric shapes of all sizes and colors (attribute blocks work well)
- old checkbooks and order books
- play money
- measuring rope made of fabric with knots tied close together to count
- scales
- compasses
- counting rods
- blocks
- simple balance
- egg timer, kitchen timer
- hourglass
- cutout cardboard numbers
- one foot-long cutout with cardboard feet attached
- cubes
- large foam dice
- labeled plastic jars filled with specific numbers of objects (jar of 149 marbles, jar of 316 feathers)

Invite children to explore, organize, categorize, and count familiar objects according to number, shape, dimension, and volume.

MUSIC SMART (MUSICAL INTELLIGENCE)

When children demand that we "turn on the music" or find themselves routinely dancing, singing, humming, or working to music, they are exercising their musical intelligence. You don't have to be a talented or gifted musician to enjoy exercising your music smart. Children of all ages have a propensity for rhythm and begin moving and listening to music at a very young age. Music has been known to relieve stress and can be a memory enhancer if played while children are doing skill-related tasks. It can relax or inspire children if used at opportune times throughout the day. It can also be used as a medium for introducing content or concepts.

With infants and toddlers, provide rhythm instruments that are age appropriate for them to explore, and play children's music by Hap Palmer, Dr. Jean, and Greg and Steve or classical works by Mozart, Schumann, Brahms, and Pachelbel. Preschoolers will also delight in learning new songs that are piggybacked onto tunes that they already know, such as singing a cleanup song to the "Farmer in the Dell" tune: "We're cleaning up our toys; we're cleaning up our toys. Hi-ho the derry-o; we're cleaning up our toys." You can also help them to make musical instruments to play in a homemade rhythm band or invite their primary caregivers or other creative musicians to come to your home or center and play for them. Use the song "We Didn't Start the Fire" by Billy Joel as a historical timeline with older schoolagers. Children can construct a timeline on butcher paper that can span the center or a room, including drawings and information about each period or person in history mentioned in the song. Assist older schoolagers in doing homework by creating raps and chants that use the concepts being studied. These can aid in memorizing new material. Also, ask musicians to give mini-performances to whet the children's appetite for learning to play an instrument. If possible, take schoolagers to places where musicians perform and practice.

Please, please, don't be shy,

It's so easy to multiply.

1 times 1 is 1, have fun.

1 times 2 is 2, for you.

1 times 3 is 3, for me.

1 times 4 is 4, get the door.

1 times 5 is 5, I'm alive.

1 times 6 is 6, pick up sticks.

1 times 7 is 7, not eleven.

1 times 8 is 8, don't be late!

1 times 9 is 9, on a line.

1 times 10 is 10, I win!

STRATEGIES

Follow the Leader (for Older Preschoolers and Young Schoolagers)

This activity works well in a large space, inside or outside. Your circle time rug can be used if children move around the perimeter as the music plays.

Create large posters with the following prompts:

- - - - - - means "follow me by hopping on one foot."

__.__.__.__.__ means "take giant steps alternating with teeny tiny steps."

〜〜〜〜〜 means "tiptoe very quietly."

ᐯᐯᐯᐯᐯ means "run in place."

_____ means "skip in line."

__|__|__|__|__|__ means "go slow, and put one foot in front of the other."

Hold up each poster, and have children practice following the visual directions.

Start the music. Children change their movements to reflect the poster displayed. A child can then become the leader, holding up posters while the others follow.

Rapping Multiplication (For Schoolagers)

In order to learn concepts more easily, have children make up silly raps or rhymes such as the following:

PICTURE SMART (SPATIAL INTELLIGENCE)

When thinking of the words *picture smart*, artists and architects come to mind. But spatial intelligence is exercised by anyone who thrives on organizing, making the environment aesthetically pleasing, reading maps, or even reading the body language of other people. Being able to make pictures in our minds is also part of being picture smart.

You can provide infants and toddlers with lots of realistic drawings and portraits in their environment; change them often to continue interest and stimulation with color and patterns. Inspire young children with bright, colorful surroundings; suspend light and airy fabrics from your ceilings and provide lots of natural light. Foster spatial intelligence in your preschoolers by providing art supplies for creating paintings, drawings, and sculptures. Allow them to help arrange or rearrange the toys on a shelf or the child-sized furniture in your center or home. Make room for dancing with scarves, small instruments such as maracas and tambourines, and wrist ribbons. For schoolagers, provide photography or videography activities as well as chess and games that require using maps.

STRATEGIES

Letter Puzzles (for Preschoolers and Young Schoolagers)

Materials: Large alphabet cutouts—one letter per child (S for Sam, etc.) and crayons, markers, paints, brushes, etc.

Have older children make large cutouts of the alphabet to share with younger children. Each child selects his own first initial. After decorating, cut each letter into a three- or four-piece puzzle for younger children, and into multiple pieces for older children. Store pieces in containers so that children can reassemble puzzles often.

Other intelligences enhanced through this activity include linguistic, bodily-kinesthetic, and logical-mathematical.

Classic Art Puzzles (For Schoolagers)

Materials: Poster size prints of art such as Picasso's *Evening Flowers* or *The Dance of Youth*, Van Gogh's *Sunflowers* or *Starry Night*, Maya Lin's Vietnam War Memorial, Diego Rivera's *Agrarian Leader Zapata*, Georgia O'Keeffe's *Red Hills and Bones*, and Monet's *Water Lilies* or *Poppies* (Hurwitz and

Day 2007). Use posters of any art that represents the cultures of the children in your care and that may be recognizable to young children (Kohl and Solga 1996).

Cut the posters into large interlocking pieces and laminate them. Distribute to children, and have them put the poster back together with and without the assistance of a picture of the painting.

BODY SMART (BODILY-KINESTHETIC INTELLIGENCE)

Children who need to move around (a lot), like to touch most things (are tactile learners), and learn better when movement is included in any activity may be tapping into their bodily-kinesthetic intelligence. Some call this "learning by doing." These children may be unable to resist touching things (more so than other children) and have trouble sitting for long periods of time. They love to run, jump, wrestle, or engage in any physical activity that includes movement at its core. Their fine motor skills may be sharpened, and their gross and fine motor coordination are well developed .

Infants enjoy large crawl spaces, and toddlers love to have room to run indoors and out. Their need to touch tangible objects is heightened, more so than for other children, and they often look for things to climb or jump from. Preschoolers with body smarts have an unusually difficult time sitting for stories, lessons, and group times. Try offering objects for them to hold or pass around to sustain their interest longer. Schoolagers are drawn to sports with lots of physical activity as well as computer games that require significant manual dexterity. Make daily plans that incorporate lots of movement opportunities for kids with bodily-kinesthetic intelligence or who are body smart.

STRATEGIES

Marching Shape Parade (For Older Preschoolers and Schoolagers)

For this activity, you'll need lots of space, such as a gym floor, playground, or parking lot.

Materials: Shapes (with corners) that are about four feet in diameter made from old sheets and a whistle.

1. Children stand in line facing the same direction. Allow them to practice movement/ marching in different directions as you blow a whistle.

    a. One short whistle blow: march to your right.

    b. Two short whistle blows: march to your left.

    c. Three short whistle blows: stop/freeze.

2. Add other whistle prompts for moving forward, backward, diagonally, etc.

3. Next, lay each shape on the ground or floor, one by one, and ask, "How many people are needed to stand on the corners?" Ask chil-

dren to stand in each corner. When the children are in place, blow the whistle to make a marching shape parade.

Other intelligences enhanced through this activity include musical, bodily-kinesthetic, spatial, and interpersonal.

Giant People Triangle

One child is positioned at a point of the triangle.

Two children stand behind the point child.

Three children stand behind two other children, and so on. Ask children to complete the triangle.

Alternate strategy: Add rhythm instruments and music. Have children march around the playground, staying in their triangle shape.

Other intelligences enhanced through this activity include musical, bodily-kinesthetic, spatial, and interpersonal.

WE SMART (INTERPERSONAL INTELLIGENCE)

Children who get along well with others and make friends easily demonstrate high interpersonal intelligence. If a child shows concern or empathy for the other children in your care or if he likes to work with or alongside others rather than alone, chances are he possesses we smart. This child may be sought out by others to play or is chosen first in a competitive game to be on someone's team. He shows large amounts of friendliness and positive interactions with peers and adults.

To foster we smart, give infants and toddlers time to bond to you as they develop this sense of intelligence. Attachment to significant adults is instrumental in children acquiring lots of interpersonal intelligence. Preschoolers need spaces to build relationships and to try out friendship making. Comfortable furniture, double-sided easels, sand and water tables for two or more children, climbing structures for more than one child, and places to sit and talk are all helpful things in a preschooler's world to foster interpersonal intelligence.

Look for schoolagers who are considered leaders by their peers. To sharpen or polish those skills, give them opportunities such as 4-H club meetings, Boys and Girls Club committee memberships, and being peer tutors for your younger children.

STRATEGIES

Communication Boxes

Place small boxes with each child's name in a common area so that everyone can give each other notes, letters, drawings, photos, and other messages (handwritten and computer-generated). For very young children, place a photograph instead of a name on the front of each box.

- Use the contents of the boxes as a group time activity, allowing children to "show and tell" what's in their boxes. Permit children to discuss their disappointment in not receiving messages, and encourage the group to think of ways that each person can receive communication through the boxes. For example, a note on a box that says "I'm lonely in here" can alert other children that a communication is hoped for.

- Make a panel/documentation board of messages selected by children, and display it in a common area.

ME SMART (INTRAPERSONAL INTELLIGENCE)

If you've noticed children in your care who have a good sense of self and who understand others, they may have strong intrapersonal intelligence. They prefer to play alone, avoid large groups or crowds, and have high amounts of efficacy and self-worth. They are able to express their feelings to get their needs met and often show significant amounts of independence, which is often mistaken for "strong will." If you've ever labeled a child as "marching to the beat of a different drummer," you've probably cared for a child with lots of intrapersonal intelligence. Consider that her strong will might be a way of showing that she has lots of me smart. Channel this behavior into opportunities for her to make decisions about her world.

To remember the difference between intrapersonal intelligence and interpersonal intelligence, I use the "a" in intra- to remind me that someone possesses this when they are comfortable with themselves or like to be *alone* a lot. I use the "e" in interpersonal intelligence to remind me that someone possesses large amounts of this when they are comfortable being with *everyone*.

STRATEGIES

Sticky-Note Journaling (for Preschoolers to Schoolagers)

Materials: Sticky notes in sizes from small to large (five by seven inches) and journals or diaries to house sticky notes.

Place the sticky notes in a basket. Encourage kids to make notes to themselves, doodle, draw, write poems and stories, and record events each day in their journals. Use circle time to share something from their journals. Remember to keep the groups very small to maintain a high level of interest during show-and-tell.

NATURE SMART (NATURALISTIC INTELLIGENCE)

Kids with naturalistic intelligence are drawn to nature—being outside, recognizing and classifying animals, and observing insects, the weather, and plants. If the kids in your care want to be outside more than inside, even on a hot or rainy day, or spend their inside time looking at, talking about, or making plans for the animals in your program, their nature smarts are strong.

Take infants and toddlers outside to enjoy the activities that you've planned as well as the outdoors in general. Hang mobiles and wind chimes for them to experience movement and wind as well as flower baskets for them to experience color and texture. Let preschoolers help plant flowers and vegetables in small outdoor gardens. Hang bird feeders and fill bird baths with water; take nature walks, and teach the names of animals and birds that are indigenous to your area. Schoolagers can plan activities outdoors that include games and sports, climbing-wall activities, gardening, and bird watching.

WONDER SMART (EXISTENTIAL INTELLIGENCE)

In military families, children are often more exposed to the concept of death than other children. If children are tuned in to the media, death may become a constant in their lives, as they see and hear about the dangers associated with military jobs. Even if parents don't address it with children directly, schoolagers can begin to wonder if their military parent or parents will ever be coming home. Existential intelligence is apparent in children who have many questions about life and death, as well as a keen sense of wonderment about humanity in general. Find books about death that portray it as part of the life cycle and help them to understand it (see chapter 9 for suggestions). Answer their questions about life and death, and ask primary caregivers to join you. Help them to focus on living, and direct them to the small but important things that we all encounter every day. Older children may wonder about "what's out there" or about life on other planets. Guide them to books that will give them a better understanding.

Planning Your Family Child Care Program around Multiple Intelligences

If yours is a family child care home, you can use MI theory to plan effectively and according to the strengths and needs of the children in your care. Beginning with an objective that has been developed from a national or state standard, think of ways that you can bring the objective to life through an activity that is based on one or more intelligences. To ensure that your program is well balanced, plan activities that address all intelligences every day, and make sure the children have vested interests in the program planning. Indoor and outdoor play can address the intelligences. Try color coding your daily plans to make certain that you are not offering too much physical play and not enough opportunities for art or music or vice versa. Listen to children to determine what their propensities are. They usually are prompt in telling adults what they like to do, and from their requests you may be able to get some idea of what their intelligence needs are.

The theory of multiple intelligences can provide a framework for developing military child and youth programs, either in center-based or home-based care. MI theory focuses on children's strengths rather than dwelling on their weaknesses. It is also important to remember that the intelligences work together rather than separately, and as a result, you can plan activities that enhance many intelligences at once.

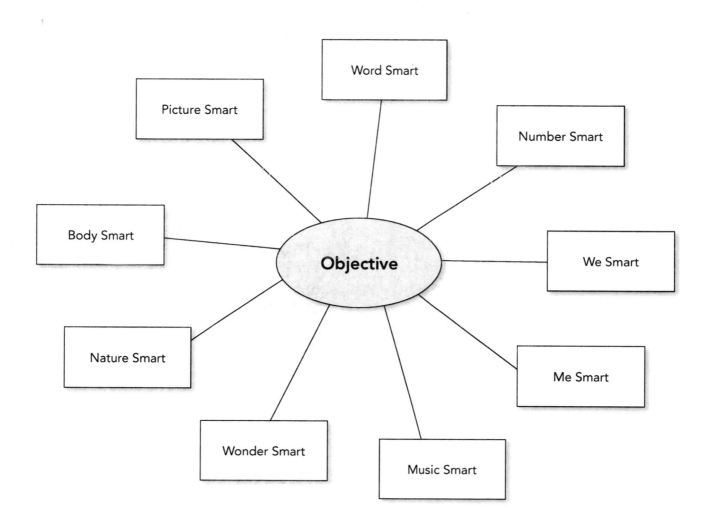

Multiple Intelligences at a Glance

SPATIAL INTELLIGENCE, OR PICTURE SMART

A child with this intelligence

- prefers an aesthetic or visual environment;
- enjoys or is drawn to art: color, shape, line, and form;
- has a sense of direction and distance;
- builds elaborate block structures;
- prefers Lego blocks to books;
- enjoys painting and sculpting (anything with color, line, and shape).

LINGUISTIC INTELLIGENCE, OR WORD SMART

A child with this intelligence

- is sensitive to words, meanings, and sounds;
- enjoys listening to and telling stories;
- enjoys reading or looking at books;
- enjoys jokes and riddles;
- enjoys rhyming books;
- has an extensive vocabulary.

BODILY-KINESTHETIC INTELLIGENCE, OR BODY SMART

A child with this intelligence

- shows coordination in physical activities such as sports and dance;
- enjoys engaging in gross motor activities such as climbing, swinging, jumping rope, throwing a ball, hopscotch;
- uses her whole body to solve a problem;
- would rather be moving than sitting still (active rather than passive).

MUSICAL INTELLIGENCE, OR MUSIC SMART

A child with this intelligence

- enjoys listening to or playing music;
- enjoys singing or humming;
- recognizes tones;
- composes music;
- plays an instrument;
- engages in lots of rhythmic activities such as fingerplays, rhymes, and songs.

LOGICAL-MATHEMATICAL INTELLIGENCE, OR NUMBER SMART

A child with this intelligence

- enjoys anything with numbers;
- enjoys puzzles, both printed and tangible;
- is an investigator;
- asks lots of questions about how things work;
- likes computers and technology of any kind.

INTRAPERSONAL INTELLIGENCE, OR ME SMART

A child with this intelligence

- enjoys being or playing alone;
- is self-directed and self-motivated (sets personal goals);
- self-reflects or can describe his own strengths and weaknesses;
- is sought out by others for help and advice;
- is self-disciplined (when older).

INTERPERSONAL INTELLIGENCE, OR WE SMART

A child with this intelligence

- enjoys meeting and being with people;
- prefers crowds or groups over being alone;
- makes friends easily and is outgoing;
- forms lasting relationships;
- engages in activities that afford opportunities to be with other children or adults;
- shows leadership ability at a young age.

NATURALISTIC INTELLIGENCE, OR NATURE SMART

A child with this intelligence

- enjoys the outdoors for the sake of being with nature (camping, hiking, walking outside);
- enjoys gardening and growing things inside and outside;
- enjoys tending to plants and animals;
- is curious about the names of plants and animals.

EXISTENTIAL INTELLIGENCE, OR WONDER SMART

A child with this intelligence

- is curious about life after death;
- asks lots of "what if" questions;
- engages in wonderment and spiritual concepts;
- has concern for global perspectives (people around the world and their situations).

Reggio Emilia

The philosophy of educators in the town of Reggio Emilia, Italy, has drastically affected the way child care providers around the world look at caring for children. Although it is not a curriculum, aspects of Reggio teaching are being used in quality programs for U.S. children. In 1945, the people in Reggio Emilia, a small city in northern Italy, used money from the sale of military equipment to rebuild the schools that had been destroyed during World War II. Over time, they created a system that offered free education for children from the age of three months to six years. Today, education is still free there, where about 160,000 people live. The many schools in this area are influenced by the late Loris Malaguzzi, the founder of the Reggio movement (Edwards, Gandini, and Forman 1998).

The Reggio philosophy of education has shown us another way to care for children; it places children, teachers, and parents at the center of the curriculum. Teachers in Reggio Emilia believe in the importance of play but stress that adults are to be participators more than facilitators of play. Parent participation is also considered essential in creating the adult-child relationships that will sustain emotional and social development in children.

Learning about their world is not only valuable but an integral part of the Reggio philosophy. Encourage children to know about their world, such as the dress or uniforms that their parents wear to work, items that their parents use at work, and places that their parents go to work. For example, a military child might attend an orientation about what their parents do on the job. Many branches offer days when children are invited to an event that highlights the military person's life.

Carla Rinaldi, author and teacher of Reggio principles, stated that the children of Reggio have rights as well as needs, and teachers are the authors of pathways for children. In other words, through observation, documentation, illumination of the process rather than the product, and an interpretation or analysis of the process, teachers serve as the channel to children's learning. According to Rinaldi, Reggio schools are family driven, and parents' expectations are vital to the program, as they actively participate in the process of learning *with* their children rather than about their children. Cultural influences are tremendous, and the whole town becomes the classroom, as children visit scenes and sites to make discoveries and to plan new projects. Most important, the lesson plan is not to supersede the rights of children (Rinaldi 1988; Edwards, Gandini, and Forman 1998).

The U.S. government provides a commitment to quality child care that is equal or parallel to that of Reggio Emilia. In fact, many of our military programs for children are already providing or showcasing Reggio principles by using good practices. If you are caring for military children off an installation, you may not be familiar with many of the military child care initiatives that already incorporate Reggio principles. This section highlights some ways that the Reggio approach can help children soar to new heights of creativity and learning.

Children as the Center of the Child Care Program

One of the most admirable attributes of military care providers and administrators is that they are continuously seeking ways to improve the care they offer (Tomlinson and Brittain 2007). Reggio Emilia is one approach that offers a tradition of excellence in working with children.

Jean Piaget, John Dewey, and Lev Vygotsky (Mooney 2000) are three important theorists whom American educators draw from in designing child care programs. All three encouraged putting children's interests and innate ability to create at the forefront of our care. They all agree that children are active learners and require environments that facilitate cognitive and emotional growth, alone and with their peers. Italian teachers from Reggio Emilia, or *pedigogista*, also draw from these theorists and put children's needs for developmental growth at the height of their philosophy, but Reggio teachers look at the child in terms of having rights versus needs. Children are seen not in terms of their deficits or inabilities, but rather in terms of their strengths and possibilities (much like MI theory).

Good listening is an important element of the Reggio approach. When a child speaks, slow down to really hear what the child is saying rather than formulating an answer to the question before the child has finished speaking. As children speak, you can gain valuable information about their interests and hobbies. This information can then be used to plan your curriculum, all because you were a good listener.

I've observed time and time again a provider sitting with children and being really engaged in activities with them, rather than moving from place to place, policing or monitoring the activities of all children. This interaction sets a positive tone, and the provider thus prioritizes the quality of activities rather than how many goals can be achieved during a day. Children become more engaged in the process of their investigations when the provider can attend rather than supervise.

Investigations: The Hundred Languages of Children

Teachers in Reggio Emilia have a saying, "You don't know it until you can express it." Thus, children are encouraged to express their thinking in a hundred different ways or languages through their investigations, explorations, and projects. At the heart of this approach is thoughtful dialogue and discussions about the children, which are common between teachers and parents. They share ideas in order to foster the creativity and expressiveness that they have seen and that are part of the children's lives. Most impressively, Reggio children are encouraged to bring their interests to school from home and from school to home; they craft projects that express and explain the journeys that have been taken throughout the process. Projects can be in the form of sculptures, drama, songs, poetry, dialogues, paintings, and photography, among others—all "languages" the child may use. The various materials available to children to aid in the expression of thought are endless.

I've been reminded of the Reggio approach over and over when visiting military child care—in family homes, school-age programs, and child development centers. Children's interests are often the basis of the curriculum, and providers plan activities based on children's ideas. The idea for traveling documentation boards (page 126) that showcase military children's works was born out of a training I conducted for many installations, as I visited the Hundred Languages of Children exhibit and knew that military kids were creating artifacts that were culturally important to the people of their area. The exhibit houses reproductions of photographs, drawings, and projects made by the children of Reggio Emilia, Italy, and travels around the world, giving others a tangible sense of the Reggio schools. The "languages" refer to all the ways that children communicate through graphics, such as drawing, sculpting, and painting to name only a few (Edwards, Gandini, and Forman 1998). In caring for military children, you can create your own exhibit of "languages" consisting of children's drawings, projects, recordings, and paintings.

Environment as a Third Teacher

In the Reggio approach, the environment or third teacher is often given as much thought and attention as the curriculum itself—often becoming an extension of the curriculum during planning time. The importance of the environment cannot be underestimated. Ask anyone what her preschool care was like, and she will often refer to the environment as well as to the people who were there. "I remember that it had a yellow door that had a sun painted on it." "It was an old brick building, but the atmosphere was warm and inviting." "Mine had a reading loft that my friend Jessica and I used to climb into every day during centers time." This space truly has a voice and speaks to everyone who passes through.

Within the environment, Reggio Emilia uses light as an artistic medium in as many ways as possible—through windows, inside glass walls, and with mirrors and shiny glass objects placed all around (Fraser and Gestwicki 2002). Colored, transparent film on windowpanes provides "transparency" (115), and mirrors are hung where children can see their reflections. Painted translucent panels, prisms, kaleidoscopes, and light boxes are all used to integrate the arts across the curriculum rather than approach it as a discrete area of learning (Krogh and Morehouse 2007). Problem solving extends to the visual arts as well, and children are encouraged to hypothesize or make guesses about their projects when in process, not just at the end when they are asked, "What can you tell me about this picture?"

Each Reggio school has an *atelierista*, a person with visual arts training who works directly with the children, and these children's works are usually beyond what is expected of four- and five-year-old children in U.S. care. Lilian Katz and Sylvia Chard, longtime observers and proponents of Reggio schools, write that preprimary children communicate their ideas, feelings, understandings, imaginings, and observations through visual representation much earlier than most U.S early childhood educators typically assume (Katz and Chard 2000). The likely reason for the children's increased development is because of their constant association or relationship with the "artist in residence." Studios (*atelieri*) or workshops for children, teachers, and parents are available for long-term projects. Materials are available for children and parents to use. This characteristic of the Reggio approach may be one of the easiest to model and implement in military child care. The following strategies will help you incorporate Reggio principles into your program's environment.

STRATEGIES

Entryways

Create an inviting entry with plenty of natural light (windows or inside glass) for children, providers, and parents. Live plants and fresh flowers, authentic pictures of children taken while working and playing, and adult furniture such as sofas or big comfortable chairs can be added to create a welcoming environment for all. Live plants (placed in front of mirrors if possible), fresh flowers, reduced clutter, and additional mirrors can all provide an open and respectful environment for children and parents.

Museum

Create a "museum" area that showcases children's works. Tape recorders can be set up to allow parents and children to listen to children's conversations or dialogues; video cameras or computers can be available to view children's works in action. Hang frames that can be replenished as new works (artwork and photos) are prepared by children in your care. Create display panels that can accommodate multidimensional works such as collages.

Block Centers

Use nonbreakable mirrors or reflective material as a base for children's block building to add interest and provocation. Add mirrors to the walls of the block center to provide depth and to facilitate awareness when building with blocks. Move the block center to an area with natural light, and hang prisms so that bits of color will wash over the block center.

Artists

Provide space for experts from many artistic fields to visit to draw, paint, play a musical instrument, tell stories, dramatize, sculpt, sing, etc. Retired military personnel, local artists, and current military personnel (civilian and military) can provide a wealth of untapped talent and skill for military kids.

Documentation

Documentation is "a verbal and visual trace of the children's experiences and work, and opportunities to revisit, reflect, and interpret" (Fraser and Gestwicki 2002, 11). In other words, photographs or a series of snapshots, written observations, artwork, and daily journaling can provide documentation of an ongoing process during which children carry out an idea or interest. These visuals not only trace the work of the child but also give the parents and teachers an idea of the direction the child is taking.

Reggio children question and engage in a type of follow-through that demonstrates their thinking and ability to form hypotheses. Documentation of these actions can show just how deep the learning goes; it can be in the form of photographs and artwork placed on display in the school or elsewhere. A record of learning can help us see the connections children made during the process of the project activities. In the Reggio approach, we are reminded that documentation is about more than capturing the end product of an activity or experience. It also captures the activities in process and represents all the different stages of a project's development. A web of "hypotheses, observations, predictions, interpretations, planning, and explorations" (Fraser and Gestwicki 2002, 129) serves to make the child's learning visible. With such documentation, primary caregivers and teachers are aware of the child's plans as well as the progress and challenges during the child's journey through the plan. The process that children must go through to decide what to include in the documentation is inspiring. The documentation becomes a portrait of a child's careful planning and thinking.

The Reggio approach involves three steps in documenting children's work: observation, interpretation, and analysis. All three take place on two levels—that of the child observing his world and that of the adult observing the child.

STRATEGIES

Documentation Boards

Documentation boards can be made by compiling photographs, transcripts of conversations, and pieces of visual art. Display the boards wherever children are cared for and where all can easily view them. In order to present the children's findings to their parents and the wider community, transfer the documentations onto display boards—freestanding or wall mounted. Allow the boards to "travel" as you find locations frequented by families, such as local businesses, and ask for space to display the boards. Plan field trips to the places of business so that children can see their work on display.

Teaching Kids to Question: Beginning a Project

When you teach kids to question, an idea for a project gets off the ground. You begin to provoke children to extend their thinking about something that has happened in real life, developing the idea into an open-ended project that is full of possibilities for exploration and discovery. These provocations can also occur by chance. For instance, when a child sees a rainbow in the sky, this could provoke her into talking about the rainbow to her parents or teachers. Then the adults incite the child to explore the interest more and think a concept through to the point of understanding and expression. The child in turn begins to make predictions about her interests.

STRATEGIES

Researching and Investigating

Children can easily become researchers or investigators with scaffolding or assistance from you. A product or visible symbolic representation such as a clay sculpture of a building is the direct (and sometimes indirect) outcome of an idea that has come to fruition from days, weeks, or even months of deliberations or conversations with peers or adults about buildings and their shapes, sizes, and forms. Help older children extend their investigations into a topic of interest, such as the children in Iraq, or help younger children with a topic such as dinosaurs. Allow time for thinking, planning, and questioning as you allow the children to provide leadership on the investigations. Assign each child a task that brings more information to the research project. Provide access to resources such as books, magazines, adult experts, and the Web.

Investigations of the Authentic Environment

David Elkind writes of a "trickle down curriculum," or one that was being pushed down on children from a developmentally inappropriate perspective (2006). The Reggio approach, on the other hand, promotes a curriculum that emerges or is born out of an authentic experience such as a trip to the neighbor-

hood park, birds building nests outside a school window, or a visit from a local artist or craftsperson. It attempts to create opportunities for children's thinking to catapult or propel their learning. This authentic experience sets the stage for thinking about and then acting on those thoughts and reflections of the experience. The thoughts become words, the words become symbols, and the symbols take the form of paintings and crafts, sculptures, dramas, and songs, to name a few.

Children as Researchers: The Project Approach

Loris Malaguzzi used the word *progettazione* to describe the core of the curriculum in Reggio Emilia schools, as it includes flexible planning done by parents, teachers, and children (Edwards, Gandini, and Forman 1998) and is built with strong cultural influences from the community. Out of this reflexive planning may come projects with children based on their interests. American educators Judy Helm, Sylvia Chard, and Lilian Katz refer to the children who engage in a project approach as "young investigators" (Helm and Katz 2001; Katz and Chard 2000, 1) making inquiries about their chosen topic just as researchers would. Rather than choosing a theme as a topic of inquiry for the children, the project approach mirrors the *progettazione* by working with children, listening to and observing them to find out their interests, and then reflecting on their works and words about their projects. Katz and Chard define the project approach as one in which the young child has greater decision-making power and initiative within an in-depth investigation about a particular topic. A whole class, a small group, or an individual child can take on a project to investigate over a period of time (Katz and Chard 2000). Military child care as well as family child care and after-school programs can use projects as a way of capturing the interest of all children in the program.

In American schools, we often say that we follow a theme until the children no longer show interest. But perhaps the children's interest wanes because the teacher fails to scaffold or lure them forward into new facets of the projects. Developing a curriculum around the project approach takes time and consultation with other providers and trainers, but these extra steps are worth taking. The following ideas may help in sustaining children's interest and luring them forward to develop and complete a project.

Think BIG! Rather than thinking of particular themes to explore such as "rodeo," "beach," and "bears," think in terms of multiple levels of investigation that encompass all areas of curriculum—math, science, social studies, language, and art (Wurm 2005). Instead of studying planes—types of planes, names of planes, and history of planes— plan a more in-depth journey into all facets of planes. The interests of the children should generate the ideas, with the adults scaffolding the learning. The ideas often begin small and then grow as the children investigate and work on the project, with assistance from the adults.

Consider how many languages of the children can be incorporated into the project in the form of stories, photographs, videos, dramatizations, audio recordings, songs, etc.

Keep the end result *out* of mind. If it is truly a divergent (open-ended) project with the children constructing knowledge as they go along, the end is not readily in sight.

Avoid setting a time limit on projects. Divergent thinking takes time to explore and explode! While children often make time lines in order to project which steps will be taken, it is not necessary to attach time limits to teach each stage or phase.

Try to move away from the idea of "planned curriculum" or "curriculum planning," in which you make all the decisions about what the children will learn on a daily basis.

Capitalize on large and small group times to facilitate the planning of the *progettazione.* Use project or topic webs to kindle and inspire children's thinking. A *web* is a simple drawing with a circle at the center containing the main idea and "branches" shooting off from the circle; the research questions related to the main idea are written on the branches. Webs help children brainstorm their ideas and make connections with others who may have similar interests. Children can make their own webs or you can get them started by brainstorming a topic with them.

To incorporate projects into the daily schedule, provide uninterrupted blocks of time for children to plan and develop their interests into projects. You will need to set aside forty-five-minute to sixty-minute project times at least once per day. Review time is needed after each project work time for children to assimilate their own ideas and share them with others. Helm and Katz (2001) suggest that you ask visiting experts to share their knowledge as well as field questions from children as they work on their projects. You can also provide books on project topics as well as assist children to do research on computers and in libraries.

PROJECT APPROACH PROCESS

Stage 1: The topic emerges. Help the children use a web to explore and find a topic.

Stage 2: Research the topic. Support the children in investigating other similar projects (for example, field trips).

Stage 3: Review the topic. Involve all children and adults in the program in the review.

Stage 4: Continue on or disband the topic. Allow the children to decide to proceed with the current topic or start a new one.

Stage 5: Do the project. If the children have decided to continue the project, allow them to continue researching and to begin bringing the topic to life in any of the hundred languages.

Stage 6: Document findings on the topic. Assist the children in assembling the documentation of the topic and sharing it.

In this chapter, I have provided strategies for your programs from two approaches to curriculum in early childhood, the theory of multiple intelligences and the Reggio Emilia philosophy. Each is unique, but both, at their core, allow children to be creative thinkers. They also provide opportunities for children to work from within, with a high degree of independence and problem solving. I am not suggesting here that you completely redo your curriculum to base it entirely on either approach, but I do recommend that you reexamine and reevaluate the approach that you currently use to determine if it fosters the kinds of growth that you want in your children. It is important to take even small steps to ensure that your program places children's rights and needs first.

CHAPTER SEVEN

Developing Partnerships:
Families and Providers Working Together

Working together for the benefit of children is a universal expectation of all providers and parents—whether children are in Department of Defense Schools or civilian child care in centers or family homes. When deployment occurs, you may find yourself working not only with a lone parent but also with primary caregivers: grandparents, aunts and uncles, other family members, older siblings, friends, and neighbors who will be helping care for young children in the absence of their parents. Because they become the primary source of care during deployment, you may develop relationships with people other than the child's parents. This often requires patience and understanding but is very rewarding as you become part of a circle of caring adults providing for the needs of military children.

Primary Caregivers as Partners

Partnering with military primary caregivers is critical in providing quality programs for their children. When military children and their parents experience separation, grief and loss, relocation issues, loss of friends and extended families, and the stress of starting all over again, they need our support. Parents of children in Reggio Emilia schools understand the stress that families face, and they eliminate a great deal of it by creating a support structure that begins with orientation and establishes trust between new families and the schools (Fraser and Gestwicki 2002). In other words, before parents leave their child in care for the very first time, they have already established a relationship with the school and their child's providers. You can learn from this philosophy by including parents and other primary caregivers in all aspects of care for their children.

In addition to asking primary caregivers to continue dialogues at home that their children begin at school regarding projects and journeys of inquiry, there are other ways to create a more inclusive environment for families in your program. Note: if you face financial or space constraints, you can modify these ideas and implement the changes on a smaller scale.

- Provide meeting rooms for small groups of primary caregivers to hold undisturbed recreational activities (such as a quilting, cake-baking, or sewing/knitting party) and professional meetings (such as parent-teacher meetings).
- Schedule a once-a-semester, monthly, or biweekly meeting for primary caregivers to get to know one another and exchange phone numbers and other information.
- For primary caregivers under extra stress, provide brochures, resources, and materials such as local phone numbers for doctors, hospitals, counselors, housekeepers, and babysitters.
- Provide a newsletter on a weekly, biweekly, or monthly basis in order to maintain regular links between school and home. Ask primary caregivers to help with writing and/or publishing.
- Schedule cooking clubs for primary caregivers who want to visit while cooking a week's or month's worth of meals. They may also wish to share meals.
- Encourage primary caregivers to express their ideas and to ask questions by providing an e-mail address. Be sure to check it regularly.
- If you have a gymnasium, open it to primary caregivers and guests for use before or after school. For example, some military installations and community gyms sponsor basketball leagues for adults, with games before and after school-age programs begin and end.
- Create a quiet room for primary caregivers to get a cup of coffee or cold drink and to relax. Furnish the room with soft furniture, reading materials, a lending library with fiction and nonfiction books, Internet/e-mail access, and television with cable for before- or after-school drop-off and pickup. Many parents will be away from these luxuries all day while on the job or on missions.
- Ask for input from parents and primary caregivers before making major program decisions. Create task forces based on the skills, knowledge, and interests of the important adults in the lives of the children in your care.
- Accept that conflict is a necessary part of working together and that through differences in opinions, an appreciation for exposure to a variety of opinions can occur between providers and primary caregivers.

As an installation mechanic, John was on the flight line all day performing a special mission. His wife, Pam, was deployed in Iraq. Their two-year-old daughter, Macy, was in care at the installation's child development center. The mission was expected to be completed well before John needed to pick up Macy by the center closing time of 6 PM. Unfortunately, his mission ran longer than anticipated, and he wasn't able to let the center know he would be late. He arrived at the center after 6 PM. The director and staff welcomed him and assured him that Macy was okay and waiting for her daddy.

This scene happens over and over with U.S. military men and women on and off installations around the world. Setting clear expectations and understandings is essential, as parents, primary caregivers, and child care providers have to work together to take care of children. Each needs to understand and appreciate how important everyone's contributions are to the children and to the family-provider relationship.

Family-centered care involves recognizing and embracing the diverse characteristics of the families for whom you provide care. This includes recognizing each family member's area of expertise and abilities or capabilities and drawing upon those often, building networks of support, communicating and consulting with parents about their children, and listening attentively to primary caregivers. One of the best gifts you can give children is to develop sincere relationships with their parents and primary caregivers. You have an added challenge in working with military families who endure additional stress many of us cannot imagine.

Family-Centered Environments

You have an enormous responsibility in setting a welcoming atmosphere for parents and their children. Most parents care more about being welcomed than about beautiful surroundings, expen-

sive furnishings, or the latest curriculum. It can't be overemphasized how important a welcoming atmosphere is to building bridges with parents and primary caregivers before any problems may arise.

STRATEGIES

Family Involvement

Provide a welcoming environment that keeps primary caregivers interested in their children's daily experiences by promoting communication. Relationships with primary caregivers are strong predictors of the success of a child in a child care program, and you can capitalize on that connection not only by involving primary caregivers in your plans but also by encouraging them to participate in advocacy groups or advisory committees.

Family Friendliness

Strive for family friendliness in your program. Place easels, clipboards, or whiteboards outside your classroom so that parents can see the current events or reminders when they drop off or pick up their children. For instance, posting "Don't forget the chili supper tonight at 6:30" in the morning will help remind a primary caregiver who got the note last week and has totally forgotten about the supper. Signs about upcoming events placed on large standing easels outside the front entrance are family-friendly reminders as well. "Don't forget that picture day is tomorrow!" will ensure that little ones aren't left out!

Providing a Family-Centered Environment

Provide a place where families feel welcome and are encouraged to linger (Keyser 2006):

- Offer adult-sized comfortable furniture.
- Offer adequate space for good-byes.
- Respect cultural diversity by appreciating the home language of each family and honoring and supporting the home values and cultural

norms by sharing photos, objects, and activities (such as stories and songs) and reading books about the cultures of each family (NAEYC 1995).

- Provide family mailboxes for daily communication.

- Create and distribute a weekly or monthly newsletter.

- Provide primary caregivers with an e-mail address for communicating with you.

- Make entrances easily accessible for people with disabilities.

- Provide a family resource area that is filled with books on parenting, discipline and guidance, and other topics of interest.

- Provide brochures and flyers on local resources such as pediatricians, social workers, and take-out menus.

Communicating with Primary Caregivers

Use a balance of verbal and written communication to let primary caregivers know what their children are doing in your program. Keeping them informed is the cornerstone of care. When children enter your program, ask their parents or primary caregivers which method of communication is best for them—written or verbal. Offer to send e-mails or make phone calls for special events, scheduling parent meetings, and ongoing communication for issues, concerns, or even celebrations. Everyone has particular likes and dislikes and will respond positively to your willingness to accommodate their preferences.

Verbal Communication

Consistent daily contact between caregivers and primary caregivers builds a sense of trust and the basis for a relationship that can last through deployment. Make time each morning and afternoon to meet and greet primary caregivers of the military children in your care. If you are not on duty at both times, make sure you are available at one of the times. Much vital information can be exchanged during these transitions, such as when a dad lets you know that his daughter stayed up late the night before to wait for her mom's plane to land and she may be a bit cranky today. You have gained valuable information that you can use in working with that child. A face-to-face meeting is also the best way to let primary caregivers know of an important incident, such as a toddler receiving a bite or a school-age child getting in a fight with a peer. If you have spent time building the bridge of trust with primary caregivers prior to the incident, your words will be received as sincere and caring.

PRIMARY CAREGIVER MEETINGS
Make meetings comfortable and something everyone looks forward to. Schedule regular meetings to just "catch up" or share celebrations of the child from time to time. Then, when it is necessary to have private, uninterrupted conversations, you and the primary caregivers won't be so anxious. During meetings, discuss documentation of the child's development through observation records, progress reports, behavioral plans, or learning portfolios. Some teachers like to invite the child to meetings about celebrations; others like quiet time with the parents. Reflective listening works well with primary caregivers, just as it does with children. After all, the best communication occurs when one per-

son genuinely cares about and tries to understand what the other person is saying.

Begin with a question such as, "What would you want everybody to know about your child?" As you listen to the answer, try to empathize, as deployment is stressful on the adults as well as the children. After the primary caregiver starts talking, use reflection comments, such as "You seem very proud of your child," or "I share your concern," or "You are worried that he is getting in trouble a lot at school." Avoid roadblocks with primary caregivers by verifying what they are trying to say before you ask another question. Warning, admonishing, moralizing, and judging don't work well with children and certainly won't be well received by primary caregivers. Even if the conversation becomes intense, remember that reflective listening requires both parties to be working to find a common solution.

STRATEGIES

Primary Caregiver Meetings

- Be prepared by having current and adequate documentation of the child's development on hand, such as checklists, portfolios, anecdotal notes, and samples of the child's work.

- Learn to recognize the primary caregiver's feelings by listening carefully to what he or she says.

- Clarify the primary caregiver's thoughts and feelings by saying what you think you heard. For example, "I think I hear you saying that you feel sad a lot of the time since the deployment, and you think that is carrying over to your children."

- Express empathy with the primary caregiver, and offer assistance. For example, "It must

be frustrating to instantly become a single parent because of deployment. How can I better help your child?"

- Show interest in the primary caregiver's words. Maintain good eye contact; refrain from planning your next "attack" or question before the parent finishes talking. Nod encouragingly, and remain attentive.

- Empathize with the primary caregiver's point of view. It may take more than one meeting to address serious challenges with the child, especially if a parent is also dealing with serious challenges related to the loss of a spouse through deployment.

Written Communication

Several types of written communication, such as bulletin boards, newsletters, calendars, and personal notes, keep primary caregivers informed. E-mail, suggestion boxes, and phone calls are also important because they provide back-and-forth opportunities for parents to communicate with providers as well.

The best child care programs and schools boast that frequent and consistent contact with parents is the key to a successful program. Lack of communication between parents and teachers can hurt a program just as much as consistent negative contact. It's best to open lines of communication before an incident occurs, and to continue to communicate when dealing with a problem. Consistent communication builds trust. The following letter is an example of written communication. Feel free to copy it and share it with parents.

Dear Parents,

Thank you for entrusting us with your child. We are honored that you have chosen us to be the care providers at such an important time in your child's life, and we take our responsibility very seriously.

We have an open-door policy. Please feel free to stay as long as you like or drop by at any time. We know how busy you are and will do our best to keep you informed through weekly (or monthly) newsletters, direct communication each day, bulletin board information, and the parent nook in our building. We are all in this together, and any information you have regarding the care of your child is important to us and will be kept in confidence. Should changes occur in your family such as deployment, divorce, illness of any family member (especially your child), or death, please know that we are here to help. We will alert you if anything should or might change here.

Finally, we know that we are offering a service to you and want you to feel that you are getting your needs met on a daily basis. Please let us know how we can improve what we do or meet the needs of your child in another way. Again, we are interested in building a strong bridge between your home and ours.

Sincerely,

Daily Child Reports

Information sheets that report on a child's day are excellent forms of communication. Primary caregivers need to know how the day went for their children when they come to pick them up, and you need to know anything that might have affected the children outside of child care. This exchange of information helps you provide the best care. If drop-off and pickup times are too busy and not conducive to discussing the child's day, written communication may be the only way that you and the primary caregivers can exchange information.

The sample daily report shown here is published by Redleaf Press. Have the primary caregiver complete the top portion of the report, and you should complete the bottom portion at the end of the day for the primary caregiver. A clipboard hanging by the entrance will provide a visual reminder for primary caregivers to complete the form each day. For privacy, have the primary caregiver place the form in a designated file or spot where you can retrieve it. Pockets, file folders, and mail slots are a few ways to assure primary caregivers that you respect their privacy as well as the privacy of the children in your care.

Bulletin Boards

Bulletin boards or display boards can be used to communicate with primary caregivers. Change the information often to keep it up-to-date; it will become a written bridge of communication between you and the primary caregivers. Here are some ideas for successful bulletin boards to use in your program:

- Place bulletin boards in a visible place for parents, such as the foyer, entrance, or sign-in or sign-out spot.
- Place a "For Families" sign on the portion of the board that is for them.
- Enlarge articles or notes for primary caregivers on a photocopier, or print notes in large type so they are more visible.

Toddler Daily Report

Parents, please complete this section.

Child's name

Today my child seemed
- Active as usual
- A bit fussy
- Other

Last night my child slept
- Soundly
- Restlessly

Today my child woke up at
_____ AM/PM

Today my child ate
- Breakfast before coming
- Nothing before coming

Today, please note for my child
- Diet changes
- Activities to avoid
- Medication
- Other

Parents, here is information on your child's day.

Today your child
- Showed curiosity and interest in surroundings
- Found own play area or activity
- Was happy and played well
- Enjoyed activities
- Needed more attention
- Was tired
- Did not participate much

Today your child ate
- All
- Most
- A little
- None

During naptime your child
- Slept
- Rested quietly
- Was restless

Today your child
- Wore diapers
- Wore underpants
- Used the potty
- Had a BM
- Toileting comments

Please bring
- Extra clothes
- Other

Comments

Redleaf Easy Forms

- Make the boards colorful and appealing through the use of backgrounds and borders.
- Keep information current, and change it as soon as it expires in order to keep primary caregivers checking the board. Nothing turns the eye away more than an announcement that expired two weeks ago.
- Attach a folder of articles or brochures to the board for primary caregivers to take away with them to read at a later time. Useful takeaways include timely articles from early childhood journals.
- Create entire bulletin board displays on critical topics such as biting, readiness, literacy, and play.
- If you are using the Reggio Emilia approach, you can document children's work on the bulletin boards.

- In a multiclass program, use individual bulletin boards outside each classroom to provide information and daily news about each class.
- For an additional way to inform primary caregivers (especially those who are always in a hurry), place easels outside but close to the entrance to hold bulletin boards, whiteboards, flip charts, or chalkboards.
- Avoid using bulletin boards just for payment reminders. Positive quotes about parenting, reminders of important events, and authentic children's quotes are all conducive to primary caregiver involvement and attention.

Newsletters

Primary caregivers love newsletters that contain real information, such as calendars with school and community events that can be posted on the refrigerator as an extra reminder. Ask primary caregivers to assist in publishing the newsletter or to help prepare items to be included such as recipes, garage- or yard-sale ads, babysitting services, and volunteer services.

As a child care teacher of four-year-olds, I prepared my lesson plans in newsletter format each week in order to keep parents informed on the skills and concepts that we were learning. I also included upcoming events and news about parties, center closings, field trips, birthdays, births in families, grandparent news, book fairs, recipes, and words to songs we were singing. Newsletters can

- enhance communication between primary caregivers and providers;
- supply current information;
- provide an authentic medium for children to showcase their work;
- provide a medium for primary caregivers to communicate with one another.

Personal Notes

Personal notes can be like little pieces of gold to parents. I've seen parents save them for long periods of time, revisiting them to enjoy the good feeling all over again as they read, "Andy is adjusting so very well—he's playing with the other children and has begun sharing!"

It only takes a minute to write a sentence or two, but the benefits are enduring. It may be just the thing to brighten the day of a parent who is feeling the pressures of being left alone with his children. The parent who is deployed overseas can receive the note in a care package from home. You would be surprised how many grandmothers have personal notes on their refrigerators! Keep a weekly grid such as the one below to remind you whose parent or primary caregiver you've written notes to.

MONDAY	Keri Blake
TUESDAY	Ron Mary
WEDNESDAY	Sam Carol Melissa
THURSDAY	Max Amy Laura
FRIDAY	Lilly Jeff

Signs

Primary caregivers appreciate handy signs that are pertinent to the child's day. Just as children need environmental print to foster reading and writing skills and to provide visual communication, primary caregivers also can benefit from this form of communication. Here are a few suggestions for environmental print for primary caregivers:

- sign-in sheets for kids and primary caregivers (side-by-side on clipboards or whiteboards)
- menus for the week or month posted in the entryway or outside the classroom
- word of the week
- saying of the day
- upcoming field trips
- weekly lesson or activity plans
- list of local babysitters
- daily news flash such as "Sam's mom had a baby girl today!" or "Judy's dad returned from deployment last night!"

Electronic Communication

In addition to posting a routine chart in the kitchen to gently remind each child what will happen next, a family child care provider also maintains a password-protected Web site with pictures and stories of each of the children in her care. Military parents as well as other family members (including grandparents) and primary caregivers can access the site at any time to read the latest news from the program. A video camera provides live footage of the child care program through the Web site as well. It's just one more way of keeping the deployed connected to the world they have left behind. The provider has received a tremendous positive response to her efforts to keep parents informed.

E-mail is a mainstay of communication for many parents and teachers, as most of us either have computers and e-mail accounts or have access to them. You can use e-mail to send out daily or weekly reminders, personal notes, and electronic newsletters. Remember that deployed parents may not have instant access to e-mail, and it may take weeks to get a response.

If you aren't interested in maintaining a Web site or aren't able to, then a blog (Web log) or a wiki (see chapter 8 for information on blogs and wikis) may be just the thing. There are several free sites where you can set up a discussion board or forum for military parents to use to communicate with each other. The content on a wiki can be changed by anyone, but the content on a blog can only be changed by the creator. If you want to have more control over the site, you should choose the blog as your medium. Photos and graphics can be added to either kind of site, and password protection is optional. Of course, primary caregivers who do have not access to the Internet will need to have opportunities to participate through other means of communication.

STRATEGIES

Build a Web site for Kids and Primary Caregivers

Many companies offer free hosting for teachers and care providers. A Web site is a great way to keep primary caregivers informed and encourage them to interact with the child and the program. Notes that get lost in transit can now be posted in private on the Web site. Whole group or class notes can be posted there as well. You can house reminders for upcoming events in one place that a primary caregiver can easily check at a moment's notice. If computer access is challenging for military parents for security reasons, make a computer at your program's arrival area accessible to parents. They can check for messages, schedules, progress reports, and so on, when they drop off or pick up their child. On installations, most military parents have computers at home, and can check the Web site there as well.

―――――――

Electronic Feedback

Give parents and primary caregivers opportunities to provide feedback electronically. Many of the old suggestion boxes that graced the entrances to child care centers have been replaced by electronic invitations with feedback, online surveys, blogs, and wikis. Knowing that many centers had not had much luck with suggestion boxes for a long time, and after seeing several placed in high-traffic areas in child care centers, I asked at one center if there were a lot of responses in the boxes. "Hardly ever," a provider told me. "I don't know why we keep them—I guess because we're expected to." A provider who had tried an online survey site with her parents reported that it worked extremely well, giving her feedback more quickly than ever before. She could even set the controls so that the feedback was anonymous. (Note: most military parents use e-mail, but primary caregivers other than parents may not.)

Program-to-Home Activities for Kids and Primary Caregivers

Send the content home! Primary caregivers can keep up with learning objectives for their children with traveling suitcase libraries that come home for the week, outfitted with activities for the primary caregiver and child to complete together. These learning activities can give primary caregivers a chance to sit down with their children and find out what they are learning in child care. Activity bags that contain an item from each area or domain of development (social-emotional, language and literacy, cognitive, and physical) can be prepared for all ages, from infants to schoolagers.

Make bags out of a strong fabric that will hold up under frequent use, or use a small rolling suitcase to hold heavier items. Always include a checklist so that primary caregivers can remember to put all the items back into the bag. Let all children take turns "bagsitting" for a night or a weekend. Try the following ideas for bags in different learning areas, and watch children smile as they take them out the door!

LANGUAGE AND LITERACY

- children's books such as *Flat Stanley* (J. Brown 2003), *Goodnight Moon* (M. W. Brown 1991), and *Caps for Sale* (Slobodkina 1987). Books should match age and stage development of the child.
- a puppet that accompanies a book, such as a bunny for *Goodnight Moon* (M. W. Brown 1991), a monkey for *Caps for Sale* (Slobodkina 1987), or a bear for *Brown Bear, Brown Bear, What Do You See?* (Martin 1992)
- reading buddies such as a Traveling Dolly or Traveling Wally (large female and male doll puppets) and a notebook for parents or kids to record adventures during Dolly's or Wally's visit
- instruction or idea sheet
- magnetic letters
- books on tape and tape player
- puzzles

COGNITIVE (THINKING) SKILLS

- sample letters or directions that child and parents can read together
- alphabet cards, drawing and writing pads, markers, stickers, crayons
- mini whiteboard and dry-erase markers
- puzzle books
- small microscopes
- musical instruments
- CDs and tapes
- DVDs

SOCIAL-EMOTIONAL SKILLS

- Send disposable cameras home for children to take photos of special events, such as the birth of a sibling, a birthday party, or a homecoming or reunion.
- Take photos of children and send them home in a photo album or scrapbook. Leave a few pages blank for the child to add more photos to bring back to your program to share.
- Make survival kits for the car and send them home with the children. Include jokes and riddle books, books on tape, and printable travel games to play with children or that children can play together, such as "I Spy," "Car Bingo," "Radio Bingo," and others that can be found at www.disneyfamily.com.

PHYSICAL SKILLS

- puzzles that are theme related
- instructions for scavenger hunts that are theme related
- dominoes
- small parachute and activities to do with the parachute
- number cubes for rolling and counting

Note: avoid using bags as positive reinforcement (a reward) for good behavior, as their purpose is to provide quality activities that all primary caregivers can do with their children—strengthening the relationship between child care and home.

STRATEGIES

"Visiting" the Deployed

I watched a woman snap a photo of her nephew Max riding a carousel horse at a local shopping mall. But her nephew lived in Maine, and we were in Texas! She explained that the picture of her nephew's face attached to a cardboard body was his teacher's version of the main character in the book Flat Stanley *(J. Brown 2003). She had received the Flat Max in the mail with a letter that asked her to take it to interesting places in her area since the real Max was not able to visit. She showed me several pages of photos from places Flat Max had visited so far—the zoo, dining out, near some Texas longhorns, and a professional basketball game. What a great idea for military kids, I thought. They may not be able to visit the places where their military parents work or are deployed, but maybe their flat selves could!*

In 2006, the Maine National Guard provided Flat Daddies and Flat Mommies for the families of each member who was deployed to Iraq or Afghanistan. Photos of Guard members (from the waist up) were enlarged to life-size; they were then cut out and glued to foam board. Families left behind when the Guard was deployed took the Flat People everywhere. The project was a tremendous success.

Any local or online photocopy store can make a Flat Dad or Mom. The family members left behind can have one copy, and the deployed parent can have a copy to take with her when she is deployed.

Benefits of Strong Relationships between Families and Programs

Direct involvement of primary caregivers in child care programs can often build strong relationships between providers and primary caregivers and is decidedly better for the children both in the short and long term. A primary caregiver can't begin too soon—child care programs are ripe with possibilities for families to make vital contributions. The main thing that primary caregivers can remember to do is to talk to their kids—intentionally and attentionally. Share with primary caregivers how to ask *intentional* questions such as how the child's day went and then really pay *attention* to the answer. Remind primary caregivers to pause after asking questions so the children have time to think about their answers. You can model this technique for primary caregivers as they arrive and depart each day or while they visit for longer periods.

Use the following information to help keep busy primary caregivers informed and engaged with you and their children.

Arriving and Departing

Primary caregivers have a need to be affirmed or noticed when they drop off or pick up their child. For example, once you've communicated with a primary caregiver through a simple "Hello, Ms. Jackson. How is everything today?" she is much more comfortable in leaving her child with you for the whole day. And you thought it was just the child who needed your attention!

Separation is one of the most difficult adjustments that children must make when entering care for the first time. New surroundings, people, and peers, as well as the idea of being away from Mom or Dad, is often too much to manage. Deployment of a parent compounds the problem, often making the child even more frightened of leaving the remaining primary caregiver. Helping the child learn to cope with the new setting is one of the biggest challenges you will face in caring for young children. Let's take a closer look at the stages a toddler or early preschooler will go through in separating from a parent.

RETREAT STAGE

If the child retreats to a primary caregiver's arms after entering the classroom, take the first step and offer to take the child after the primary caregiver gives him a hug and says good-bye. Partings are difficult, but sometimes all a child needs is a bit of additional contact with the primary caregiver. Ask the primary caregiver if she has an extra moment to stay. If not, try redirecting the child with a favorite toy or taking him gently and guiding him to the next activity.

ONLOOKER STAGE

Allow the child time to adjust while in the primary caregiver's arms or lap. The primary caregiver might begin talking about other children and activities that are taking place in the classroom or mentioning available toys.

INSPECTION STAGE

The child inspects or looks over the classroom and the children who are playing. The child continues to stay in the primary caregiver's lap but is calm and focused on the activity going on in the setting.

SELECTION/RETRIEVAL STAGE

The child gets out of the primary caregiver's arms and selects a toy, then runs back to the primary caregiver. The child may repeat this stage, getting more and more toys as he practices being away from the primary caregiver for longer and longer periods of time.

PROVIDER CONTACT STAGE

Approach the child and make contact by using a language lure, such as: "Do you want to play [the most powerful word in a child's universe]?" or "I have some more puppets in the closet—let's get a new one out." (Novelty is key here, so be willing to get a new or novel toy out to interest the child.)

> **TIP**
>
> Recycle toys often by putting them away after children have played with them for a few days. Bring them back out on occasions such as this one to provide the extra motivation a child needs in order to detach from a parent.

PRIMARY CAREGIVER DEPARTURE STAGE

Twenty-month-old Gracie entered her classroom in the arms of her dad, crying and saying, "No, stay!" The provider was busily feeding breakfast to the other toddlers, with her back to the door of the classroom. Gracie continued to cry as her dad (still holding her) put her bag in her cubby. There was still no contact between Dad, Gracie, and the provider. Dad appeared frustrated, put Gracie down, and said, "I'll try to pick you up early today, honey." As Dad drove away from the center, he looked back to see Gracie standing at the window, still crying.

Children who get upset when having to detach from their primary caregivers are showing a healthy sign of attachment. Rather than looking on the incident with Gracie and her dad as one of difficulty, the provider might use the following phrases:

- "It's Gracie! We are so glad that you came and brought your dad."
- "Look, Gracie. Everyone is eating breakfast!"
- "Can you show your dad where to put your things?"

- "We are going to make smoothies. Wash your hands so you can help."
- (To Dad) "Do you have any special instructions for us today? Be sure to write them down too."
- "Gracie, can you look in my pocket?" (The provider wears an apron with large pockets for special times like this.)

While observing in many military child care centers as well as family child care programs, I've noticed that primary caregivers are often in a hurry when dropping off and picking up their children. It will take some time to educate and encourage primary caregivers to come a little early in order to prevent abrupt departures, which are especially important to avoid because of the deployment/separation issues that are present in military care. Separation issues are only compounded by rushed primary caregivers, especially when at least one parent is already missing from the home because of deployment.

STRATEGIES

Easing into the Environment

Provide a rocking chair or other comfortable chair in front of a large, wall-mounted mirror that the child can see while in the primary caregiver's lap (while the primary caregiver's back is to mirror). Encourage the primary caregiver to stay as long as he likes, in order for the child to become at ease in the environment.

Barriers to Relationships with Families

What if a primary caregiver's values or parenting style seems to oppose yours as a care provider? What if you have done everything that you think is possible to build bridges with primary caregivers, and it isn't working? Perhaps there is one primary caregiver who just isn't responsive.

Cultural differences can become barriers in building a healthy and close family-provider relationship. Embrace the diverse cultures that are represented by the children in your care. Gather information as soon as possible about a child's heritage and traditions so that you can include those in your program planning. For example, Yoshi's mom is Japanese but his dad is American. He brings many cultural traditions to your program from both parents. Since his mom speaks limited English, Yoshi often translates for her and asks her to stay at his preschool program to "learn English better." As a provider, you can honor his request to have his mother share his experiences by including her as much as possible. Her ability to speak Japanese with the children can add a wonderful dimension to your program as you foster respect for cultural diversity.

Too little time and job stress are obstacles that get in the way of strong relationships between primary caregivers and providers. Workdays are getting longer, and leisure time is getting shorter. Children who were once cared for in the home are now cared for in programs and child care centers for up to ten hours per day.

Different values and a lack of understanding of the program can prevent primary caregivers and providers from finding common ground and can contribute to a perceived lack of respect on both sides. Military parents want the same things non-military parents do: access to high-quality care that is affordable and accessible. They also need flexible hours as well as care for mildly ill and special needs children. They may need twenty-four-hour and extended or long-term care when deployed or on special training exercises and missions. If you know the challenges that military parents face, you can break down many of the barriers by offering care that meets their needs or by assisting them in finding excellent care for extended child care. You can be successful in working with military parents if you frequently set learning goals for yourself that include working with parents in challenging times,

continuing to initiate conversations and communication with parents (written and verbal) during trying times, planning ahead for challenges, such as long term deployments or short separations during upcoming training missions, and persevering as you face barriers that require understanding on the part of you the provider and the parents.

As you explore ways to work with parents and primary caregivers more effectively, take time to consider your assumptions about them and how those assumptions guide your beliefs and practices. Reflect on the following questions: Do you embrace diversity, and does your program reflect your beliefs about inclusion? Do you know every primary caregiver's name? Can you learn one significant thing about each one so that there is always a familiar connection? Do you consider challenges with parents opportunities for professional growth? Do you meet often with primary caregivers or just on scheduled visits? Does your program do more than place a welcome sign on the door to communicate to families that they are welcome? The barriers to family-provider relationships can be torn down as you practice strategies for developing partnerships with the parents and other primary caregivers of military children.

CHAPTER EIGHT

Staying Connected

Staying connected to family members and friends is of great importance to children in military families. It takes a creative effort to continue a close relationship with a deployed parent or with the folks "back home."

their parents and must leave friends and family behind as they relocate with the military parent to new installations and communities worldwide.

As parents locate and relocate throughout their military careers, their children are often expected to move when parents have been called up for duty. There are countless children who are "serving" with

Awaiting a flight out of Tokyo, I spoke with a military mom who was traveling with her eight-year-old daughter to her next assignment as a radio operator in Iceland. As I spent my entire childhood living within a one-mile area in east Texas, it seemed surreal to me that an eight-year-old had already lived in Germany and Japan and now would be attending school in Iceland. "What's the hardest part about moving?" I asked the mom. "Leaving her friends. But with e-mail and video cameras and instant messaging, she's gonna be okay. She's done this before, and it's not so hard now that we have all this technology." The little girl nodded and smiled.

As children of military parents relocate, they must cope with instant, as well as planned, national and international moves. Because the U.S. military makes an effort to keep families together whenever possible, children are more mobile now than ever before. Yet the problem for military children is two-pronged: losing their parents because of deployment or active-duty separation and leaving friends and family behind when relocating. Staying connected with those left behind or with parents who are serving in the armed forces is important to their well-being and sense of self. Military children know the importance of respecting the jobs their parents do, but they also know the difficulty in leaving familiar faces and places behind.

Children who are left behind with relatives or friends when their parents deploy face an extremely difficult form of separation. Even if parents are not engaging in direct warfare, they may be serving on installations thousands of miles away for a year or more. Reservist children may be hit the hardest. They may not have had the experience of many military children—their parents have held conventional, nonmilitary jobs until being called up for duty. These children may be unfamiliar with military culture or what to expect. What they see on the nightly news suddenly becomes a real portrayal of what may happen to their parents. Staying connected becomes fundamental. Knowing that they are loved, even in the absence of the active-duty parent, can transcend the fear and anxiety in military kids. Let's explore how they can continue to communicate—to stay connected to deployed parents or to those they have left behind after a move.

Find maps of the countries or states where the children's deployed parents are working. Do research on the people who live there, especially the children. Discuss how they are alike and different from the kids in your care. What is the geography like? What kinds of foods do they eat? Do they have special games that they play? What are their programs like? By answering any or all of these questions, you will help make the area where their parents are deployed seem less far away or unreal to military kids.

STRATEGIES

Locating the Deployed Parent

Help children figure out where their deployed parent is serving. Use a distance calculator such as the ones found at www.deploymentkids.com or www.indo.com/distance to determine the distance between them and their parents.

Staying in Touch when Separated from Parents

It is difficult enough to deal with the absence of a loved one, but the thought of not being able to correspond with a parent, another family member, or a friend is taxing for children. Jane Bandler of Our Military Kids reports that "the psychological stress of living in a home where a parent is deployed cannot be minimized. Besides coping with the sadness

and loneliness of missing a parent, there is the 24/7 stress of worry and concern for the well-being of the parent soldier" (www.ourmilitarykids.org).

Although it takes a creative effort to continue a relationship while separated, it is well worth it. One military spouse said it best: "I will do whatever it takes to keep my children connected to their father." She knows (and the rest of us can learn) that adults must play a large role in assisting children with efforts to stay connected. Some children are motivated to stay connected in the beginning stages of deployment, but may become less engaged as the days, weeks, and months go on with irregular response from the deployed parent. For example, a child's mom may be serving in an area where e-mail or the Internet is unavailable or available only sporadically. Or, she may be in a location where any contact would compromise her safety, and no news from her is to be considered good news. It is difficult to keep children engaged in communicating when the tangible rewards of receiving return communication are sometimes impossible. In these cases, you can play a creative role in keeping the communication going.

on a secured site. If the child likes to draw or paint, use those projects as focal points of a care package.

If there is more than one child in the family, provide colored envelopes (one color per child) when sending letters to the deployed parent. Include an extra envelope of the same color with a return address so that the service member can respond in that same color. When the letter arrives, the child will instantly know it is a letter from Dad or Mom.

Create a weekly or monthly newsletter to send to the parent. Include program events, photos, and drawings.

Assist the primary caregiver in creating a calendar of upcoming events to send once a month to help the deployed parent keep track of what the family is doing day to day. Include events such as dental appointments, baseball games, ballet lessons, and pizza and movie nights as well as birthdays, christenings, trips, and performances. Ask the deployed parent to make a calendar as well to let the family know his daily activities (to the extent possible).

Have children draw pictures on magnetic paper (found in craft stores), and send them to the deployed parent. Pictures can then be attached to anything metal and will stay without nails or tape.

Trace the child's hand on posterboard twice. Send the tracings to the deployed parent, and ask that she trace her hand over one hand and return it so that the child has a picture of them "holding hands."

STRATEGIES

Creative Connections with Deployed Parents

Focus on the interests of the child. Take photos of the child doing something he likes, and send them to the parent, or post them

Staying Connected to Family and Friends Left Behind

It is important to keep children engaged in productive, authentic, and significant activities while a parent is deployed away from the family or the family has moved away from home because of deployment. Younger children cannot fathom the element of time, and a year may mean an eternity to them.

While conducting a provider training in Alaska, my Southern accent was a giveaway. One care provider said, "You sound like my family back home in Texas!" I nodded yes, as it is always fun to meet others from my home state. "My kids miss their grandparents in McKinney so much that I would like to stow them away in that big props suitcase of yours over there and send them back with you. We haven't been home in over a year." "How do you and the kids stays connected with them?" I asked. "We talk just about every day. Our phone bills are outrageous!"

Kids need a support system to strengthen and sustain their sense of self. The family of origin is an important part of a child's life, and connections should be maintained at all costs, even if it sometimes means "outrageous" telephone bills. But there are also inexpensive ways to keep relationships with family members and friends strong. In one program, schoolagers e-mailed friends they had known at other installations in other countries. A provider remarked that it made the transition easier for them when relocating. Children often rely on the friendships they make in installation communities, since they are separated from family during deployments. Children who reside in communities away from installations also need strong support systems and often rely on family and friends in other parts of the state or country. The following strategies are for children who are living in countries or states away from their friends and extended family.

STRATEGIES

Keeping Children Connected with Family Members Back Home

Create a time capsule to "freeze" time for deployed family members. Time capsules are a great way to preserve or commemorate important events in their absence. The capsule can be as simple as placing some memorabilia in a taped box or buying a waterproof container to house your treasures for a long time. Use the following ideas as a guide to preserving treasures and treasured moments in the anticipation of homecoming:

- Decide on the length of time that your capsule will represent according to each individual child in your care.

- Choose a container that will appropriately house the child's contributions. (You can even make an online time box.)

- Include photographs (black and white work best), drawings, newspaper clippings (copied on acid-free paper if you want to preserve them for a long time), journal entries, news of world events, and anything else the child would like to save for Mom or Dad.

You can also help children create family trees. Ask their deployed parents or primary caregivers to contribute information about the people in their family. Use visuals such as trees, pyramids, or charts with boxes for the information on each person in the child's family. Large charts can be placed on posterboard so that the child can add new comments or graphics as he acquires more information.

Start with the child in the first box or tier and concentrate on only two or three generations in the beginning. Have the children think carefully about (or get to know more about) the closest members of their families rather than learning about people who died a long time ago. When possible, request a photograph of each important family member. Find out likes and dislikes of the closest members, and put pictures by their names that tell their stories in more than words.

Using Technology to Keep in Touch

Technology has become a mainstay of environments for military children, as the number of children needing to stay connected to their parents and others around the world has increased in recent times. Technology has improved military family communication tremendously over the past few years. What once was a difficult challenge is now as easy as sending e-mail. E-mail and instant messaging are the fastest ways to stay in touch, but kids are also using webcams, podcasts, video or vodcasts, family Web pages, blogs, wikis, and lots of other technological media to keep in touch.

Children's interest in computers and other electronic devices may be the key to helping them stay connected when they are hesitant to begin a long-distance relationship or keep one going as the weeks and months wear on. At one time it was a question of *whether* to include computers and the Internet in our environments for children; now it is a question of *how* to best include them, authentically and appropriately. As tools for communication, computers and other kinds of technology can boost a child's ability to correspond with loved ones and friends. Electronic devices also increase the opportunities for problem solving, critical thinking, cognitive and language development, cooperative learning, documentation of their work, and outlets for creativity.

Collaborations

The distance between children and their deployed family members or friends who have moved to other installations or entered civilian life is no longer a barrier to communication. Technology can remove obstacles easily and provide the tools for continued collaboration. Communicating with friends and family members on the other side of the installation or the other side of the world is simple and fast.

STRATEGIES

Keeping Kids Interested and Engaged in Networking

Instant messaging is free with messaging services such as MSN (www.msn.com), Yahoo! (www.yahoo.com), and Google mail (www.gmail.com), to name just a few. You will need to sit with young children and type for them. Schoolagers can type their own messages but still need supervision and technological assistance.

Telephone software allows kids to make calls from a computer to their friends and family anywhere or to call the United States from military installations overseas—for free or at little cost. Skype (www.skype.com) and Google Talk (www.google.com/hangouts/) are two popular voice chat services that offer kids the ability to stay in touch for a small fee.

The ePals Web site (www.epals.com) offers SchoolBlogs, in2Books, and SchoolMail to schoolagers (kindergarten to twelfth grade). With children's need to maintain relationships with distant family and friends, Internet pen pal sites are crucial.

Digital cameras and camcorders are especially exciting tools for school-age children in your care. They are easy to use (with supervision) and provide almost instant feedback or playback of the recorded event. If you want your schoolagers to complete a tutorial before they pick up the camera, you can download a guide at http://k-12.pisd.edu/multimedia/peripherals/camera/camera.htm. Ask older schoolagers to visit your program and take photos and videos of infants, toddlers, and preschoolers, or you can use the cameras to document activities with younger children and their parents.

- Take pictures of children on a particular day of each month to include in a calendar for an end-of-the-year gift for parents.

- Make a video or photo journal of special events such as field trips, holiday festivities, and presentations. Play the video at an open house.

- Take lots of pictures of kids, and store them on your computer to use as graphics in flyers, brochures, newsletters, etc. Schoolagers can also assist with this project.

- Take photos of each child to use in greeting cards. Group photos are also great for get-well and good-bye cards.

- Take photos of each child on the first day of attendance. Prepare a bulletin board of all the photos.

- Create a "Good-bye Board" in order to remember those who have moved away.

- For the children left behind to view, make a video scrapbook of each child before the child moves to another installation. Make a copy for the child's parents as well.

- Make videos of the whole group for the child who is leaving so she can remember the friends from this installation or community.

- Take photos on nature walks, and use photo editing software such as Paint Shop Pro or Microsoft Photo Editor to create photo collages.

- Take random photos throughout the year, and make a PowerPoint presentation with music or sounds for parents to view at an open house or parents' night.

Video letters are great fun for children to exchange once they have moved to other installations and left friends behind. Send them over the computer, or load them on a CD-ROM and send them in the mail.

Online educational games can be played with a friend or a parent at sites such as Fun Brain (www.funbrain.com/kidscenter.html). There are also games such as "Balloon Pop!" for preschoolers and older toddlers to play with an adult. Kids can play games independently and then compare scores. Some game sites, such as those for chess, can be accessed from more than one location, permitting two kids or a parent and child in different locations to play together.

Electronic greeting cards can be sent for free from some sites and are quick and easy to use. Fun Brain has cards to send too.

Podcasts (portable on-demand broadcasts) are digital media files that can be broadcast, much like programs on the radio, but via the Web or on a portable media (MP3) player. Many school-age children have players and can download podcasts to listen to.

- Step 1: Select a podcasting educational site for children, such as www.poducate me.com.

- Step 2: Have children listen to podcasts of their favorite topics, such as fishing, kite flying, musical instruments, or dog training. There are literally hundreds of podcasts available. They can be found on the World Wide Web at www .pbskids.org/dragonflyTV, www.classics forkids.com, www.kids.gov, and www2 .scholastic.com, as well as many more.

- Advanced step 3: Encourage kids to explore sites such as www.poducateme .com that give simple directions in learning to make podcasts.

- Advanced step 4: Publish podcasts on a kid-safe and kid-friendly site such as kid-cast.com (www.kid-cast.com).

E-mail is the most common form of communication outside of cell phones and postal mail. It is a great way to send greetings to loved ones, but remember that it is not a private means of communication. Keep in mind that service members may not be able to receive some content on military computers. Save jokes and pictures for password-protected blog and wiki sites. One suggestion is to number e-mail messages you send to active-duty members of the military, as they sometimes receive them all at once, especially if they are serving on ships. Don't be alarmed if you do not get an instant response. No news may be good news.

Webcams can be found on laptops and some desktops and can be purchased as extra hardware for many PCs. One mother reported that being away from her children would be impossible if she did not have a webcam so she can see them every day. Webcams can be tricky to use with time differences around the world, but they offer a great way to stay visually connected with friends and family.

Blogs (short for *Web logs*) are Web sites you can create for free. They need to be maintained with current information, like an online diary. People use blogs to post their thoughts on particular topics; readers can post comments. Blogs also allow the owner to post images and links to other Web pages and to add podcasts. Blogs are chronological, and the most recent news or post will always appear first on the home page, with older posts accessed with a click from other pages.

Wikis are Web pages that house information on a more permanent basis and can be changed by anyone who has access. Unlike blogs, they are not chronological. Many users like their appearance and the fact that many other users can participate in developing the wiki. Many wiki sites are free.

Social networking Web sites such as MySpace and Facebook are free, password-protected sites that can be accessed from any computer with Internet access. You can upload and share pictures with your loved ones as well as messages. These sites may be reducing the need for personal Web sites.

Internet Safety Tips

As the children in your care use the Internet to connect with loved ones, use safety precautions. Monitor and limit children's time on the Internet. Use timers to provide specific start and stop times rather than allowing children to do endless surfing. Monitor what the child is viewing on the Internet. Set controls so that inappropriate sites are unreachable. Web sites such as www2.scholastic.com, www.kidsnewsroom.org, and www.fbi.gov/kids/k5th/safety2.htm have safety tips to ensure safe surfing on the Web.

Offering children ways to stay in touch with their loved ones is crucial, as children need to get news firsthand from their parents rather than hearing it from someone else. Older children need to be able to send and receive greetings, and technology is a wonderful tool that allows them to stay connected. A letter or e-mail addressed directly to the child can help her to know that someone is thinking about her, even though her parent may be far away.

CHAPTER NINE

Special Issues

Over one hundred thousand children in military families are facing life changes in greater degrees than ever before. More members of the military, especially reservists and National Guard members, are deployed now than before the terrorist attacks on September 11, 2001.

Children whose parents were wearing "civvies" rather than fatigues prior to the events of September 11 are watching their parents being deployed to unfamiliar places and for unknown periods of time. The dad who has never missed a soccer game will now miss a whole year (or more) of his daughter's life, and the mom who was her son's biggest fan at baseball games will now be absent for the next season. Adults without children who work with youth in their community are leaving many kids behind as well. For example, a teacher who is a reservist worked with three hundred kids on a weekly basis. When she left to work as a communications expert in Iraq, her deployment was so dramatic and affected so many young people that it was reported on the local news. Her sister told me, "She didn't just leave my two sons [her nephews], she left so many kids [who] adore and miss her."

Children may live on an installation in a military town or in an area that is heavily populated with military families, or their parents may be reservists, so that they are geographically separated from anything military. They may have one or both parents in the military or another family member or friend in the military. If they have one or both parents in the military, they may stay with family or friends in their present locations or move somewhere new to live with family or friends. This may be their first experience with deployment and separation or the second or third experience. One woman I knew reported that out of the twenty-two years that her father was in the military, she was with him a total of eleven years.

Children who grow up in the military are often accustomed to the drill—pre-deployment, deployment, sustainment, and reunion, before being deployed a second or even a third time. Absence of the parent is not easy but becomes the norm. The children of reservists and guard members, on the other hand, are accustomed to absences of one weekend per month while their parents are in training and two weeks in the summer. Being away from their parents for extended periods of time may be unthinkable as well as frightening.

This chapter addresses several special issues, including extended deployments, repeat deployments, and the deployment of both parents. I also discuss the challenge that arises when single parents are deployed, and what happens when military children face the death of a military parent. Last, I discuss child abuse, which can become a real issue due to the trauma and stress that military life can bring. I offer strategies for you to use when confronting any of these special challenges.

Extended Deployments

Extended deployments have been more common since the war on terror began in Afghanistan, and especially so during the Iraq War, or Operation Iraqi Freedom. Military downsizing and the lack of a draft have led to multiple deployments. When the countdown of the long-awaited return of the deployed parent is interrupted by news of an exten-

sion of the parent's tour of duty, children's anticipation of a happy homecoming is disrupted, and new plans must be made to weather the longer period of separation. With the news, hopes are dashed or at least put on hold until a new return date is announced. Children feel a sense of betrayal. At times like these you must continue to provide coping strategies so that the child's emotional health is not in jeopardy. Helping children accept the idea that their parents are still at work or have to work longer before coming home can give them a sense of peace.

STRATEGIES

Support Children through Extended Deployments

Plan a visit to the point of return (airport, pier, etc.) with flags, tokens from home, etc. Allow children to select small gifts for the parent who is returning.

Put on a puppet show about extended deployments. Use large puppets that all children can use to later reenact the story. If you have children of multiple ages in your care, the older ones can put on the show for the younger children.

Hero packs are often given to the youngest heroes—children of deployed service members. Make your own hero packs to distribute; fill them with items such as a disposal camera, writing paper, thank-you notes, small stuffed animals (to keep or to send to parents), and gift certificates. You may also contact Operation: Military Kids for hero packs. Depending on availability in your state, they have two versions: one for younger children (ages three to eight) and one for older kids (ages nine to eighteen). See the Web site www.operationmilitarykids.org for more information.

Ask older military children to speak to younger military children about their deployed loved ones. They can tell stories of past experiences with deployment as well as give advice and describe ways they have learned to cope. Capitalize on the experiences of the teens and older schoolagers in your area. Speak Out for Military Kids (SOMK), sponsored by Operation: Military Kids, raises community awareness about deployment and the issues that families face while separated from loved ones. SOMK provides opportunities for military kids to have speaking opportunities and gain leadership skills.

Chapter 2, Offering Emotional Support, is full of ways to help kids, including infants and preverbal toddlers.

Repeat Deployments

When children understand that once their parents return from a tour of duty, a repeat deployment is possible, they may be frightened. Learning to cope with the fear, sadness, and anxiety is crucial to the emotional well-being of military children. The emotional trauma of deployment is magnified for children who know the dangers of the work their parents do to protect their country. Although deployments and repeat deployments vary according to the units served and the missions that military members are on, children only see that a loved one will not be around for events such as school plays, picnics, parties, saying good night, and teaching them how to cook or play baseball. Learning how to cope while parents are working far from home and how to pass the time until they return is challenging for kids, but you can help.

STRATEGIES

Support Children through Repeat Deployments

Installation chaplains often stay behind their units in order to work with the families left behind, especially the children. Encourage parents and primary caregivers to contact installation chaplains for assistance by phone or e-mail when children are hurting due to repeat deployments of their loved ones.

Give children a special journal to record their thoughts as much as possible. Provide special pens to write with or stickers that can be placed on each page of the journal as a story starter or thinking "button." Assign different colors of markers or pens for particular feelings, such as red for angry and blue for sad. Also, encourage younger children to draw in their journals.

Provide scrapbooking materials that will allow children to express feelings and connect with the deployed parent or other loved one when they return. The scrapbook can be shared or presented to the parent as a gift.

Mobile technology labs (MTL) are now available through Operation: Military Kids in many areas for children to connect with deployed parents or other family members. The labs contain laptops, digital cameras and video cameras, printers, scanners, laminators, and software for children to use in making connections. Request that an MTL come to your area, or if that isn't possible, create your own lab with equipment you have available.

When Both Parents Are Deployed

When both parents are deployed, caregivers need information about family support organizations that provide services and programs to improve the quality of life for military families. Each branch of the military has its own organization that provides such support services for families. Local installations house the organizations and are available for primary caregivers to use in the absence of the parents. Communities in which reservists live often have online as well as face-to-face support groups that are active for each military reserve group. Here is a list of military support organizations:

- Army: Army Community Services Center (ACSC)
- U.S. Marine Corps: Family Services Center (FSC)
- Navy: Fleet and Family Services Center (FFSC)
- Air Force: Airman and Family Readiness Flight Center (AFRFC)
- National Guard: Family Assistance Center (FAC)

STRATEGIES

Supporting Children when Both Parents Are Deployed

Ask the nearest command of a military branch, Veterans of Foreign Wars (VFW) post, or American Legion to "adopt a school" in order to build community between the military and civilians who are caring for military children. Activities such as tutoring, bringing a skill or talent to your program, being a "big brother or big sister" to children left behind, or volunteering in your program are all great ways to build strong relationships while assisting in the care of children whose parents are deployed.

Contact the military support group or groups that represent the children in your care.

Make service member collages using large poster frames, and hang them in the hallways or on classroom walls to honor the military parents who are deployed. Include photos, newspaper clippings, letters to the parents from children, drawings, and any other remembrances.

Get to know military time. The twenty-four-hour clock that is used by all military personnel is often confusing for civilians. Learn the basics of telling military time; it is common for a military parent to write or speak "military time."

Tips to convert from conventional time to military time:

12:00 AM (midnight) to 12:00 PM (noon)

Delete the colon, and use all four numbers.

Before 10 AM, add a zero (7:00 AM to 0700), pronounced "oh seven hundred."

12:00 PM (noon) to 12:00 AM (midnight)

Delete the colon.

Add twelve hours to the conventional time; 1 PM becomes 1300 hours, and 7 PM becomes 1900 hours.

When Single Parents Are Deployed

Single parenting is a difficult job, and when the parent works in the military, it gets even tougher. When a single parent is deployed, the children may or may not be able to accompany the parent. If deployment will confine the parent to an installation job, child and youth care may be available. In other cases, single military parents must find substitute care for their children. Many service members report that their ex-spouses care for their children, while others leave relatives or family friends in charge.

STRATEGIES

When Single Parents Are Deployed

Here are some ideas to help you keep connections with the parent as strong and as frequent as possible (adapted from www.militaryhomefront.dod.mil):

Career Day: It is a myth that all deployed military parents are in the infantry or do ground fighting. Hold a Career Day in which you invite local civilians who do the same jobs that military service members perform, such as electricians, computer technicians, doctors, firemen, attorneys, and nurses, to come to your program to talk about their work. Ask them to bring items for show-and-tell. Help children compare the jobs that civilians do with the jobs their parents do. Provide props for children to use in dramatic and role playing. The following Web site lists the many jobs in each branch of the military: http://usmilitary.about.com.

Child-dictated letters: Take dictation from nonwriters, and compose a letter for them to send to their deployed parent. Provide stickers and markers for the child to "dress up" the letter or to personalize it. Assist the child in making a mark for her name if she is unable to write it.

Photo books: Ask the deploying single parent for photos before he leaves. Make a photo book for the child to look at (as often as she wants) while the parent is gone. Take time to discuss the photos, and talk about each one with the child. To keep a conversation going about the parent, add new photos as often as possible.

Communication: Build a strong bond with the noncustodial parent or the family member who is left behind with the child by exchanging e-mail addresses and phone numbers, times available to meet, opportunities for volunteering in your program, and frequent verbal communications.

Cookbooks: Make the deployed parent's favorite recipes. Allow children to assist if possible. Assemble a cookbook of parents' favorite recipes, and make copies for every parent. Send copies to deployed parents.

Crossword puzzles: Assist older children in making crossword puzzles to send to their parents. Using Braille or writing in Morse code is fun to do as well. "Come home soon" or "I miss you" in code is always a welcome greeting to a parent who is serving far from home.

Benefits of Military Life for Children

If you are not familiar with military life or did not grow up in a military family, you may find it difficult to understand the benefits that military life can bring to children. Being a part of a larger community of other military service members extends the family unit. If a child and his family are deployed to installations far from their family of origin, the new military family often becomes their extended family. Also, being in the military fosters maturity and independence in children. Military children may have more flexibility, as many have moved more than once in their young lives, and being a military child often builds resiliency and strengthens family bonds (Operation: Military Kids 2007).

Why Parents Leave Their Children Behind

"Why would you take a job that requires leaving your children behind?" is a question that military parents hear often. While it may be difficult for nonmilitary parents to understand, those whose jobs take them to the most remote places in the world as peacekeepers or peacemakers, in combat and support, have good reasons. Many of them serve because they want to build a world where their children will be safe from terror and free to make choices about their lives as they grow older. These parents' patriotism may govern what they do with their lives, as they want to keep America (and other countries) free, especially when it comes to preventing more acts of terror on U.S. soil.

One airman serving in Iraq commented that he joined the armed forces "because we are fighting for good people who just want the same peace and happiness that we tend to easily take for granted." Another stated that she felt she was "providing acts of kindness to those less fortunate around the world—building schools, providing medical care." And finally, another service member reported that he stayed in the service because he wanted to "take part in something greater than myself, in that I was serving our nation and helping to free the oppressed who live under regimes of terror." Yes, they find it extremely difficult to leave their children, but military parents seem to have tremendous passion for their work and its larger purpose.

Deployment Checklist for School-age Kids

It is hard to say good-bye to your dad or mom when he or she deploys. Kids need to be deployment ready—just like Mom and Dad. To get ready and make it easier to be apart, try the following ideas (adapted from http://navyreserve.navy.mil).

BEFORE YOUR PARENT GOES ON DEPLOYMENT	STAYING IN TOUCH
☐ Let your parent know you love her. ☐ Talk to your parent about how you feel about his leaving. ☐ Ask your parent to tell you about her job. If possible, go see her workspace. ☐ Make a "date" to spend time alone with your parent. Do something special, just the two of you. ☐ Have a picture taken of you and your parent. Keep one copy, and send one with your deploying parent. ☐ Make or buy something special that your parent can take on the deployment. ☐ Talk to your parents about rules, responsibilities, chores, and allowance. Make sure everyone understands what is expected during the deployment. ☐ Plan ways to celebrate special occasions even though you're apart.	☐ Make sure you stay in touch. This takes planning in advance. Talk to your parent about writing letters, talking on the phone, and sending e-mails. ☐ Keep a list of what you want to ask or tell your parent so you will remember when you write or talk to him. ☐ Buy copies of the same book. As both of you read it, you can share your thoughts and ideas with each other. ☐ Keep your parent up to date on what's going on with you (in school, sports, and so on). ☐ Send drawings or photographs. ☐ Burn a copy of your favorite CD, and send it. ☐ Send your schoolwork. ☐ Bake cookies, and mail a batch. ☐ Make an audio or video tape. ☐ Cut out articles or comics from the newspaper that you know your parent would like. ☐ Write a review of a movie you saw. ☐ Send your parent sports scores. ☐ Keep a journal or scrapbook to share when your parent returns.

It's okay to feel sad or mad sometimes. It's not easy to have your parent far away. But if you are feeling bad a lot or are taking it out on others, talk to your parent, teacher, coach, or other adult friend about your feelings. Adults can help!

Remember that your mom or dad is still your parent even though he or she is deployed. Your parent loves you and cares about you.

FAMILY CARE PLANS

Family Care Plans ensure that the family's needs are cared for during deployment, especially when there are children involved. A Family Care Plan consists of documents that instruct the guardians of their children and also provides power of attorney. Enrollment forms for medical and health insurance must be in order prior to deployment so that the primary caregivers can continue getting the best care for military children. Single parents and military couples must complete a Family Care Plan prior to deployment, so if you are caring for a child whose single parent or both parents have been deployed, know that plans are in place to assist you. More information about Family Care Plans can be found on the Web sites of each branch of the military.

Month of the Military Child

Since 1986, April has been celebrated as the Month of the Military Child. It is during this time that military installations around the globe focus on activities and programs to celebrate and show support for children. It is a time to celebrate the military child within the family and to bring attention to the challenges that military children face on a daily basis. Military family advocacy personnel are available for training, presentations, and workshops in schools, child care centers, and one-on-one meetings with parents. Programs are available in many areas and are aimed at providing support for spous-

es or providers who are caring for deployed service members' children.

April is also National Child Abuse Awareness and Prevention month. Child abuse occurs in all kinds of families, at all levels of society, and across all cultures. Stress in the family is commonly understood to be an important factor in or cause of child abuse. During deployment, stress and depression are common for both children and parents. Because you are associated with children in military families, it is important for you to know that recent findings regarding child neglect occurring during deployment show that it occurs at higher rates when one parent is left behind after the other is deployed (Rentz, Martin, Gibbs, Clinton-Sherrod, Hardison, and Marshall 2006).

Back-to-back and extended deployments can increase the chances of child neglect and abuse. Research has shown that of the abuse that occurs, rates are higher during deployment (Gibbs, Martin, Kupper, and Johnson 2007). Military families also face the unique stress of cyclical adjustment and readjustment to a changing family structure as a parent leaves and returns. You need to be proactive and recognize early signs of family distress and perhaps suggest support services provided at the installation. Families of reservists and guard members who are unaffiliated with military installations may need extra support, especially since many community members are unaware of the resources available to military families.

Children at Risk

Following are signs to look for when determining whether children need additional support or intervention:

- low weight for age and/or failure to thrive and develop
- untreated physical problems such as sores, rashes, and untended illness (chronic runny nose, etc.)
- extreme anxiety about being abandoned, when it is not age appropriate
- lack of adequate supervision for the child's age
- constant hunger
- lack of hygiene, continuous dirty appearance
- consistently picked up late or brought late to care or school
- extreme longing for adult affection
- poor or pale complexion and poor hair texture

Parents or Caregivers at Risk

The following are signs to look for to determine whether primary caregivers (parent or other adult) may need additional support or intervention:

- is unable or unwilling to provide adequate food, shelter, clothing, medical attention, or safe home conditions
- leaves child(ren) without appropriate supervision
- abandons child(ren) for short or long periods of time
- is not nurturing and often avoids physical contact

STRATEGIES

Guarding against Child Abuse and Neglect

- Military children are heroes too. They are "serving" during this difficult time and have stresses and challenges that are sometimes difficult for parents or other primary caregivers left behind to deal with. Help the children's primary caregivers to keep the focus on serving the children.
- Visit the Web site www.militaryonesource .com, or call 800-342-9647.
- Many military branches have added additional social workers and psychologists to help families in crisis.
- Encourage parents or primary caregivers to hold regular family meetings and keep discussions open and honest. They shouldn't be afraid to talk about their fears and should allow children to voice theirs as well.
- Remind primary caregivers that they are not alone! Share with them these two Web sites that offer support strategies and resource materials: www.militaryhomefront.dod.mil and www.childwelfare.gov.
- Suggest that they contact the command ombudsman for the deployed parent's installation or unit and ask for help. Counseling is available. Find out if there is a twenty-four-hour hotline to call in case emergency help is needed in coping with the stresses of raising a family alone.
- Recommend parenting classes that include information about shaken baby syndrome.

Death and Grief

Although military children are typically healthy, strong, and resilient, they are also at risk for emotional trauma in the event that one or both parents are lost during active duty and deployment. Children's stages of development and their environment strongly influence their conception of death. Religion, culture, and ethnicity are also powerful predictors of how they will handle the stress of learning that they have lost a very important person in their lives. There is no right or wrong way to grieve or to heal, and healing takes time. Children cannot be expected to "get over" the loss of someone they love. Normal grief reactions in children include symptoms such as stomachaches and headaches, lack of concentration, clinginess, excessive crying, irritability, and regression in behavior.

One of the most important ways that we can help children to grieve is to be completely honest when we communicate with them and to allow them to experience grief and sadness without shame or guilt. Refrain from statements such as, "Your mommy would not want you to be sad" or "It's going to be okay tomorrow." The following list can help you know what to do for and say to children when someone dies.

STRATEGIES

Talking to Grieving Kids

- Talk about the deceased with children— mention their favorite things to do, favorite foods, etc. "Your dad loved mashed potatoes, didn't he?" Recall or tell stories about the deceased, and ask children to tell stories often.

- Be honest about the death and how it occurred. Offer as much information as the child can understand: "Daddy died in his plane," or "Mommy died in her car in an accident."

- Encourage children to ask more questions if they do not understand—as often as they need to.

- Encourage families to involve children in funeral or memorial planning.

- Help them to understand that they are not responsible for the death of their loved one.

- Provide good touches and hugs.

- Reassure children that it is normal to feel sad and that it may take a long time to feel better. Children (like adults) will grieve and heal in their own way and in their own time.

- Honor their religious traditions regarding life after death or the nonexistence of life after death. Avoid presenting your own religious beliefs if that is not the wish of the remaining parent or guardian.

- Plan activities to celebrate the deceased loved one's birthday or special occasions such as Memorial Day.

Helping Kids Grieve

- Use nationally known centers for children and grief such as The Dougy Center (www.dougy.org) and the Alcove Center for Grieving Children and Their Families (www.thealcove.org). These have suggestions for books, group meetings, and resources in your local area.

- Suggest that the remaining parent or guardian contact the Tragedy Assistance Program for Survivors (TAPS, www.taps.org), a nonprofit organization that provides services to all who have lost a loved one who was serving in the armed forces. TAPS counselors are available twenty-four hours a day, seven days a week at 800-959-TAPS (8277) or by e-mail at info@taps.org. Everyone there has experienced death and grief.

- Learn the name of a chaplain or the family support center for the installation or command nearest you to share with the parent or guardian. For instance, chaplain care and grief recovery hotlines are available for many armed service branches.

- Provide books about death that are age appropriate, such as the ones for preschoolers and early schoolagers listed at the end of appendix A.

- Acquire books to learn about procedures and activities to do with children when they have lost a loved one:

  o *35 Ways to Help a Grieving Child* (The Dougy Center 1999)

  o *Helping Children Cope with Death* (The Dougy Center 1998)

  o *What about the Kids? Understanding Their Needs in Funeral Planning and Services* (The Dougy Center 2004b)

  o *After a Death: An Activity Book for Children* (Lindholm and Schuurman 2007)

  o *Never the Same: Coming to Terms with the Death of a Parent* (Schuurman 2004)

  o *A Tiny Boat at Sea: How to Help Children Who Have a Parent Diagnosed with Cancer* (Smith 2000)

  o *Waving Goodbye: An Activities Manual for Children in Grief* (The Dougy Center 2004a)

  Note: The above titles are available online at The Dougy Center (www.dougy .org).

- Plan a Memorial Day Service for the children in your care. Have them bring mementos of their deceased parents, write poems about them, tell stories, show photos, etc.

- Provide a tracking checklist for the kids in your program in order to initiate and maintain appropriate responses to children who have suffered a loss. The chart on the following page is one example for you to use.

Do's and Don'ts When Working with Kids Whose Parents Are Deployed

It is not appropriate to expect children to recover from tragedy or to go through deployment by themselves. As an important adult in their lives, you can always show them that you are filled with hope for the future, no matter what tragic events have occurred. Children deserve our best. Teaching them to be empathetic and to care for people they do not know, as well as to envision what someone else's life is like, will go a long way in helping them to understand why their parents serve in the armed forces. They will also be able to make their own choices about how they can make the world a better place.

Caring for Kids in Crisis

Child's name: Date of crisis:

Date of birth: Classroom or grade:

Parent or guardian of child:

Description of crisis:

Resources provided:

Books

Group meetings

One-on-one or impromptu discussions

Counseling or referral to outside agency (describe)

Describe follow-up activities planned for child at one month and later.

Events planned for future times of concern (birthday of loved one, important holidays, and other events):

Event   Date

Event   Date

Event   Date

Do's

- Allow children to show their full range of emotions: fear, sadness, anger, pain, and empathy.
- Show your empathy for children and their families in other countries as well as in our own country during disaster and war.
- Encourage children to take action to reduce stress or to move forward by writing letters or joining positive groups or organizations, such as Boys and Girls Clubs and 4-H.
- Help them to use their gifts and talents through creative outlets.
- Be askable and tellable—allow questions about the unexplained or unmentioned. Allow them to tell you about unpleasant events to discover misunderstandings and misinformation.
- Gently guide children to a place in your program's environment where they feel secure and safe.

Don'ts

- Don't assume that kids don't know something just because they don't talk about it. Kids today know much more than we think, use the Internet in record numbers, and are exposed to news and events at much faster speeds than ever before. Make a point to bring up important issues that you know affect them on a daily basis.
- Don't expect children to take care of a stressed or grieving parent.
- Don't expect military children to share their feelings before a large group if they are not comfortable doing so.
- Don't expect children to "get over it" if you avoid acknowledging what they are going through.
- Don't expect that when a deployed parent returns, that is the end of any issues the

DO TAKE CARE OF YOURSELF

It isn't easy caring for someone else's children. The responsibilities are enormous, and the rewards are not immediate. It's important to remember that your work makes a difference in the life of a child. It doesn't matter if you are an entry-level provider or a seasoned veteran, you must take care of yourself before you can benefit others. There are two aspects of taking care of yourself: professional and personal.

In order to improve professionally, consider joining a local organization in which providers meet to discuss and learn about child care. Topics will range from becoming a provider to being a child's first reading teacher. Find out if there is a local child care agency with resources such as toys and materials that you may borrow and opportunities to attend child care training.

The responsibility of keeping children safe while helping them learn can be overwhelming and take a toll on your personal well-being. Emotional resiliency is required in order to manage daily stress from fatigue, excitement, disappointment, and constant decision making. It may be as simple as finding someone you can use as a sounding board. In any event, take care of your physical and emotional needs first, and then you will be much better at caring for military children. Abraham Maslow (1970) created a needs hierarchy that begins with physiological needs for safety, water, and food and then progresses to mental and emotional needs, including safety and security. If these needs go unmet, our ability to give to others is severely impaired. What does this mean for you? Take care of yourself! Make a weekly plan or schedule that includes personal time for yourself.

children have been facing because of the separation.
- Don't express anti-war sentiments in front of the children.

This sentence is from an actual e-mail I received from a deployed mom in Iraq, three weeks after sending her an e-mail: "Sorry this e-mail is so late but I've actually been quite busy." She and her husband are both serving in the Army in Iraq and are one of the few couples who are fortunate enough to live together. They left two children back home with grandparents. This situation is more common than many of us realize and happens for various reasons. As busy as her job keeps her, she was delighted to share her family photos with us and to connect with people back home.

We can all feel proud of military parents, as we hope for their safe return. Their children are in our charge, and we will do our best to provide for their well-being.

Afterword

Inside and Outside Perspective

As an educator, I wrote this book from an etic perspective, or that of an observer and researcher. The emic or insider's perspective is equally important, as it is made up of years of experience in direct care of military children and working with families. Many of you have a dual role: not only do you care for military children, but you were a military child once or you are part of a military family now. Your experiences and beliefs are important. I hope I have done justice to them.

Caring for military children is complex, and one size does not fit all. Each branch of the military comes with its own set of protocol and has its own culture; each one is distinctive and unique, but all are interwoven when it comes to children being respected and revered. As we respect one another's views from the inside and the outside, we can build community. We can provide caring environments that hold to our beliefs that children come first.

When I began writing this book, my desire to provide a voice for children's needs in military families was strong, and that has not changed. My work with teachers and providers of military children was filled with passion, and my need to provide a book that was directed purposefully for them was fervent. That, too, has not changed. As I have researched the topics within this book and listened to your stories, my enthusiasm for finding strategies to enable you to do the best work possible for children in military families has found its own voice.

Best Practices

It was my intention to provide best practices for children in military families, but most of the strategies that are shared in this book are developmental-ly appropriate for all kids so that military children are never singled out or treated as being isolated or different from other children. The practices and strategies found here are by no means comprehensive, and you as a provider may use hundreds of other ideas every day that are equally as good and important to children and their families.

The Web is filled with excellent resources for child care providers, and I have included many sites in this book that feature appropriate, enriching activities for you and the children in your care. Web sites for symphonies and museums contain experiences for children that are unparalleled to anything I have experienced in my lifetime. Each military branch has created a Web site for military families, and these are also excellent resources for you to use. But please use all Web sites mentioned in this book judiciously, and preview each one for use by children, as links and content change rapidly on the Web.

I hope that *Deployment: Strategies for Working with Kids in Military Families* will inspire you to explore innovative ways to work with military kids as you expand your own professional knowledge. As a participant and leader in your field, you have many opportunities to become a member of professional associations, attend professional conferences, and read professional journals that will assist you as you work with kids in military families. It has been my pleasure to write and an honor to have you read these pages. I hope that I have served children in military families well.

Appendix A

Children's Books

Bedtime or Naptime Books

Boynton, Sandra. 1997. *Snoozers: 7 short bedtime stories for lively little ones.* New York: Little Simon.

Brown, Margaret Wise. 1991. *Goodnight moon.* Pictures by Clement Hurd. New York: HarperFestival.

———. 2005. *The runaway bunny.* New York: HarperCollins.

Fox, Mem. 1997. *Time for bed.* Illustrated by Jane Dyer. San Diego: HarcourtBrace.

Hoban, Russell. 1995. *Bedtime for Frances.* New York: HarperTrophy.

Lloyd-Jones, Sally. 2006. *Time to say goodnight.* New York: HarperCollins.

McBratney, Sam. 1994. *Guess how much I love you.* Somerville, MA: Candlewick Press.

Rathmann, Peggy. 2004. *10 minutes til bedtime.* London, UK: Puffin Books.

Books for Storytelling and Retelling

Cowley, Joy. 1990. *Mrs. Wishy-Washy.* San Diego: Wright Group.

Galdone, Paul. 1981. *The three billy goats Gruff.* Boston: Houghton Mifflin.

Marshall, James. 2000. *The three little pigs.* New York: Penguin Young Readers Group.

Slobodkina, Esphyr. 1987. *Caps for sale.* New York: HarperTrophy.

Wood, Audrey. 1984. *The napping house.* New York: Harcourt Brace.

Books for Babies (Birth to Eighteen Months)

Brown, Margaret Wise. 2005. *The runaway bunny.* New York: HarperCollins.

Hamsa, Bobbie, and Tom Dunnington. 1985. *Animal babies.* A Rookie reader. Chicago: Children's Press.

Hill, Eric. 1983. *Where's Spot?* New York: Puffin Books.

Katz, Karen. 2007. *Peek a baby.* New York: Little Simon.

Kunhardt, Dorothy. 1976. *Pat the bunny.* New York: Golden Books.

Martin, Bill. 1996. *Brown bear, brown bear, what do you see?* Pictures by Eric Carle. New York: Holt & Company.

Concept Books

Bond, Rebecca. 2007. *The great doughnut parade.* Boston: Houghton Mifflin.

Carle, Eric. 1996. *The very grouchy ladybug.* New York: HarperCollins.

Hoban, Tana. 1973. *Over, under, and through.* New York: Simon & Schuster Children's Publishing.

———. 1996. *Shapes, shapes, shapes.* New York: HarperCollins.

Hutchins, Pat. 1989. *The doorbell rang.* New York: HarperCollins.

Lewis, J. Patrick, and Bob Barner. 2007. *Big is big (and little, little): A book of contrasts.* New York: Holiday House.

Lift-the-Flap Books

Beeler, Selby. 2004. *How many elephants?* Somerville, MA: Candlewick Press.

Bunting, Jane. 1993. *My first ABC.* London: Dorling Kindersley.

DK Publishing. 2003. *My first number book.* New York: DK Preschool.

Hiaasen, Carl. 2005. *Hoot!* New York: Random House Children's Books.

Myers, Christopher. 1999. *Black cat.* New York: Scholastic.

Rhyming Books

Dillon, Leo, and Diane Dillon. 2002. *Rap a tap tap: Here's Bojangles—Think of that!* New York: Scholastic.

Guarino, Deborah. 1997. *Is your mama a llama?* New York: Scholastic.

Langstaff, John. 1973. *Over in the meadow.* New York: Harcourt Children's Books.

Martin, Bill. 1989. *Chicka chicka boom boom.* New York: Simon & Schuster Children's Publishing.

Trapani, Iza. 1998. *The itsy-bitsy spider.* Watertown, MA: Charlesbridge Publishing.

Westcott, Nadine Bernard. 1998. *Miss Lucy had a baby (The lady with the alligator purse).* New York: Little, Brown Young Readers.

Williams, Sue. 1996. *I went walking.* New York: Harcourt Children's Books.

Picture Books

Barchas, Sarah E. 1993. *I was walking down the road.* New York: Scholastic.

Barrett, Judith. 1982. *Cloudy with a chance of meatballs.* New York: Simon & Schuster Children's Publishing.

Brown, Marcia. 1997. *Stone soup.* New York: Simon & Schuster Children's Publishing.

Brown, Margaret Wise. 1994. *Big red barn.* New York: HarperCollins.

Burton, Virginia Lee. 1978. *The little house.* Boston: Houghton Mifflin.

Carle, Eric. 1989. *The very busy spider.* New York: Penguin Young Readers Group.

———. 1996. *Have you seen my cat?* New York: Simon & Schuster Children's Publishing.

De Paola, Tommie. 1997. *The art lesson.* New York: Penguin Young Readers Group.

Eastman, P. D. 1960. *Are you my mother?* New York: Random House Children's Books.

Fox, Mem. 2007. *Where the giant sleeps.* New York: Harcourt Children's Books.

Freeman, Don. 1968. *Corduroy.* New York: Viking Books.

Galdone, Paul. 1985. *The little red hen.* Boston: Houghton Mifflin.

Kalan, Robert, and Byron Barton. 2002. *Jump, frog, jump!* New York: HarperFestival.

Keats, Ezra Jack. 1996. *The snowy day.* New York: Penguin Group.

Mayer, Mercer. 1992. *There's a nightmare in my closet.* New York: Penguin Group.

Pfister, Marcus. 2004. *Rainbow fish.* LaVergne, TN: North-South Books.

Piper, Watty. 1990. *The little engine that could.* New York: Grosset & Dunlap.

Rosen, Michael. 1997. *Going on a bear hunt.* Illustrated by Helen Oxenbury. New York: Aladdin.

Taback, Simms. 2000. *Joseph had a little overcoat.* New York: Viking Penguin.

Urbanovic, Jackie. 2007. *Duck at the door.* New York: HarperCollins.

Willems, Mo. 2003. *Don't let the pigeon drive the bus.* New York: Hyperion.

Wood, Audrey. 1984. *The napping house.* New York: Harcourt Brace.

Wood, Audrey. 1994. *Quick as a cricket*. Illustrated by Don Wood. New York: Scholastic.

Ziefert, Harriet. 1995. *Gingerbread boy*. New York: Young Readers Group.

Zion, Gene. 2006. *Harry the dirty dog*. New York: HarperCollins Children's Books.

Chapter Books for Schoolagers

Ada, Alma Flor. 1995. *My name is Maria Isabel*. New York: Aladdin Paperbacks.

Gantos, Jack. 2004. *What would Joey do?* New York: HarperCollins.

Hamilton, Virginia. 2000. *Second cousins*. New York: Blue Sky Press.

Lester, Allison. 2005. *Are we there yet?* La Jolla, CA: Kane/Miller Book Publishers.

Lowry, Lois. 2002. *The giver*. New York: Random House Children's Books.

Norton, Mary. 2003. *The borrowers*. Illustrations by Diana Stanley. Fiftieth anniversary edition. Orlando, FL: Harcourt.

Pinkney, Andrea Davis. 2000. *Let it shine: Stories of black women freedom fighters*. New York: Harcourt.

Selznick, Brian. 2007. *The invention of Hugo Cabret*. New York: Scholastic Press.

Spears, Elizabeth George. 1972. *The witch of Blackbird Pond*. New York: Random House Children's Books.

Taback, Simms. 1999. *Joseph had a little overcoat*. New York: Viking Press.

Taylor, Mildred. 1976. *Roll of thunder, hear my cry*. New York: Dial Books for Young Readers.

Warner, Gertrude Chandler. 1990. *The boxcar children*. Morton Grove, IL: Albert Whitman.

Wright, Betty Ren. 1995. *The dollhouse murders*. New York: Scholastic.

Yep, Laurence. 2003. *The magic paintbrush*. New York: HarperCollins.

Antibias Books

Carlson, Nancy. 1992. *Arnie and the new kid*. New York: Putnam Books.

Doros, Arthur. 1997. *Abuela*. New York: Pearson.

Hines, Anna Grossnickle. 1999. *Daddy makes the best spaghetti*. New York: Clarion Books.

Hoffman, Eric. 2002. *Best best colors/Los mejores colores*. St. Paul: Redleaf Press.

Paek, Min. 1988. *Aekyung's dream*. New York: Children's Book Press.

Polacco, Patricia. 1994. *Pink and say*. New York: Philomel Books.

Vigna, Judith. 1996. *Black like Kyra, white like me*. Morton Grove, IL: Albert Whitman & Company.

Zolotow, Charlotte, and William Pene Dubois. 1985. *William's doll*. New York: HarperTrophy.

Multicultural Books

Adoff, Arnold. 1973. *Black is brown is tan*. New York: Harper & Row.

Cheltenham Elementary School. 1991. *We are all alike: We are all different*. New York: Scholastic.

Hoffman, Mary. 1991. *Amazing Grace*. New York: Dial Books.

Kissinger, Katie. 1994. *All the colors we are*. St. Paul: Redleaf Press.

Say, Allen. 1991. *Tree of cranes*. New York: Houghton Mifflin.

Sung Yung Shin. 2004. *Cooper's lesson*. San Francisco: Children's Book Press.

Williams, Vera B. 1982. *A chair for my mother*. New York: Greenwillow.

Books about Deployment

Andrews, Beth. 2007. *I miss you! A military kid's book about deployment.* Illustrated by Hawley Wright. Amherst, NY: Prometheus.

Ferguson-Cohen, Michelle. 2002. *Daddy, you're my hero!* New York: Little Redhaired Girl Press.

Madison, Ron. 2004. *Ned and the general: A lesson about deployment.* Illustrations by David Cavolo. Johnstown, PA: Ned's Head Productions.

Robertson, Rachel. 2005. *Deployment journal for kids.* St. Paul: Elva Resa Publishing.

Thomas, James, and Melanie Thomas. 2004. *My dad is going away, but he will be back one day: A deployment story.* Victoria, B.C.: Trafford Publishing.

Books on Death for Preschoolers and Early Schoolagers

Brown, Laurie Krasny, and Marc Brown. 1998. *When dinosaurs die: A guide to understanding death.* Boston: Little, Brown.

Brown, Margaret Wise. 2008. *The dead bird.* New York: William Morrow.

Bunting, Eve. 1982. *The happy funeral.* New York: HarperCollins Children's Books.

Clifton, Lucille. 1988. *Everett Anderson's goodbye.* Illustrated by Ann Grifalconi. New York: Henry Holt.

Coerr, Eleanor. 1989. *The Josefina story quilt.* New York: HarperTrophy.

Cohen, Miriam, and Ronald Himler. 1984. *Jim Dog's muffins.* New York: Dell Yearling.

Fassler, Joan. 1983. *My grandpa died today.* New York: Shawnee Press.

Gould, Deborah, and Cheryl Harness. 1987. *Grandpa's slide show.* New York: Viking Kestrel Picture Books.

Hermes, Patricia. 2008. *You shouldn't have to say good-bye.* Naperville, IL: Sourcebooks Jabberwocky.

McWhorter, Gay. 2003. *Healing activities for children in grief.* Gay McWhorter Self Publishing.

Mellonie, Bryan. 1983. *Lifetimes.* New York: Bantam Books.

Mundy, Michaelene. 1998. *Sad isn't bad: A good-grief guidebook for kids dealing with loss.* St. Meinrad, IN: Abbey Press.

Owens, Karen. 2002. *Child and adolescent development: An integrated approach.* Belmont, CA: Thomson Learning.

Parker, Marjorie, and Janet Wilson. 2002. *Jasper's day.* Tonawanda, NY: Kids Can Press.

Patterson, Katherine. 1989. *Park's quest.* New York: Puffin Books.

Romain, Trevor. 1999. *What on earth do you do when someone dies?* Minneapolis: Free Spirit Publishing.

Silverman, Janis. 1999. *Help me say goodbye: Activities for helping kids cope when a special person dies.* Minneapolis: Fairview Press.

Stickney, Doris, and Gloria C. Ortiz. 2004. *Water bugs and dragonflies: Explaining death to young children.* Cleveland: Pilgrim Press.

Thomas, Pat. 2001. *I miss you: A first look at death.* Hauppauge, NY: Barron's Educational Series.

Varley, Susan. 1992. *Badger's parting gifts.* New York: HarperTrophy.

Vigna, Judith. 1991. *Saying goodbye to daddy.* Morton Grove, IL: Albert Whitman.

Viorst, Judith, and Erik Blegvad. 1987. *The tenth good thing about Barney.* New York: Aladdin Books.

Appendix B

Web Sites

What Caregivers Can Expect

MILITARY HOMEFRONT
www.militaryhomefront.dod.mil
This site houses the official Department of Defense information for quality-of-life initiatives and is designed to help troops and their families as well as those who care for their children during deployment and times of separation.

NATIONAL AFTERSCHOOL ASSOCIATION
www.naaweb.org
NAA's mission is to be the leading voice of the after-school profession and is dedicated to the education and care of children and youth during after-school hours with developmentally appropriate programming. This Web site describes activities and events useful in planning after-school programs.

NATIONAL ASSOCIATION FOR THE
EDUCATION OF YOUNG CHILDREN
www.naeyc.org
NAEYC is dedicated to improving the well-being of all young children (birth through age eight).

NATIONAL ASSOCIATION FOR FAMILY CHILD CARE
www.nafcc.org
NAFCC works to support family child care providers.

NATIONAL NETWORK FOR CHILD CARE
www.nncc.org
This site provides opportunities for child care providers to connect with each other and grow together while caring for children.

Emotional Support

NATIONAL MILITARY FAMILY ASSOCIATION
www.nmfa.org
This site that provides resources and support to spouses and children in military families.

SESAME STREET WORKSHOP:
TALK, LISTEN, CONNECT
http://archive.sesameworkshop.org/tlc
This bilingual (Spanish/English) site has resources for adults and videos for children ages two to five to help children whose parents are deployed and whose parents return from deployment with injuries.

Promoting Learning through Play

DISNEY FAMILY.COM
www.disneyfamily.com
This resource contains family fun coloring pages, printable travel games and puzzles, crafts, and holiday and seasonal activities.

KIDS.GOV
www.kids.gov
This U.S. government site has educational resources for school-age children and teachers.

NATIONAL INSTITUTE OF ENVIRONMENTAL
HEALTH SCIENCES
kids.niehs.nih.gov/games/songs/index.htm
This site houses sing-along activities and ideas that are educational and appropriate for children.

Music and Literacy Programming

CREATING MUSIC
www.creatingmusic.com
Creating Music allows children to create music in a safe environment that includes composing, performing, playing music games, and solving music puzzles.

DALLAS SYMPHONY ORCHESTRA
www.dsokids.com
This site has activities and information for children and teachers, including an instrument encyclopedia.

FUN BRAIN
www.funbrain.com/kidscenter.html
This engaging site gives kids the chance to play games and learn fun facts about just about everything. Games include word games like Scramblesaurus and Grammar Gorillas.

NATIONAL ASSOCIATION FOR MUSIC EDUCATION
www.menc.org
This Web site of the world's largest arts education organization addresses all aspects of music education.

PUTUMAYO
www.putumayo.com
Putumayo sells a wide range of world music for children and adults. The company also has teacher's guides available to use in connection with the music.

SAN FRANCISCO SYMPHONY KIDS' SITE
www.sfskids.org
This site provides opportunities for children to explore and investigate orchestral instruments.

TEACHER OZ
www.teacheroz.com/music.htm
This site includes an overview of music periods and genres.

Multiple Intelligences and Reggio Emilia

NORTH AMERICAN REGGIO EMILIA ALLIANCE
www.reggioalliance.org
NAREA is inspired by the education programs in Reggio Emilia, Italy. NAREA serves as a resource and facilitator for educators in North America.

WOLF TRAP INSTITUTE FOR EARLY LEARNING THROUGH THE ARTS
www.wolf-trap.org
This site provides innovative arts-based teaching strategies and services to early childhood teachers, caregivers, parents, and their children.

Developing Partnerships

CHILDREN AND DEPLOYMENT
www.25idl.army.mil/deployment/ACS/childdep.pdf
This PDF from the Army's Web site contains important information regarding children and deployment and can be downloaded and provided to parents as a ready-made flyer.

Staying Connected

DEPLOYMENT KIDS
www.deploymentkids.com
This resource for kids contains information about deployment places and time zones, a distance calculator, and lots of games.

EPALS
www.epals.com
This is an online home for global collaboration and meaningful learning.

GOOGLE TALK

www.google.com/hangouts/

This free service can help children stay connected to parents during deployment through chat, instant messaging, and phone connections.

KID-CAST

www.kid-cast.com

On this safe and kid-friendly Web site, kids can publish their own podcasts for other kids to enjoy.

SKYPE

www.skype.com

Skype is revolutionizing the way we can communicate with each other during travels to other parts of the world. Calls via computer are free to people using Skype and inexpensive to land lines in most countries.

Special Issues

THE ALCOVE FOR GRIEVING CHILDREN AND FAMILIES

www.thealcove.org

The Alcove supports children and families who are grieving the death of a loved one. Although the support services are primarily for Southern New Jersey residents, the Web site's information is applicable to anyone who has suffered a loss.

CHILD WELFARE INFORMATION GATEWAY

www.childwelfare.gov

This site provides access to information and current resources to support and preserve families.

THE DOUGY CENTER FOR GRIEVING CHILDREN AND FAMILIES

www.dougy.org

The Dougy Center was the first organization in the United States to provide peer support for grieving children. Much information and encouragement can be found here.

MILITARY CHILD EDUCATION COALITION

www.militarychild.org

This organization helps military kids through transitions from school to school by offering partnerships and networking between military installations and local school districts.

TRAGEDY ASSISTANCE PROGRAM FOR SURVIVORS

www.taps.org

This site is America's frontline resource for all who are grieving the death of a loved one serving in the Armed Forces. It provides a twenty-four-hour hotline.

Glossary

AD: Active Duty

ADT: Active Duty Training

APO: Army Post Office

AT: Annual Training

AWOL: Away without Leave—to be absent from the military without appropriate leave or permission

BAH: Basic Allowance for Housing

Billeting: Lodging on an installation or post

Bravo Zulu: A job well done

Brief: Instructing service personnel for a specific job or operation

CDC: Child Development Center

CO: Commanding Officer—senior person in charge of a command

Coast Guard: A branch of the U.S. military administered by the Department of Homeland Security

Commissary: Grocery store on an installation or post where service members and their families can make purchases at lower prices (usually) than in stores off the installation

Debrief: To give a verbal report after a mission has been completed or accomplished

Deployment: Sending of personnel and equipment to an area of military operation

DoD: Department of Defense—the Army, Marines, Navy, and Air Force are administered by this government department

DoDS: Department of Defense Schools

Duty: Work period that usually lasts for twenty-four hours

EFMS: Exceptional Family Member Services—services to family members with special needs

Family Member: Person receiving support from a service member

Family Support Center: Support organization that provides programs and services to improve the quality of life of military personnel and their families; also known as Family Support Center, Community Service Center, and Work-Life Center

FAP: Family Advocacy Program—addresses problems of family neglect, violence, and sexual assault; provides education on parenting, anger and stress management training, crisis intervention treatment, and follow-up when violence has occurred

Geedunk: Snacks—candy, cookies, chips, etc.

IG: Inspector General—helps service members and families to resolve problems if the chain of command has failed

JAG: Judge Advocate General—the legal office for military personnel

Leave: Time off with pay and authorization

Liberty: Short period of authorized leave of absence

MP: Military Police—an Army term for armed or security forces

MWR: Morale, Welfare, and Recreation—the department that offers recreational programs as well as support and entertainment to military service members and their families

NCO: Noncommissioned Officer or enlisted personnel between the ranks of E4 and E9

OCONUS: Outside the Continental United States

Ombudsman: Spouse of a member of the command who is appointed by the Commanding Officer to serve as official liaison between family members and the command

OOD: Officer of the Day—a duty usually lasting only twenty-four hours

PCS: Permanent Change of Station (change of permanent station)—a move or transfer

POC: Point of Contact—designated contact person for a particular project or event

Quarters: A place of residence—can be a house, an apartment, a barracks, or a tent

Remote Assignment: An assignment to a military installation or other activity in the United States for which military and civilian medical or dental facilities accessible to that installation are inadequate to support needs of assigned personnel or their families; also, being stationed at an installation a minimum of fifty miles or one hour of driving time from the nearest military facilities

Service Member: A member of one of the branches of military service: Army, Air Force, Coast Guard, Marines, Navy, National Guard, or Reserves

Sponsor: Military member or DoD civilian with dependents

TDY: Temporary duty

Theater: A geographic military theater of operations such as Europe or the Pacific

TRICARE: Medical insurance for families of active-duty, retired, and deceased members of the military

Unaccompanied Tour: An overseas assignment without the presence of dependents endorsed by the appropriate overseas military commander

USAFE: United States Air Forces in Europe

USAREUR: United States Army Europe

References

Armstrong, Thomas. 1999. *7 (seven) kinds of smart: Identifying and developing your multiple intelligences.* New York: Penguin Putnam.

Awdry, Wilburt. 1990. *Happy birthday, Thomas!* Illustrated by Owain Bell. Based on the railway series. New York: Random House.

Bandler, Jane. 2007. The importance of maintaining childhood routines during times of stress and sacrifice. McLean, VA: Our Military Kids, Inc. www.ourmilitarykids.org.

Bjorklund, David F. 2005. *Children's thinking: Cognitive development and individual differences.* 4th ed. Belmont, CA: Thomson/ Wadsworth.

Bowlby, John. 1973. *Attachment and loss.* New York: Basic Books.

———. 1988. *A secure base: Parent-child attachment and healthy human development.* New York: Basic Books.

Brown, Jeff. 2003. *Flat Stanley.* Pictures by Scott Nash. New York: HarperTrophy.

Brown, Margaret Wise. 1991. *Goodnight moon.* Pictures by Clement Hurd. New York: HarperFestival.

Byrnes, Deborah, and Gary Kiger, eds. 2005. *Common bonds: Anti-bias teaching in a diverse society.* 3rd ed. Washington, DC: Association for Childhood Education International.

Carle, Eric. 1974. *The very hungry caterpillar.* New York: Collins Publishers.

———. 1996. *Have you seen my cat?* New York: Simon & Schuster.

———. 1997. *Today is Monday.* New York: Putnam Juvenile.

———. 1998. *Draw me a star.* New York: Putnam Juvenile.

Cole, Joanna, and Stephanie Calmenson. 1990. *Miss Mary Mack and other children's street rhymes.* New York: HarperTrophy.

Coles, Robert. 2004. *The story of Ruby Bridges.* Illustrated by George Ford. New York: Scholastic.

Copple, Carol, and Sue Bredekamp, eds. 2009. *Developmentally appropriate practice in early childhood programs serving children birth through age 8.* 3rd ed. Washington, DC: NAEYC.

Corsaro, William. A. 1985. *Friendship and peer culture in the early years.* Norwood, NJ: Ablex Publishing.

Crews, Donald. 1996. *Freight train.* New York: HarperCollins.

Curtis, Jamie Lee. 2002. *I'm gonna like me: Letting off a little self-esteem.* Illustrated by Laura Cornell. New York: Joanna Cotler Books.

Department of Defense. 2004. *Profile of the military community.* http://cs.mhf.dod.mil/ content/dav/mhf/QOL-Library/PDF/MHF/ QOL%20Resources/Reports/Combined%20 Final%20Demographics%20Report.pdf (retrieved October 13, 2008).

Derman-Sparks, Louise. 1997. *Anti-bias curriculum: Tools for empowering young children.* Washington, DC: NAEYC.

Diamond, Marian Cleeves, and Janet L. Hopson. 1998. *Magic trees of the mind: How to nurture your child's intelligence, creativity, and healthy emotions from birth through adolescence.* New York: Dutton.

The Dougy Center. 1998. *Helping children cope with death.* Canby, OR: The Dougy Center for Grieving Children and Families.

———. 1999. *35 ways to help a grieving child.* Canby, OR: The Dougy Center for Grieving Children and Families.

———. 2004a. *Waving goodbye: An activities manual for children in grief.* Canby, OR: The Dougy Center for Grieving Children and Families.

———. 2004b. *What about the kids? Understanding their needs in funeral planning and services.* Canby, OR: The Dougy Center for Grieving Children and Families.

Edwards, Carolyn Pope, Lella Gandini, and George Forman, eds. 1998. *The hundred languages of children: The Reggio Emilia approach—advanced reflections.* Greenwich, CT: Ablex Publishing.

Elkind, David. 2006. *The hurried child: Growing up too fast too soon.* New York: Da Capo Press.

———. 2007. *The power of play: How spontaneous imaginative activities lead to happier, healthier children.* New York: Da Capo Press.

Epstein, Ann S. 2007. *The intentional teacher: Choosing the best strategies for young children's learning.* Washington, DC: National Association for the Education of Young Children.

Fagot, Beverly I., Carie S. Rodgers, and Mary D. Leinbach. 2000. Theories of gender socialization. In *The Developmental Social Psychology of Gender,* ed. T. Eckes and H. M. Trautner, 65–98. Mahwah, NJ: Lawrence Erlbaum Associates.

Fields, Marjorie, and Katherine L. Spangler. 2000. *Let's begin reading right.* Upper Saddle River, NJ: Merrill Prentice Hall.

Fleet and Family Support Centers of Hampton Roads, VA. Children and deployment. http://www.cnic.navy.mil/regions/cnrma/installations/nsa_hampton_roads/ffr/support_services.html.

Fogel, Alan. 2001. *Infancy: Infant, family, and society.* Belmont, CA: Wadsworth.

Frank, Anne. 1973. *The diary of Anne Frank.* Trans. B. M. Mooijaart-Doubleday. London: Heron.

Fraser, Susan, and Carol Gestwicki. 2002. *Authentic childhood: Exploring Reggio Emilia in the classroom.* Albany, NY: Delmar.

Frost, Joe L., and Eric Strickland. 1985. Equipment choices of young children during free play. In *When children play: Proceedings of the International Conference on Play and Play Environments,* eds. Joe L. Frost and Sylvia Sunderlin, 93–101. Wheaton, MD: Association for Childhood Education International.

Frost, Joe L., Sue C. Wortham, and Stuart Reifel. 2005. *Play and child development.* 2nd ed. Upper Saddle River, NJ: Prentice Hall.

Gardner, Howard. 1983. *Frames of mind: The theory of multiple intelligences.* New York: Basic Books.

———. 2006. *Multiple intelligences: New horizons in theory and practice.* New York: Basic Books.

Gibbs D. A., S. L. Martin, L. L. Kupper, and R. E. Johnson. 2007. Child maltreatment in enlisted soldiers' families during combat-related deployments. *JAMA: the Journal of the American Medical Association* 298 (5): 528-35.

Goleman, Daniel. 1995. *Emotional intelligence: Why it can matter more than IQ.* New York: Bantam.

Harper, Piers. 2004. *Little owl.* New York: Cartwheel Books by Scholastic.

Helm, Judy Harris, and Lilian Katz. 2001. *Young investigators: The project approach in the early years.* New York: Teachers College Press.

Henniger, Michael L. 2005. *Teaching young children: An introduction.* Upper Saddle River, NJ: Prentice Hall.

Hines, Anna Grossnickle. 1999. *Daddy makes the best spaghetti.* New York: Clarion Books.

Hort, Lenny. 2003. *The seals on the bus.* Illustrated by G. Brian Karas. New York: Henry Holt.

Hurwitz, Al, and Michael Day. 2007. *Children and their art: Methods for the elementary school.* Belmont, CA: Thomson Wadsworth.

Hyson, Marilou. 2003. *The emotional development of young children: Building an emotion-centered curriculum.* New York: Teachers College Press.

Jacobson, Tamar. 2003. *Confronting our discomfort: Clearing the way for anti-bias in early childhood.* Portsmouth, NH: Heinemann.

Jenkins, Ella. 1989. "No more pie." On *Adventures in Rhythm* [CD]. Washington, DC: Smithsonian Folkways Recordings.

Jensen, Eric. 2005. *Teaching with the brain in mind.* Rev. ed. Alexandria, VA: Association for Supervision and Curriculum Development.

Kalan, Robert, and Byron Barton. 1995. *Jump, frog, jump!* New York: Greenwillow Books.

Katz, Lilian G., and Sylvia C. Chard. 2000. *Engaging children's minds: The project approach.* Norwood, NJ: Ablex Publishing.

Keats, Ezra Jack. 1999. *Over in the meadow.* New York: Viking.

Keyser, Janis. 2006. *From parents to partners: Building a family-centered early childhood program.* St. Paul: Redleaf Press.

Kohl, MaryAnn F., and Kim Solga. 1996. *Discovering great artists: Hands-on art for children in the styles of the great masters.* Bellingham, WA: Bright Ring Publishing.

Kostelnik, Marjorie, Anne K. Soderman, and Alice Phipps Whiren. 2004. *Developmentally appropriate curriculum: Best practices in early childhood education.* 3rd ed. Upper Saddle River, NJ: Prentice Hall.

Krogh, Suzanne, and Pamela J. Morehouse. 2007. *The early childhood curriculum: Inquiry learning through integration.* Columbus: McGraw-Hill.

Levin, Diane. 2003. *Teaching young children in violent times: Building a peaceable classroom.* Cambridge, MA: Educators for Social Responsibility.

Lindholm, Amy Barrett, and Donna L. Schuurman. 2007. *After a death: An activity book for children.* Canby, OR: The Dougy Center for Grieving Children and Families.

Marion, Marian. 2003. *Guidance of young children.* 6th ed. Upper Saddle River, NJ: Merrill Prentice Hall.

Martin Jr., Bill. 1992. *Brown bear, brown bear, what do you see?* Pictures by Eric Carle. New York: Henry Holt.

Maslow, Abraham. 1970. *Motivation and personality.* 2nd ed. New York: Harper & Row.

Mooney, Carol Garhart. 2000. *Theories of childhood: An introduction to Dewey, Montessori, Erickson, Piaget, and Vygotsky.* St. Paul: Redleaf Press.

Muro, Joel, Karen Petty, and Mavis DakoGyeke. 2006. Facilitating the transition between play in the classroom and play therapy. *Journal of School Counseling* 4 (17). jsc.montana.edu /articles/v4n17.pdf.

National Association for the Education of Young Children (NAEYC Position Statement). 1995. *Responding to linguistic and cultural diversity: Recommendations for effective early childhood education.* Washington, DC: NAEYC. www.naeyc.org/files/naeyc/file /positions/PSDIV98.PDF.

National Association for the Education of Young Children. 1996. Celebrating holidays in early childhood programs. Washington, DC: NAEYC. oldweb.naeyc.org/ece/1996/18.asp.

National Head Start Child Development Institute. 2004. *The Head Start child outcomes framework.* http://www.hsnrc.org/CDI/pdfs/UGCOF.pdf.

New York State Department of Social Services. 1993. A parent's guide to child care for school-age children. State University of New York. http://www.nncc.org/choose.quality.care/parents.sac.html.

Olsen, Henry D. 1975. Bibliotherapy to help children solve problems. *The Elementary School Journal* 7:422–29.

O'Neill, Alexis. 2002. *The recess queen.* New York: Scholastic.

Operation: Military Kids. 2007. *Ready, set, go training manual.* Washington State 4-H/Army Youth Development Project. www.4-h militarypartnerships.org/p.aspx?tabid=127.

Owens, Karen. 2002. *Child and adolescent development: An integrated approach.* Australia: Wadsworth/Thompson Learning.

Parten, Mildred. 1932. Social participation among preschool children. *Journal of Abnormal and Social Psychology* 27:243–69.

Pattillo, Janice, and Elizabeth Vaughan. 1992. *Learning centers for child-centered classrooms.* Washington, DC: National Education Association.

Pennypacker, Sara. 2004. *Stuart's cape.* New York: Orchard Books.

Petty, Karen. 1993. Group entry strategies and reciprocal social interactions of preschoolers in social contexts. Ph.D. diss., Texas A&M University.

Piaget, Jean. 1954. *The construction of reality in the child.* New York: Basic Books.

Piper, Watty. 2005. *The little engine that could.* New York: Philomel.

Raffi. 1988. *Shake my sillies out.* New York: Crown Books for Young Readers.

———. 1992. *Five little ducks.* New York: Crown Books for Young Readers.

———. 1998. *Down by the bay.* New York: Crown Books for Young Readers.

Rentz, E. D., S. L. Martin, D. A. Gibbs, M. Clinton-Sherrod, J. Hardison, and S. W. Marshall. 2006. Family violence in the military: A review of the literature. *Trauma Violence Abuse* 7(2): 93–108.

Rinaldi, Carla. 1988. The Reggio approach. Notes by Karen Petty on presentation given at NAEYC conference, Atlanta, November 16.

Rosen, Michael. 1997. *We're going on a bear hunt.* Illustrated by Helen Oxenbury. New York: Aladdin.

Sanders, Cheryl E., and Gary D. Phye. 2004. *Bullying: Implications for the classroom.* San Diego, CA: Elsevier Academic Press.

Schuurman, Donna. 2004. *Never the same: Coming to terms with the death of a parent.* New York: St. Martin's Griffin.

Schwartz, Alvin. 1999. *And the green grass grew all around: Folk poetry from everyone.* Illustrated by Sue Truesdell. New York: HarperTrophy.

Seuss, Dr. 1959. *Happy birthday to you!* New York: Random House.

Shore, Rima. 1997. *Rethinking the brain: New insights into early development.* Rev. ed. New York: Families and Work Institute.

Slobodkina, Esphyr. 1987. *Caps for sale.* New York: HarperTrophy.

Smith, Izetta. 2000. *A tiny boat at sea: How to help children who have a parent diagnosed with cancer.* Portland, OR: I. Smith.

Smith, Peter K., Helen Cowie, and Mark Blades. 2003. *Understanding children's development.* United Kingdom: Blackwell Publishing.

Taylor, Barbara J. 2005. *A child goes forth: A curriculum guide for preschool children.* 10th ed. Columbus: Merrill/Pearson.

Thomas, Alexander, and Stella Chess. 1977. *Temperament and development.* New York: Bruner/Mazel.

Thompson, Lauren. 2003. *Little quack.* Pictures by Derek Anderson. New York: Simon & Schuster Books for Young Readers.

Tomlinson, Lee, and David Brittain. 2007. Military child care ranked number one. *AF/A1 Journal* (Summer).

Trapani, Iza. 1998. *The itsy-bitsy spider.* Watertown, MA: Charlesbridge Publishing.

Wanerman, Todd, Leslie Roffman, and Cassandra Britton. 2010. *Including one, including all: A guide to relationship-based early childhood inclusion.* St. Paul: Redleaf Press.

Westcott, Nadine Bernard. 1990. *There's a hole in the bucket.* New York: Harper & Row.

———. 1998. *The lady with the alligator purse.* 1st board book edition. Boston: Little, Brown.

———. 2003. *I know an old lady who swallowed a fly.* 1st board book ed. Boston: Little, Brown.

Wolpert, Ellen. 2005. *Start seeing diversity: The basic guide to an anti-bias curriculum.* St. Paul: Redleaf Press.

Wood, David, Jerome S. Bruner, and Gail Ross. 1976. The role of tutoring and problem solving. *Journal of Child Psychology and Psychiatry* 17:89–100.

Wurm, Julianne. 2005. *Working in the Reggio way: A beginner's guide for American teachers.* St. Paul: Redleaf Press.

York, Stacey. 2003. *Roots and wings: Affirming culture in early childhood programs.* Rev. ed. St. Paul: Redleaf Press.

Zelinsky, Paul O. 1990. *The wheels on the bus.* New York: Dutton Children's Books.

Zolotow, Charlotte. 1985. *William's doll.* Illustrated by William Pène Du Bois. New York: HarperTrophy.

Photo Credits

Photo on page 98 courtesy of U.S. Army.

Photo on page 39 courtesy of U.S. Army. Photographer: Jason Austin.

Photos on pages 62 (left) and 78 courtesy of U.S. Army. Photographer: Brandon Beach.

Photo on page 159 (left) courtesy of U.S. Air Force. Photographer: Mindy Bloem.

Photo on page 123 courtesy of U.S. Navy. Photographer: Sara Bohannan.

Photo on page 17 courtesy of U.S. Navy. Photographer: Matthew Bookwalter.

Photo on page 108 courtesy of U.S. Navy. Photographer: Regina L. Brown.

Photos on pages 44 (left) and 129 courtesy of U.S. Army. Photographer: Amy L. Bugala.

Photos on pages 10, 18, and 23 (right) courtesy of U.S. Navy. Photographer: Joseph M. Buliavac.

Photo on page 14 courtesy of U.S. Army. Photographer: Clester Burdell.

Photo on page 121 courtesy of U.S. Navy. Photographer: Daniel J. Calderón.

Photo on page 116 (left) courtesy of U.S. Air Force. Photographer: Megan Carrico.

Photo on page 30 courtesy of U.S. Navy. Photographer: Michael Cortez.

Photo on page 33 courtesy of U.S. Army. Photographer: Joyce Costello.

Photo on page 99 courtesy of U.S. Navy. Photographer: Scott Dagendesh.

Photo on page 55 courtesy of U.S. Army. Photographer: Nick D'Amario.

Photo on page 132 courtesy of U.S. Air Force. Photographer: Bennie J. Davis III.

Photo on page 142 courtesy of U.S. Marines. Photographer: Michelle M. Dickson.

Photo on page 19 courtesy of U.S. Navy. Photographer: Philip Forrest.

Photo on page 34 courtesy of U.S. Navy. Photographer: Patrick Gearhiser.

Photo on page 101 courtesy of U.S. Navy. Photographer: Nicholas Hall.

Photo on page 59 (right) courtesy of U.S. Army. Photographer: Mark Heeter.

Photo on page 134 courtesy of U.S. Marines. Photographer: James B. Hoke.

Photo on page 117 courtesy of U.S. Navy. Photographer: Kristin M. Johnson.

Photo on page 97 courtesy of U.S. Navy. Photographer: Jeff Johnstone.

Photos on pages 16, 61, and 72 courtesy of U.S. Army. Photographer: Lacey Justinger.

Photos on pages 51 and 59 (left) courtesy of Lacei Koffi.

Photo on page 44 (right) courtesy of U.S. Marines. Photographer: Justin P. Lago.

Photo on page 9 courtesy of U.S. Air Force. Photographer: Marc I. Lane.

Photo on page 154 (bottom) courtesy of U.S. Navy. Photographer: Michael Lantron.

Photo on page 151 courtesy of U.S. Army. Photographer: Brandon Little.

Photo on page 79 (right) courtesy of U.S. Army. Photographer: Elizabeth M. Lorge.

Photo on page 32 courtesy of U.S. Army. Photographer: Marny Malin.

Photo on page 145 courtesy of U.S. Navy. Photographer: Julie Matyascik.

Photos on pages 48, 54, and 116 (right) courtesy of Elizabeth McCarroll.

Photo on page 83 courtesy of U.S. Army. Photographer: Sarah McCleary.

Photo on page 165 courtesy of Jacqueline McCloud.

Photo on page 43 courtesy of U.S. Army. Photographer: Lee Min-hwi.

Photo on page 146 (middle) courtesy of U.S. Marines. Photographer: C. Nuntavong.

Photo on page 22 (right) courtesy of U.S. Navy. Photographer: Seth C. Peterson.

Photos on pages 12, 31, 62 (right), and 70 courtesy of Kassidy Petty.

Photo on page 23 (left) courtesy of U.S. Navy. Photographer: Ramon Preciado.

Photos on pages 79 (left), 127, and 141 courtesy of U.S. Army. Released.

Photos on pages 49, 64, and 146 (bottom) courtesy of U.S. Marines. Released.

Photos on pages 154 (top) and 155 courtesy of U.S. Navy. Released.

Photo on page 146 (top) courtesy of U.S. Navy. Photographer: Kelli Roesch.

Photos on pages 74 and 119 courtesy of Katie Rose.

Photo on page 147 courtesy of U.S. Marines. Photographer: Antonio Rosoas.

Photo on page 102 courtesy of U.S. Navy. Photographer: Kaitlyn Scarboro-Vinklarek.

Photos on pages 63, 80, and 93 courtesy of Lyndsay Shaffer.

Photo on page 81 courtesy of Matthew Shaffer.

Photo on page 90 courtesy of U.S. Navy. Photographer: Terry Spain.

Photo on page 42 courtesy of Molly Taylor.

Photo on page 162 courtesy of U.S. Navy. Photographer: Stephanie Tigner.

Photo on page 144 courtesy of U.S. Navy. Photographer: Joshua J. Wahl.

Photo on page 22 (left) courtesy of U.S. Air Force. Photographer: Megan Ward.

Photo on page 159 (right) courtesy of U.S. Navy. Photographer: Jason R. Zalasky.

35512

OCT 06 2015

OCT 10 2015

BASEMENT

CPSIA information can be obtained at www.ICGtesting.com
Printed in the USA
LVOW09s1046280715

447925LV00007B/22/P

9 781933 653747